CALIFORNIA
THE BEAUTIFUL
COOKBOOK

AUTHENTIC RECIPES FROM CALIFORNIA

Grilled Trout (recipe page 78)

AUTHENTIC RECIPES FROM CALIFORNIA

CALIFORNIA
THE BEAUTIFUL
COOKBOOK

RECIPES BY
JOHN PHILLIP CARROLL

TEXT BY
VIRGINIA RAINEY

FOOD PHOTOGRAPHY BY
ALLAN ROSENBERG

SCENIC PHOTOGRAPHY BY
LEO MEIER

CollinsPublishersSanFrancisco

A Division of HarperCollinsPublishers

First published in the U.S.A. 1991 by
Collins Publishers San Francisco

Conceived and produced by Weldon Owen Inc.
90 Gold Street
San Francisco, CA 94133 U.S.A.
Phone (415) 291-0100 Fax (415) 291-8841

Weldon Owen Inc.:
President: John Owen
Managing Editor: Jane Fraser
Project Coordinator: Ruth Jacobson
Editor and Indexer: Frances Bowles
Proofreader: David Sweet
Production: Mick Bagnato, Stephanie Sherman
Design: Tom Morgan, Blue Design
Design Concept: John Bull, The Book Design Company
Map: Mike Gorman
Illustrations: Yolande Bull

Library of Congress
Cataloging-in-Publication Data:

Carroll, John Phillip.
    California the beautiful cookbook / recipes by
John Phillip Carroll ; text by Virginia Rainey ;
food photography by Allan Rosenberg ; scenic
photography by Leo Meier.
        p.   cm.
        Includes index.
        ISBN 0-00-215931-7
    1. Cookery, American—California style. 2.
California—Description and travel—1981-   I.
Rainey, Virginia. II. Title.
    TX715.2.C34C371991
    641.59794—dc20   90-48847

Production by Mandarin Offset, Hong Kong
Printed in Hong Kong

A Weldon Owen Production

Pages 2–3: When Ice Age glaciers scoured out the eight-mile-long Yosemite Valley, they created a mountain paradise of forests, waterfalls, lakes and majestic granite cliffs.

Right: Shopping on skates is de rigueur in Venice Beach, where it seems anything and everything is for sale.

Pages 8–9: Palm Canyon, near Palm Springs, is a rocky ravine lined with stately palms that has been used in many movie sets.

Pages 10–11: Grilled Herbed Eggplant (recipe page 170), Roasted Whole Garlic (recipe page 182) and Pesto Tomatoes (recipe page 186)

Pages 14–15: In the Owens Valley, a lonesome wilderness triumphs over the cultivated face of the Central Valley a few miles to the west.

Endpapers: Sunrise over Napa Valley vineyards

Raspberry Vinegar (left, recipe page 206) and Basil and Garlic Vinegar (right, recipe page 210)

CONTENTS

After a hard day of wine tasting in the Napa Valley, diners enjoy an outdoor meal at the Ristorante Tra Vigne in St. Helena.

CALIFORNIA, THE CULINARY HERITAGE

The strong, steady pounding of stone pestles in deeply worn mortar pits; the hiss of fire-hot rocks dropped into tight, intricately woven baskets full of water; acorn porridge bubbling over a fire—these were the sounds of early California cooking.

Even as new American cooks on the Atlantic coast were turning out plum pudding and apple pandowdy in the 1770s, California was still a land apart. Walled off from the rest of the world by scorching deserts and formidable, snow-capped peaks on one side and a rough, foggy coastline on the other, California's culinary personality bubbled along at a spicy but measured pace in the Spanish mission and rancho kitchens—until the gold rush of 1849. Once the world rushed in, the menu was forever transformed. And it is still evolving, as the bounty of California is combined with the roots of every cuisine in the world.

For generations, the acorn was the staff of life for most of the Indian tribes who lived off the isolated land that was to become California. As basic as rice to the Chinese, wheat to the Europeans, and corn to the Pueblos, the acorn meant food for all seasons. Life in this complex crescent of coast, mountain and desert revolved around gathering, storing, grinding with mortars and pestles, and leaching bitter tannic acid from the nuts. The hard-earned acorn flour was cooked into a simple mush, and the leftovers formed into cakes and baked in the sun. For accompaniments, the Indians picked wild berries from bushes that rambled along stream beds or gathered pine nuts and plucked wild onions from the ground. In the lush coastal and forested regions, they hunted deer and small game and trapped, netted or speared the abundant salmon, trout and sweet shellfish. For most tribes, farming was not a way of life. The Yumas and Mohaves, however, dropped seeds into the muddy flood plains of the Colorado River and reaped corn, pumpkins, beans and squash.

A LAND APART

Though the land had fed native Indians for centuries, it seemed barren and inhospitable to the Spanish missionaries who crossed from Baja (lower) to Alta (upper) California in 1769. They had come to establish a chain of self-sustaining missions, supported by farming. But water supplies were unpredictable at best. Farming was a struggle, and the cuttings the padres brought with them— for *chile* peppers and olives, fruit trees and grape vines, dates and nuts—took a few years to root in the dry, lonely mission outposts. But eventually these became the crops that would leave their stamp on California agriculture and cooking forever.

One by one, as the missions were settled (twenty-one in all), their orchards, vineyards, corn and wheat fields began to blossom and thrive. The adobe compounds became the equivalent of a chain of roadside inns, stretching from San Diego in the south to Sonoma, north of San Francisco. From smoky little kitchens with adjoining rooms that opened to the sky, the newly

The precipitous Big Sur coast of central California offers a grandiose panorama of land and sea. Views like this one from Highway 1 attract visitors from all over the world.

arrived padres and their Indian cooks struggled at first, but soon were feeding inhabitants and guests with homemade cheeses and cured olives, olive oil, preserves, pastries and some fine barbecues. As the stream of California travelers and traders grew, so did the more exotic supplies, such as chocolate, preserved ginger, brown sugar and coffee delivered by ships from the East Coast, Asia and Europe.

Cooks along the mission route were soon treating visitors to *champurrado*, a sweet, thick chocolate drink, and *buñuelos*—flaky pastries similar to popovers—soaked with warm syrup flavored with the sweet aniseed that still sprouts wild all over California. They served *chile* and egg dishes (more than twenty varieties of *chiles* grew in the gardens) or tender rabbit, stewed with *chiles* and tomatoes; savory stuffed onions; and boldly flavored grilled meats, rubbed with garlic and fresh herbs. They offered pumpkin and fruit preserves for the travelers to take back out on the road.

After the missions came the ranchos—private land grants given under Mexican rule in the early 1800s. Adobe houses with thick walls and tile roofs, many of the ranchos displayed a kind of frontier elegance. Often they were furnished with rawhide and whalebone furniture along with intricately carved boxes and fine laces—treasures from a booming trade in hides and tallow and the world commerce generated by whaling ships.

During this era, California was home to thousands of herds of cattle, raised for their hides, which came to be known as "California bank notes" on the East Coast, and for tallow, or rendered fat, used to make soap and candles. What was left for the *vaqueros*, or cowboys, was beef. And they ate it almost to the exclusion of everything else. Seafood would not come into favor for another generation or so. Routinely, sides of beef were charred over glowing embers of hardwood or simmered in *chile*-infused brine and shredded for *carne seca. Frijoles* and *salsa* with mounds of fresh *tortillas* were staples as well. A journal entry from the rancho days best describes that particular style of California cuisine: "How delicious that beef was . . . properly charred on the outside, pink and juicy in the center. Beans were bubbling in the deep pots and that California sauce that was always a part of the barbecue in the early days—chopped onion, tomato and green pepper, seasoned with vinegar, salt and sometimes a dash of olive oil. Where could one find anything more delicious?" Delicious it was and is—but it was only the appetizer for what was to come.

The Spanish explorers and Mexican *vaqueros* left an indelible and delectable mark on California agriculture and cooking, but the real turning point came the day gold was discovered at Sutter's Mill in 1848. It marked the beginnings of a culinary heritage as diverse as California's legendary climate and geography, with fascinating extremes. Fortune hunters and laborers from France, Italy, Germany, Chile, Switzerland, Portugal, Armenia, Spain, Ireland, Japan and China came to work the mines north and east of Sacramento. They also happened to be dairy farmers and fruit growers, fishermen, cheesemakers, winemakers and even chocolatiers, who, like Domingo Ghirardelli, stayed on to ply their trades when gold mining did not pan out. In supplying the mines, Sacramento and San Francisco became boom towns, and gustatory indulgences in their taverns and hotel dining rooms always seemed to include legendary quantities of oysters and champagne for those who struck it rich. The flip side was "grub"—dry beef and hard biscuits, at

*The Lake Tahoe area offers a year-round serene mountain retreat and
spectacular vistas such as this one of Emerald Bay.*

IDAHO

WYOMING

Great Salt Lake

SALT LAKE CITY o

o Elko

o Ely

UTAH

Lake Powell

LAS VEGAS o

Lake Mead

Soda Lake

Flagstaff o

Needles o

Lake Havasu

ARIZONA

COLORADO DESERT

DESERT

Joshua Tree National Monument

lm rings

o Indio

t. San Jacinto

Blythe o

Colorado River

PHOENIX o

Salton Sea

Coachella Canal

Brawley o

o El Centro

o Calexico

o MEXICALI

EXICO

inflated prices. The California fruit and vegetable canning industry followed on the heels of the gold rush, and bottled fruits, preserves and pickles soon became staples in the bare mining camps.

As newly arrived immigrants settled in the cities, they built brick-oven bakeries and opened storefront restaurants and specialty shops. Dairies flourished in the Central Valley and along the central coast, wineries in Sonoma and Napa, hop farms and breweries in the northern valleys and along the coasts (where the lumber business was also booming). Farms and orchards soon blossomed throughout the state. Several of the nurserymen and farmers sent back to their native countries for cuttings of plants such as the French prune and Italian artichoke and turned them into major crops. And so the gold rush, along with the advent of the railroads in the mid- and late 1800s, colored California's early regional cooking styles.

The melting pot began to bubble over as people and crops were more easily moved about by rail. Orange growers in Riverside could send crates up to San Francisco, and fresh seafood could be packed on ice and sent from the coasts and bays to inland farmers. Now California cooking reached a new level of sophistication. By 1898, a winter menu at the Occidental Hotel in San Francisco offered Sacramento River salmon, Petaluma goose, Humboldt bear, Menlo Park artichokes, baked Salinas Burbank potatoes and Santa Cruz smelt. The state's culinary heritage began evolving into an exciting but unquantifiable mélange, based on what M. F. K. Fisher described as "an agreeable tolerance of all that is good."

RANCH CHICKEN, FROG LEGS AND THE *TAMALE* MAN

As regional culinary personalities developed, the Central Valley laid claim to solid country cooking based on local and often unusual crops. Typical in the 1930s and 1940s were some decidedly California-style concoctions such as prune and peanut butter sandwiches, carrot salad with raisins, spaghetti sauce with black olives, and honey-avocado butter—all recipe suggestions offered in the *California Farmer* magazine. Putting up preserves and

Golden poppies, the state flower, grow wild throughout California—in such abundance partly because it is illegal to pick them.

condiments was, and still is, an important part of the farm and ranch cooking heritage, and nectarine butter and pickled peaches fill cupboard shelves from Fresno to Sacramento.

Also typical of the Central Valley and central coast are lusty, flavorful dishes in which imaginative combinations from earlier days are summoned to create complex flavors. Such dishes are based solely on the bounty of the land, blending ingredients that most Americans might not have considered in the early days. For example, raisins and nuts might be combined with olives and *chiles* to create sweetly pungent sauces for meats and poultry. In addition to juxtaposing flavors, native Californians have long been comfortable with foods that seem exotic to some Americans, such as avocados, artichokes, kiwifruit, pomegranates, persimmons and figs. New and unusual crops and preparations have always been encouraged and nurtured, resulting in much-loved classics from California date prune bread to crab Louis, *huevos rancheros* and Caesar salad.

While hungry ranch hands were eating California country foods in the late 1800s and early 1900s, chefs in the great hotels such as the Del Coronado in San Diego and the Palace in San Francisco were introducing patrons to a curious blend of Euro-California-inspired preparations. Broiled native quail on toast, quince fritters *au maraschino*, abalone fritters, artichoke salad and "glaced" California fruits mark the menus of the day, along with "Breast of Capon, Farcies, a la Chevaliere" and "Fried Frog Legs a la Villeroi." On city street corners outside the hotels, one could always find a satisfying alternative to the fancy foods with the *tamale* man and his portable cart of steaming hot bundles and a pot of spicy red sauce. Steam-beer joints and basic boardinghouse fare were just as common.

NEW WAVES

As Californians later became attached to the culture of the automobile (and sacrificed farmland for freeways), roadside diners begat the in-car dining culture portrayed in movies such as *American Graffiti*. Since the 1950s, neon-lit drive-ins with waitresses on roller skates expertly dispensing hamburgers, fries and thick malts have become a classic symbol of life in California, where the car reigns supreme. Around the same time, a certain culinary homogeneity set in, invading kitchens from Yreka to San Bernardino. The wave of frozen TV dinners, fondue pots and endless casseroles hit California just as it did the rest of the nation in the 1950s and 1960s. Despite the proliferation of fads and prefab foods, California remained a land apart, leading the backyard barbecue craze and raising salads to an art form.

In California, a melting pot of cultures and styles, anything goes—carefree attire, liberal attitudes, unusual hobbies and, above all, a sense of fun and frivolity.

Far away from the gourmet restaurants of urban California, this country café in Weaverville is more likely to serve simple but hearty fare.

Today, most regions offer a culinary balance of old and new and a spicy reflection of their ethnic roots. But California, being what it is, has an incredibly diverse palate. So today, a typical meal in Venice, California, might begin with *quesadillas*, be followed by crab cakes and grilled Japanese eggplant, and end with orange shortcake for dessert. It just depends on whose kitchen you visit—and on what day.

Amid all the diversity, some common denominators do reflect current styles of California cooking at its best. Often it is based on classic preparations or combinations, refined to take advantage of fresh, local foods. So you might have pistachios with a glass of late-harvest Zinfandel and a wedge of Stilton cheese. Foods grown or made in California are generally prepared in ways that enhance, rather than mask, their natural flavors. In the wine country north of San Francisco, you could expect a meal as elegantly simple as duck breast salad on greens, served with roasted garlic and a baguette. To top it off, maybe a simple wine jelly with whipped cream. Of all the current California cuisines, that of the state's several wine regions is most clearly evolving and emerging as a distinct entity. Much of it is based on the products of local food artisans and farmers, as is true with most of the world's great cuisines.

Also typical (as if such a word ever applies in California) and more recent are all the ingredients made or grown in California that have their roots in Italy, France, Spain, Eastern Europe and all of Asia, prepared with a Californian sensibility in urban centers such as Los Angeles as well as in small towns such as Mendocino, far to the north. These ingredients might be transformed into *penne* with goat cheese; black bean cake with fresh *salsa* and cilantro; crab, artichoke and avocado salads—all relatively new combinations—simple, fresh and now entrenched in California's culinary history.

California the Beautiful Cookbook is a celebration of all this delicious history and diversity. It moves from the 1700s to the end of the twentieth century, through seven regions of the state. The story is based on geography and the subtle changes that appear as deserts give way to mountains, and the strong Mexican influence meets European farm-style cooking and Asian dishes both old and new. The two hundred recipes offer a spirited, mouth-watering tour of the culinary heritage of the state so aptly charcterized by writer Wallace Stegner as "America, only more so."

Vast varieties of fish are caught from both commercial fleets and private fishing boats all along the California coast.

THE SOUTHERN COAST

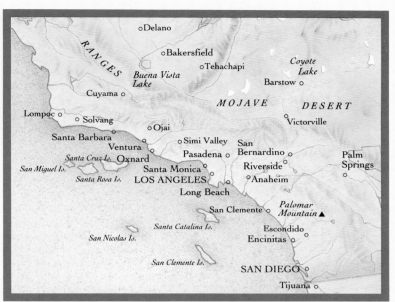

THE SOUTHERN COAST

California's south coast and inland region is drawn from the parched border where Tecate, Mexico, meets Tecate, California. Along an imaginary line about forty miles inland, the region skirts the Anza Borrego Desert and the little town of Julian, famous for its gold strike of 1870. It brushes by Riverside and the foothills of the towering San Bernardino Mountains, where deep green pines along the "Rim of the World Drive" give way to stark desert on the other side. It wraps around the gently contoured San Gabriel Mountains, the eastern border of the greater Los Angeles area. Mission San Gabriel was one of the first Spanish missions to hint at California's agricultural promise: there the padres first saw their olive trees and grapevines flourish.

North, the region continues along a coastline awash with sailboats and fishing boats. Long, lazy stretches of beach threaded with rocky coves and inlets lead to beautiful Santa Barbara. Spanish settlers called it *La tierra adorada*—the beloved land. To the east, the Santa Ynez Valley produces some of California's finest Cabernet and Chardonnay wines. To the west lies the Ojai Valley, so surrealistically beautiful that it stood in as Shangri-La in the 1937 film *Lost Horizon*.

The stunning coastal headlands at Point Conception, about one-third of the way up the twelve-hundred-mile California coastline, mark the northern stopping point of this densely populated area.

Previous pages: Sheltered beneath the golden slopes of the Sierra Madre, Santa Barbara offers a unique meeting of mountains and sea. Left: Open-air cafés along the boardwalk on Venice Beach, near Santa Monica, are the perfect places for casual and eclectic dining throughout the year.

27

SALSA TO EBLESKIVER

As throughout much of California, a Spanish-Mexican culinary influence permeates the region. It is as simple and irresistible as fresh *tortilla* chips, dipped in fiery *salsas* and eaten by the dozen, then downed with beer so icy cold it makes the throat ache. It is as comforting as plump *tamales* or cheese *enchiladas*, washed down with cool *aguas frescas*, the Mexican fruit juices served in *taquerias* everywhere. (Pink watermelon or strawberries, golden mangoes or pineapples are puréed with water and sugar to make these refreshers that are often ladled from huge earthenware pots.)

The Spanish-Mexican influence is a hallmark of many white-tablecloth dinners, too. In southern California, the tablecloth is likely to be buffeted by a breeze on some sunny deck or patio overlooking a cove of sailboats or the lights of Los Angeles. Diners may be feasting on a piquant *seviche*, rich chicken *mole* and Caesar salad.

Although Spanish culinary roots run deep and delicious, the food of southern California is as eclectic as the world that has been rushing in since the Germans settled in Anaheim, the English in Riverside and the Italians in Los Angeles.

The whitewashed port of San Diego, the first major city on the south coast, sets the pace for what is to come as the region stretches north. It hums with the excitement of a lively, fascinating selection of restaurants that reflect the world—sometimes authentically, often, California style. You might find the perfect pastrami sandwich on one block and lobster *enchiladas* on the next.

Many southern California towns are named after European cities—Naples, Valencia, Lido Isle—though, like Venice, with its bikini-clad rollerskaters whizzing by some of the wildest art and trendiest restaurants in the country, they bear little resemblance to their namesakes. Solvang, a little Danish town near Santa Barbara, is true to its heritage, both in architecture and food. It is known for plump dumplings called *ebleskiver*, cooked by descendants of Danish immigrants who established the village in 1911.

In all, the region includes eight historic Spanish missions and the largest Hispanic community in the United States. Chinese and Japanese, Thai and Vietnamese foods are becoming as familiar and appreciated as are Mexican, however. The Asian population here has grown to be the largest outside Asia.

GREATER L.A., FROM KITSCH TO SUBLIME

In the words of a former food editor for a Los Angeles newspaper, "L.A. is where people from everywhere inhabit split-level houses in split-level topography." The greater Los Angeles area, sprawling and diverse as it is, is a culinary and economic hub of the state.

It is where acres of "Valley" shopping malls meet the glitz of Beverly Hills. Palm-lined avenues lead to restaurants serving kiwifruit sorbet and goat cheese pizzas, diners serving thick chocolate milkshakes and foot-long hot dogs, often in buildings shaped like hot dogs. You might have fish *tacos* at a baseball game and some of the most exciting four-star dining in the country at dinnertime. Fleeting trends as well as firmly entrenched classics have sprouted in this metropolis—from offerings as strange as squid with blackberry sauce to the truly delicious duck sausage pizza at Spago and the staid Cobb salad, which originated at the Brown Derby restaurant in Hollywood.

But contrasts and diversity are what this region is about. Pink cotton candy and the circuslike atmosphere

Solvang, established in 1911 as the site of a Danish school, has since grown into a living re-creation of an early Danish village, complete with windmills and Danish delicacies.

of Disneyland spring up about fifty miles from the silence of Placerita Canyon, where, they say, a hungry *vaquero* named Francisco Lopez discovered gold on the roots of a wild onion he pulled from the ground in 1842—seven years before the great gold rush up north.

Today, where huge ranchos thrived in the 1800s and acres of sugar beets, bell peppers, citrus groves, barley, alfalfa and dairy ranches once flourished, a maze of freeways and suburbs crisscrosses the land. In between, pockets of several of the world's cultures add culinary texture to the life of the area. Stroll along Olvera Street, L.A.'s oldest Mexican marketplace, and you may hear the steady patting of hands as cooks make fresh *tortillas*. You will find *carnitas*—slow-cooked pork with a tender, flaky texture; wonderful fresh breads, or *panes*; candies made from *nopales*, or cactus. A few blocks away, the aroma of *dim sum* wafts from food stands in Chinatown. *Kim chee* and other Korean staples can be found on Olympic Boulevard. Los Angeles claims to have a restaurant from every country in Eastern Europe, save Bulgaria (and the only Albanian restaurant in the United States, according to its owners).

At the Los Angeles Farmer's Market, which began when farmers trucked their produce into the city during the depression, a wealth of fresh California fruits and vegetables creates a technicolor movie scene. Deep green avocados, soft yellow pears, row upon row of fresh herbs, lettuce in every curly formation and hue inspire cooks every day, in every season. Specialty produce—baby vegetables and many new or exotic items—is the province of growers and importers throughout the area.

As the world gets smaller and commerce accelerates, California is trading more of its produce and seafood than ever before—both in and out of the state. In major urban areas such as Los Angeles, everything and anything that grows anywhere in the world is now available. The bounty of produce, most of it local, may end up as crab-stuffed artichokes or Chinese vegetables, stir-fried and *chile*-peppered in a wok, or as dinner on a skewer, brushed with olive oil and grilled over glowing coals—not so different from the Spanish mission days.

The first Spanish mission was established at San Diego in 1769, when Father Junípero Serra and Gaspar de Portolá made the trek from Baja to Alta California. "All the soil is black and loamy," wrote Fray Juan Crespi, chaplain with the Portolá expedition, when they arrived, "and is capable of producing every kind of fruit and grain which may be planted." And plant they did. The missionaries were responsible for introducing countless foods—including olives, grapes, figs, *chiles*, nuts and fruits. But the early years were an incredible struggle. Mexico was far away, and the missionaries, though they brought the cuttings and seeds, were not necessarily skilled farmers.

As they learned to recognize the wild onions, garlic, berries, watercress and miner's lettuce that grew all around them, their menus improved considerably. According to one early account of Alta California: "Native wild grape and blackberry vines, heavy with small fruits, clambered riotously over the cottonwoods which grew alongside the purling streams. Black walnut and gooseberry bushes dressed the hillsides, while the unruly strawberry plants trailed the ground." Wild geese, ducks, rabbits and the occasional unlucky bear trapped in a *reata*, or rope trap, provided meat.

Mission cooks—often the native Indians—became more proficient and inventive as their plants eventually multiplied and native ingredients were combined with the new. As the missions were established and moved steadily northward, the humble adobe compounds became the equivalent of early roadside inns. They flourished during California's hide and tallow trade of the mid-1800s. The vast rangelands were used as cattle ranches, established for the sole purpose of providing leather and tallow to the rest of the country. Beef was almost a side benefit, but it was plentiful and was used to its best advantage. The choicest cuts were slashed into long strips and dipped in a red *chile*-infused brine bubbling and boiling over a fire. The beef was then dried to make *carne seca* and then shredded and used in *carne con chile* and *enchiladas*.

When the missions were secularized in 1834, land grants transformed them into private ranchos and a new style of living was introduced. For the most part, rancho cooking carried on the mission traditions of *chiles* and barbecue, chocolates and pastries that had grown up with the help of the trading ships and newfound skills of the cooks and farmers. Soon, however, it was influenced by Yankees and Europeans who did not always appreciate the kick of a hot *chile*.

BOSTON BAKED BEANS MEETS *FRIJOLES*

Railroad journeys into California changed the way other Americans thought about food forever. The Hotel Men's Mutual Benefit Association, a group of traveling professionals, recorded glowing accounts of their extensive, wide-eyed train tour through California in 1896. One such traveler, a Mr. George W. Sweeney from the Atlantic coast, candidly confessed, "I want to make particular mention of some of the dishes which have gotten the best of us on this trip. My gastronomic knowledge has been enormously increased. I have run up against such delectable concoctions as . . . *fritos, azados, tortilla de maíz* and many other palatable morsels . . . beyond ordinary analysis, which are a puzzle to scientific experts."

In San Diego, Mr. Sweeney and the other hotel men experienced their first real outdoor barbecue and a formal Spanish lunch. It included *tamales*, which were described by the visitors as "delicious, being the genuine article served after the most approved methods, and not the irresponsible hash that one buys of the itinerant vendors of the East." *Chili con carne* "was as hot as chili could make it," and all were astonished by *frijoles*—"a revelation to all who had hitherto been accustomed to the unobtrusive and unpretentious Boston Baked Bean." The south coast of California, it seems, has been pleasing and astonishing visitors, and itself, for quite some time.

Joining the river of colorful characters on the Venice Beach promenade, a Great Dane leads its owner on an afternoon stroll.

APPETIZERS, SOUPS AND SALADS

Neon beckons the hungry to a waterside café on the Santa Cruz Wharf.

APPETIZERS, SOUPS AND SALADS

The first rule is, there are no rules. California-style appetizers, soups and salads reflect the diversity that is the very essence of California cooking. Plump, fresh figs wrapped in *prosciutto*, avocado paired with local melon and shrimp, delicate almond soup or egg rolls, Cobb salad or goat cheese with tomatoes—each may be considered typical. It's all very democratic. Perhaps the only common denominator is the devotion to fresh, quality ingredients.

APPETIZERS

Appetizer menus in California's great hotels of the early 1900s, such as the Del Coronado in San Diego or the Palace in San Francisco, generally offered a selection of local products: chilled celery, olives, almonds, oysters and sardines from Monterey. Served unadorned in little dishes, they were much like Spanish *tapas*.

Today, many Californians think of appetizers as the small things you eat while waiting for the barbecue coals to reach the perfect-glow stage. And that they are, but they also might be something delicious to have with a glass of wine on a redwood deck or at a tailgate party, and they might be simple or elaborate. Regional lines are blurred. Armenian-style *dolmas* may or may not hold raisins from Fresno, and you may find them up north in Mendocino or at a Greek wedding in San Jose. Platters of fresh cracked crab legs, a San Francisco tradition, might share a party with platters of antipasto in Los Angeles.

Baskets of raw, chilled vegetables, from basic carrots and celery to *jícama* and sweet red and golden bell peppers, are often served with creamy dips, welcomed and quickly devoured everywhere. So are copious amounts of *nachos*—*tortilla* chips covered with refried beans, cheese and *chiles* and baked to melting, mouth-watering, get-your-hands-messy perfection. And then there is *guacamole*, the California paean to the avocado. The perfect *guacamole*, a true aficionado will tell you, should be slightly chunky. Hints of lime, cilantro, garlic and hot pepper sauce are all that's needed to enliven the buttery-fleshed fruit that thrives in southern California. Tradition dictates simplicity. Just scoop it up with *tortilla* chips, and enjoy with an icy margarita or a beer.

SOUPS

You are more likely to encounter a subtle cream of fresh vegetable soup, shellfish in broth or an exquisite bisque in California than most of the heartier soups. In a state with short winters and snow confined to mountain areas, it stands to reason. However, where the weather is cold—either on the foggy north and central coasts or high in the Sierras and Shasta-Cascade—hearty minestrone, bean and squash soups are ladled out generously. Fish chowders are universally loved, in all seasons.

In the balmy southern coastal areas and the summer heat of the Central Valley, fragrant strawberries, peaches or melons turn up in delicate fruit soups (originally a Scandinavian tradition). Savory cold soups, made with puréed avocados or tomatoes, as in classic *gazpacho*, are passed around in mugs or offered in tall stemmed glasses, garnished with sour cream or yogurt. The Central Valley also inspired cream of olive soup and almond soup that has just a touch of sherry.

Now, more than ever, Asian restaurants north and south offer some of the most tantalizing soups in Califor-

Previous pages: Cucumber and Tomato Salad (left, recipe page 36)
and Chicken and Watercress Soup (right, recipe page 45)

32

nia: chicken and watercress, hot and sour, and hundreds of pork and seafood soups. Thai and Vietnamese cooks have seduced Californians with coconut milk and lemon grass in savory soups of pineapple and exotic mushrooms. All the ingredients are available to adventurous cooks, but most prefer to enjoy these soups in restaurants where the cooks are producing the authentic foods of their native countries. Another soup most fans leave in the capable hands of a restaurant is *menudo*, a bracing concoction that appears on many California-Mexican menus and is known as a traditional hangover cure. In its most authentic form, it includes tripe, veal knuckles, garlic, *chiles* and hominy, simmered in a sturdy broth.

SALADS

Never is there an excuse for a mediocre salad in California. Freshness is a way of life in every season, and even the smallest towns have access to the bounty. You need not live on a farm or near an orchard, because the produce comes to you, through local farmers' markets or giant supermarkets. In fact, the array of produce in California markets astounds some visitors. In many areas, markets routinely carry ten types of greens—Romaine, escarole, butter lettuce, watercress, arugula and *frisée* to name just a few. Bell peppers of gold, red and green; eight varieties of melon; entire sections of fresh herbs—all inspire cooks to raise salads to an art, and are a source of pride throughout the state.

Salads in California range from the simplicity of Sonoma field greens dressed with a choice of specialty vinegars and oils, to free-for-alls where sprouts, sunflower seeds, carrots, raisins, pasta, ham, turkey, seafood and cheese turn a salad into a full-tilt meal. Often, the salad is the meal. Chicken, shrimp or crab salad in chilled avocado halves is a California classic—a delicious example of local ingredients in a dish that suits a Mediterranean climate and light, informal style.

Possessing some of the most sought-after hearts in the vegetable world, artichokes ripen in a field near Castroville.

Cobb and Caesar salads, made with crackling crisp greens, are year-round standards. In the fall, apples from Watsonville or Sebastopol might be tossed with walnuts, watercress and a light dressing to make a picnic salad. Winter might bring a garlicky parsley salad or Green Goddess dressing, thick and rich with mayonnaise, spooned over sturdy greens. Cooks also make dressings with honey, yogurt, poppy and sesame seeds, herb and fruit vinegars and a variety of oils, from olive to walnut.

The first and last word on salads is quality—in every element. Good oil and vinegar and impeccably fresh ingredients make all the difference. Greens should have crunch and bite, and dressing should just coat the greens, not drench the salad.

The thunderous roar of the Pacific Ocean eight hundred feet below creates a dramatic atmosphere for dining at the Nepenthe restaurant, a Big Sur landmark since the 1940s.

Southern California

QUESADILLAS

These easy-to-make filled tortillas can be done indoors in a skillet, or outside on the grill. As an appetizer, they are good preceding a Mexican dinner. On the lighter side, quesadillas with a green salad make a fresh, fast and simple lunch.

2 large tomatoes, peeled, seeded and chopped
2 garlic cloves, minced (finely chopped)
3 tablespoons chopped fresh cilantro (coriander/Chinese parsley)
salt
freshly ground black pepper
3 large green (spring) onions, chopped
2 cups (8 oz/250 g) shredded Cheddar or Monterey Jack (mild melting) cheese
8 flour *tortillas* (see recipe, page 146)
salsa (see recipes, page 207)
sour cream

❧ In a bowl toss together the tomato, garlic, cilantro and salt and pepper to taste. Stir in the green onion and cheese.
❧ Spread one-eighth—about ⅓ cup (3 fl oz/80 ml)—of the tomato-and-cheese mixture over half of each *tortilla* and fold the other side over, forming a semicircle.
❧ Place the folded *tortillas* in a hot, ungreased skillet and cook over moderate heat for about 2 minutes on each side, or grill

about 6 in (15 cm) from hot coals, turning once or twice. When the cheese begins to melt and the *tortillas* are lightly browned, they are done.
❧ Remove and cut each into 3 wedges. Serve with *salsa* and sour cream.

SERVES 4–8

Southern California

GUACAMOLE

When avocados were inexpensive, this used to be called mantequilla de pobre (poor man's butter), because of its rich smoothness and buttery texture. Now it is more of a luxury. An authentic guacamole, with small chunks of tomato and avocado, makes a good dip for tortilla chips and a perfect topping for homemade enchiladas, tacos and tostadas.

3 or 4 large, ripe avocados, about 1½ lb (750 g)
1 large tomato, peeled, seeded and chopped
1 large garlic clove, minced (finely chopped)
¼ cup (2 fl oz/60 ml) fresh lime juice
2 tablespoons chopped fresh cilantro (coriander/Chinese parsley)
1½ teaspoons salt
½ teaspoon freshly ground black pepper
½ teaspoon hot red pepper (Tabasco) sauce

❧ Peel and pit the avocados. Mash them coarsely with a fork; they should not be too smooth. Stir in the tomato, garlic, lime juice and cilantro. Season with salt, pepper and pepper sauce.

MAKES ABOUT 4 CUPS (32 FL OZ/1 L)

Santa Barbara

AVOCADO AND CHICKEN SALAD

This chicken salad is different because the avocado is puréed and combined with mayonnaise to make a subtle pale green dressing. Though the salad is good as it is, chopped almonds, walnuts or apples may be added.

1 avocado
½ cup (4 fl oz/125 ml) mayonnaise
1 tablespoon lemon juice
1 tablespoon Dijon mustard
1 tablespoon chopped fresh tarragon or 1 teaspoon dried tarragon
salt
freshly ground black pepper
3 cups (1 lb/500 g) diced, cooked chicken
4 celery stalks, finely diced
8–10 large butter lettuce leaves
2 tablespoons chopped parsley

❧ Peel and remove the pit from the avocado. Put it in a bowl and mash with a fork until almost smooth. Blend in the mayonnaise, lemon juice, mustard and tarragon. Season with salt and pepper to taste. Add the chicken and celery and combine thoroughly.
❧ Season with additional salt and pepper if necessary.
❧ Arrange the lettuce leaves around a platter or shallow bowl, mound the salad in the center and sprinkle with parsley.

SERVES 4

Avocado and Chicken Salad

*Guacamole (top right)
and Quesadillas (bottom)*

Central Coast

APPLE AND WALNUT SALAD

The flavors and textures of various nut, fruit and lettuce combinations make them interesting and compatible in salads. This salad goes well with all kinds of meats, hot or cold, and with cheese makes a good main course for a picnic.

¼ cup (2 fl oz/60 ml) vegetable oil or olive oil
2 tablespoons walnut oil (see glossary)
2 tablespoons cider vinegar
½ teaspoon dried thyme or 1 teaspoon chopped fresh thyme
salt
freshly ground black pepper
1 small head chicory (curly endive), washed, stemmed
   and dried, about 4 cups (6 oz/185 g)
1 bunch watercress, washed, stemmed and dried, about
   1 cup (4 oz/125 g)
2 Golden Delicious apples, cored and cut in wedges
1 cup (4 oz/125 g) toasted walnut pieces
2 tablespoons chopped parsley

🐟 In a tightly capped jar shake together the oils, vinegar, thyme and salt and pepper to taste. Toss the chicory and watercress with half the dressing. Toss the apples with 2 tablespoons of the remaining dressing.
🐟 To arrange the salad, spread the greens on a large platter, place the apples over the greens and scatter the walnuts on top. Spoon on the remaining dressing and sprinkle with chopped parsley.

SERVES 4

San Joaquin Valley

CUCUMBER AND TOMATO SALAD

With bread and butter this makes a good luncheon salad, unusual because the cucumbers are dressed with a little soy sauce, giving them Chinese overtones. The combination of tomatoes and chilled cucumbers is also good tossed with hot pasta, for an interesting contrast of hot, cold and crunchy.

3 large English cucumbers
salt
2 tablespoons soy sauce
5 tablespoons (2½ fl oz/75 ml) olive oil
2 tablespoons red wine vinegar
freshly ground black pepper
3 large ripe tomatoes, about 1 lb (500 g), thinly sliced
½ teaspoon dried oregano or ½ tablespoon chopped
   fresh oregano
2 tablespoons chopped parsley

🐟 Peel the cucumbers, halve them lengthwise and scrape out the seeds. Cut crosswise into ½-in (12-mm) pieces. Toss them in a colander with ½ teaspoon salt and let them stand for about 20 minutes to drain. Rinse well and pat the slices dry with a towel.
🐟 Toss the cucumber in a bowl with the soy sauce, 2 tablespoons of the olive oil, 1 tablespoon of the vinegar and pepper to taste. Refrigerate for about 1 hour, tossing occasionally.
🐟 Arrange the tomato slices overlapping on a platter. In a tightly capped jar shake together the remaining 3 tablespoons of oil, the remaining tablespoon of vinegar, the oregano and salt and pepper to taste. Pour over the tomatoes. Drain the cucumbers of their excess dressing, arrange them over the tomatoes and sprinkle with parsley.

SERVES 4–6   *Photograph pages 30–31*

Apple and Walnut Salad

blend in the artichoke purée. Add the half & half or cream and season with salt and pepper to taste. Stir in the lemon juice, and the tarragon or parsley. Serve hot or chill thoroughly and serve cold.

MAKES ABOUT 6 CUPS (48 FL OZ/1.5 L)

Southern California

NACHOS

An informal Mexican appetizer, nachos are brought out on a big platter and are almost a meal in themselves. Set the nachos on the table, with pitchers of beer and margaritas, and let guests help themselves.

6 cups (8 oz/250 g) *tortilla* chips
2 cups (1 lb/500 g) warm refried beans (see recipe, page 185)
2 cups (8 oz/250 g) grated Cheddar or Monterey Jack (mild melting) cheese, or a mixture
½ cup (4 oz/125 g) peeled and chopped hot green *chiles*
4 large green (spring) onions, chopped
sprigs of fresh cilantro (coriander/Chinese parsley)(optional)
tomato *salsa* (see recipe, page 207)

❧ Preheat the oven to 400°F (200°C).
❧ Spread the *tortilla* chips on a large pie pan or other ovenproof platter. Spoon the beans over the chips in dollops; do not smooth them out so as to cover the chips completely. In a bowl toss together the cheese, *chiles* and onion and spread over the beans.
❧ Bake for 5 to 10 minutes, until the cheese is melted and the dish is hot. Serve with sprigs of cilantro and *salsa*.

SERVES 4–6

Los Angeles

EMPANADAS

In New England, gravy and chopped leftovers are "hashed" together in a skillet; in the West, Spanish settlers used similar ingredients to make small savory turnovers. The following filling is very good, though only a suggestion, and you can alter it with other vegetables, meats, fish and poultry, depending on what you have on hand.

BASIC DOUGH

3 cups (12 oz/375 g) all-purpose (plain) flour
1 teaspoon salt
1 cup (8 oz/250 g) vegetable shortening (vegetable lard) or lard
7 to 8 tablespoons (about 4 fl oz/125 ml) water

FILLING

2 tablespoons butter
1 onion, chopped
2 garlic cloves, minced (finely chopped)
½ lb (250 g) ground (minced) beef or lamb
⅓ cup (3 fl oz/80 ml) meat gravy or heavy (double) cream
2 teaspoons chili powder
1 teaspoon ground cumin
2 tablespoons chopped parsley
½ teaspoon salt
½ teaspoon freshly ground black pepper

❧ To make the dough, combine the flour and salt in a bowl. Drop in the shortening or lard and, using your fingertips or a pastry blender, cut the fat into the dry ingredients until the mixture resembles coarse crumbs or old-fashioned soap flakes. Add the water, a tablespoon at a time, stirring well with a fork after each addition; add enough so that the dough is cohesive,

Artichoke Soup, garnished with lemon zest and fresh tarragon

Castroville

ARTICHOKE SOUP

A delicate and elegant soup to serve hot or cold, and a good way to begin a fancy dinner. It is worth starting with fresh artichokes and cooking and trimming their bottoms. There is no shortcut for this job, but you have a delicious soup as a dividend.

8 cooked artichoke bottoms, chokes removed (see recipe for Palace Court salad, page 44)
4 tablespoons (2 oz/60 g) butter
1 medium onion, chopped
2 celery stalks, chopped
1 garlic clove, minced (finely chopped)
3 tablespoons all-purpose (plain) flour
4 cups (32 fl oz/1 l) chicken stock (see glossary)
1 cup (8 fl oz/250 ml) half & half (half cream and half milk) or heavy (double) cream
salt
freshly ground black pepper
2 tablespoons lemon juice
1 tablespoon chopped fresh tarragon or parsley

❧ Purée the artichoke bottoms in a food processor or pass them through a food mill. You will have about 1⅓ cups (11 fl oz/330 ml) of purée; set aside.
❧ Melt the butter in a large saucepan, add the onion, celery and garlic and cook gently for about 10 minutes. Add the flour and cook, stirring, for about 2 minutes, then whisk in the chicken stock. Bring just to a boil, stirring frequently, then

but not sticky. On a lightly floured surface, roll it as thick as a pie crust, about ⅛ in (3 mm), and cut into 4-in (10-cm) rounds. Continue rerolling and cutting the scraps until all the dough is used. You should have about 24 rounds. Set them aside on waxed (greaseproof) paper or a floured surface and cover loosely with plastic wrap.

To make the filling, melt the butter in a skillet over moderate heat, add the onion and garlic and cook gently for about 10 minutes. Scrape the vegetables into a bowl and return the pan to heat.

In the same pan, cook the meat until it loses its pinkness, breaking it up with a spatula as it cooks. With a slotted spoon, transfer to the bowl with the onion and add the gravy or cream, chili powder, cumin, parsley and salt and pepper to taste. The mixture should be moist, but not runny.

Heat the oven to 425°F (220°C).

Brush the edges of each circle of dough with water and place a heaping teaspoon of filling on one side. Fold the other side over and press firmly with the tines of a fork to seal. Prick the top of each turnover twice with fork.

Place on an ungreased baking sheet and bake for about 20 minutes, until lightly browned. Serve warm or at room temperature.

MAKES ABOUT 24 TURNOVERS

Los Angeles

GAZPACHO

Of Spanish heritage, this dish is really a salad in soup form. (According to James Beard, a recipe for "gaspacho" appeared under salads in Mary Randolph's book, The Virginia House-wife, *in 1836.) It depends on good ripe tomatoes, in season, and a cook patient about wielding a knife—the food processor tends to do a coarse, uneven job of chopping. It is good for a picnic or barbecue.*

3 lbs (1.5 kg) tomatoes
2 garlic cloves, minced (finely chopped)
2 English cucumbers, halved, seeded and diced
½ medium green bell pepper (capsicum), minced (finely chopped)
½ medium red bell pepper (capsicum), minced (finely chopped), or more green pepper
1 medium red (Spanish) onion, minced (finely chopped)
2 celery stalks, minced (finely chopped)
¼ cup (2 fl oz/60 ml) olive oil
¼ cup (2 fl oz/60 ml) red wine vinegar
2 cups (16 fl oz/500 ml), more or less, tomato juice
salt
freshly ground black pepper
hot red pepper (Tabasco) sauce

Peel the tomatoes and cut them in half horizontally. Working over a colander set in a large bowl, scoop out most of the seeds and juice from the insides. Discard the seeds, which will remain in the colander, but save the juice in the bowl. Finely chop the tomatoes and place them in the bowl with their juice.

Add the garlic and combine well, then stir in the cucumbers, peppers, onion and celery.

In another bowl, whisk the olive oil and vinegar together, then add 2 cups (16 fl oz/500 ml) of tomato juice. Add this mixture to the vegetables and stir to blend. If necessary, add more tomato juice to obtain the consistency of soup, not salad. Season with salt, pepper and pepper sauce to taste. Chill thoroughly before serving.

SERVES 12

Nachos (left), Gazpacho (center) and Empanadas (right)

Visalia
OLIVE-STUFFED DATES

Many good things may be tucked inside a bacon-wrapped date: green or ripe black olives, whole almonds, or the rosemary walnuts on page 202. The sweet and salty flavors are good together and satisfying with drinks. Soak the wooden toothpicks in water for an hour, and they will not burn in the oven.

6 thick slices of bacon
24 large, moist pitted dates
24 pitted green or ripe black olives

🐿 Heat the oven to 425°F (220°C).
🐿 Cut each slice of bacon in half crosswise and lengthwise. Make a slit in each date and insert an olive. Wrap in a piece of bacon and secure with a wooden toothpick.
🐿 Place on a rack set on a baking pan and bake for 12 to 15 minutes. Serve warm.

MAKES 24 MORSELS

Central Valley
SALTED NUTS

These nuts are simple and irresistible. They keep well, so while you are at it, make more than you need and keep them in a tightly covered jar.

2 tablespoons olive oil or walnut oil (see glossary)
2 cups (8 oz/250 g) walnut or pecan halves, or almonds, or a
   mixture of nuts
2 teaspoons coarse or kosher salt

🐿 Heat the oven to 350°F (180°C).
🐿 Pour the oil onto a baking sheet and set in the oven for a few minutes to heat. Add the nuts to the oil and toss to coat. Sprinkle with salt and return to the oven, tossing and stirring frequently, for 15 to 20 minutes, or until the nuts are a light brown. Watch them carefully and do not let them burn.

MAKES 2 CUPS (8 OZ/250 G)

Olive-stuffed Dates (top) and Salted Nuts (bottom)

Southern California
CAESAR SALAD

A classic salad that originated in Tijuana, Mexico, in the early twenties. Like many simple dishes, it depends on the quality of fresh ingredients. Use just the tender, small hearts of Romaine lettuce, with leaves up to 7 inches long, saving the outer leaves for another salad. The croutons should be homemade. Anchovy has crept in and out; the original salad contained none, though a little does seem to bring out the flavor.

CROUTONS

⅓ cup (3 fl oz/80 ml) olive oil
3 cups (5 oz/155 g) firm-textured French bread cubes
2 garlic cloves, minced (finely chopped)

Caesar Salad

SALAD

2 large or 4 small heads Romaine lettuce
2 eggs
6 tablespoons (3 fl oz/80 ml) olive oil
2 teaspoons mashed anchovy fillets
3 tablespoons, or more, lemon juice
salt
freshly ground black pepper
½ cup (2 oz/60 g) freshly grated Parmesan cheese

❧ To make the croutons, heat the olive oil in a skillet over moderate heat. Add the bread cubes and toss them about for several minutes, until they are golden on all sides. Add the minced garlic and a dash of salt and, off heat, toss for a minute or two more. Spread on absorbent paper towels to cool.

❧ Wash the lettuce leaves and dry them well. You will need 6 to 8 small leaves per person. They may either be left whole or torn into bite-sized pieces. Place them in a bowl and refrigerate.

❧ Boil the eggs for 1 minute. Stir the oil and anchovy together.

❧ To assemble the salad, pour the oil-and-anchovy mixture over the lettuce and toss to coat. Add 3 tablespoons of lemon juice, sprinkle with salt and pepper and toss again. Break in the eggs and toss until the egg disappears. Sprinkle with the cheese and croutons and toss again to combine.

❧ Taste and add more salt and pepper if necessary, or drops of lemon juice.

SERVES 4

41

Merced

PISTACHIO CHEESE WAFERS

Savory, crisp wafers that taste of butter and cheese, these, like ice-box cookies, are sliced and baked from a piece of refrigerated dough. Serve them with drinks, soups or salads. Freeze the dough if you plan to keep it for more than five days.

½ cup (4 oz/125 g) butter, at room temperature
2 cups (8 oz/250 g) grated Cheddar cheese
1 cup (4 oz/125 g) all-purpose (plain) flour
1 teaspoon salt
½ teaspoon freshly ground black pepper
¼ teaspoon cayenne pepper
1 cup (4 oz/125 g) coarsely chopped pistachio nuts

❧ In a food processor or with an electric mixer, beat together the butter and cheese. In a separate bowl combine the flour, salt and black and cayenne pepper. Add to the cheese mixture and beat until blended. Stir in the pistachios.
❧ Turn the dough onto a floured surface and divide it in half. Push and pat each piece into a fairly even log shape about 1 in (2.5 cm) across. Wrap in plastic wrap and chill until firm.
❧ Preheat the oven to 350°F (180°C) and set out ungreased cookie sheets.
❧ Cut the chilled dough into ¼-in (6-mm) slices and place them about 2 in (5 cm) apart on the baking sheets. Bake for about 10 to 12 minutes, until golden around the edges.
❧ Transfer to a rack to cool, then store airtight.

MAKES ABOUT 48 WAFERS

Santa Barbara

AVOCADO AND TOMATO SOUP

Anything flavored with bacon is wonderful with avocados—it brings out their flavor. This soup tastes especially fresh because, except for the onion, it is not cooked at all. Pistachio cheese wafers (see previous recipe) are delicious with this.

2 tablespoons olive oil
1 medium onion, minced (finely chopped)
3 medium avocados
2 cups (16 fl oz/500 ml), more or less, chicken stock
   (see glossary)
½ cup (4 fl oz/125 ml) heavy (double) cream
2 tomatoes, peeled, seeded and finely chopped
1 tablespoon lemon juice
1 teaspoon salt
¼ teaspoon freshly ground black pepper
sour cream or yogurt
6 slices of bacon, cooked crisp and crumbled

❧ Heat the oil in a small pan, add the onion and cook gently for about 5 minutes. Peel, pit and chop the avocados.
❧ Purée them in a food processor, then add 2 cups (16 fl oz/500 ml) of the stock and blend until smooth. Blend in the cream and the cooked onion.
❧ Transfer the mixture to a bowl and stir in the tomatoes and lemon juice. Season with salt and pepper.
❧ Chill thoroughly.
❧ If the soup seems too thick, thin it with a little more stock. Top each serving with a spoonful of sour cream or yogurt and sprinkle with bacon.

MAKES ABOUT 6 CUPS (48 FL OZ/1.5 L)

Los Angeles

COBB SALAD

This version of chef's salad was originally prepared by Bob Cobb, in 1936, at the Brown Derby Restaurant in Hollywood. It is a wonderful salad, but only as good as its ingredients, so it depends on the best—and some tender, loving care in the preparation. Do not regard it as a catchall for leftovers.

¾ cup (6 fl oz/180 ml) olive oil
3 tablespoons red wine vinegar
salt
freshly ground black pepper
6 cups (1 lb/500 g) chopped iceberg lettuce
2 cups (3 oz/90 g) chopped chicory (curly endive)
1 cup (4 oz/125 g) watercress sprigs
3 hard-boiled eggs, peeled and chopped
2 tablespoons chopped parsley or chives, or a mixture
3 large tomatoes, peeled, seeded and diced
2 cups (12 oz/375 g) finely diced cooked chicken breast
½ cup (4 oz/125 g) crumbled blue cheese
1 avocado, peeled and diced
8 slices of bacon, cooked and crumbled

❧ To make the dressing, combine the oil, vinegar, 1 teaspoon salt and ½ teaspoon pepper in a tightly capped jar. Shake vigorously until blended; set aside.
❧ In a large bowl toss together the lettuce, chicory and watercress sprigs; refrigerate while you continue. In a small bowl, toss the eggs with the parsley or chives, a sprinkling of salt and 2 tablespoons of dressing. In another bowl, toss the tomatoes with 2 tablespoons of dressing and season lightly with salt and pepper. In another bowl, toss the chicken with 2 tablespoons of dressing, seasoning it also with salt and pepper.
❧ Pour the remaining dressing over the greens and toss to combine. Season them with salt and pepper if necessary. Spread the greens in a shallow mound and arrange the eggs, tomato, chicken, cheese, avocado and bacon attractively on top. Take to the table and toss just before serving.

SERVES 8–10

Pistachio Cheese Wafers (left)
and Avocado and Tomato Soup (right)

Cobb Salad

Green Goddess Dressing (top left) and Palace Court Salad (center)

PALACE COURT SALAD

This, to my mind, is a simple and perfect salad—crabmeat in an artichoke bottom. Originally made at the Palace Hotel in San Francisco, its fresh ingredients offer an appealing contrast in texture, flavor and color. Like all dishes from famous places, it has spawned variations through the years, many of them far more complicated than the original. Though the following system for cooking the artichoke bottoms appears fussy, it does prevent them from darkening and should be done well in advance.

⅓ cup (1½ oz/45 g) all-purpose (plain) flour
6 cups (48 fl oz/1.5 l) water
¼ cup (2 fl oz/60 ml) lemon juice
1 teaspoon salt
4 large artichokes
½ lb (250 g) crabmeat
2 celery stalks, finely diced
2 tablespoons minced (finely chopped) onion
2 tablespoons chopped parsley
⅓ to ⅔ cup (about 4 fl oz/125 ml) mayonnaise
salt

freshly ground black pepper
4 cups (10 oz/315 g) shredded iceberg lettuce
2 large tomatoes, thickly sliced
2 hard-boiled egg yolks, finely chopped or grated
Green Goddess dressing or Louis dressing
  (see recipes, page 45 and 68)

❦ To cook the artichokes, place the flour in a large, nonaluminum saucepan. Slowly whisk in the water, then add the lemon juice and salt. Set over medium heat and bring to a boil, stirring frequently. Watch it carefully, and do not let it boil over. When the mixture boils, turn the heat to low.
❦ In the meantime, trim the artichokes: pull off the tough outer leaves, then with a small, sharp knife, cut away and discard the remaining inner leaves to expose the thistlelike choke in the center. Trim the artichoke bottoms so that they are reasonably neat and, as you are done, drop each one into the simmering liquid. Cover the pan partially and cook for about 35 to 45 minutes, or until the artichokes are tender when pierced.
❦ Let them cool for about an hour in the cooking liquid, then rinse them under cold water. Scrape out and discard the choke. Refrigerate the bottoms, covered, until you are ready to assemble the salad.

❧ Toss the crabmeat with the celery, onion and parsley, and fold in just enough mayonnaise to moisten, then season with salt and pepper to taste.

❧ Spread the iceberg lettuce on a platter, or divide it among four salad plates. Lay the tomato slices on the lettuce and set the artichoke bottoms on top of the tomatoes. Spoon the crab mixture into the artichoke bottoms and sprinkle with the egg yolk. Pass the dressing at the table.

SERVES 4

San Francisco
GREEN GODDESS DRESSING

There are many versions of this thick tarragon-flavored mixture, reputedly first served at the Palace Hotel in San Francisco and named in honor of George Arliss, when he was appearing in the play The Green Goddess. *Sharp and flavorful, it is good on sturdy greens, such as Romaine, chicory and iceberg lettuce.*

3 anchovy fillets, mashed
1 small green (spring) onion, finely chopped
2 tablespoons chopped parsley
1 tablespoon chopped fresh tarragon or 1 teaspoon
    dried tarragon
1 cup (8 fl oz/250 ml) mayonnaise
2 tablespoons white wine vinegar
2 tablespoons chopped chives
salt
freshly ground black pepper

❧ Place the anchovy and onion in a small bowl and mash them together with the back of a spoon. Add the parsley and tarragon and blend well. Stir in the mayonnaise. Add the vinegar and chives and season with salt and pepper to taste. If the dressing is not acid enough, add a little more vinegar.

❧ Chill thoroughly before using.

MAKES ABOUT 1½ CUPS (12 FL OZ/375 ML)

San Francisco
CHICKEN AND WATERCRESS SOUP

Chinese cooks have a wonderful ability with food—they seem able to extract so much flavor from a few simple ingredients. This soup displays the same quality: it is much more than the sum of its parts. Whenever I make it, I'm impressed by how good it is. With a strong, homemade stock to flavor the soup, you could even omit the diced chicken.

6 cups (48 fl oz/1.5 l) chicken stock (see glossary)
4 large green (spring) onions, thinly sliced
2 eggs
1½ teaspoons soy sauce
2 cups (½ lb/250 g) watercress leaves
½ cup (3 oz/90 g) finely diced cooked chicken
salt
freshly ground black pepper
a handful of fresh cilantro (coriander/Chinese parsley)
    leaves (optional)

❧ Bring the stock to a boil, add the green onion and cook for 3 minutes. Beat the eggs with the soy sauce just until combined, and slowly pour the mixture into the boiling stock, stirring gently, so the egg sets in long threads. Stir in the

watercress leaves, and chicken if you wish. Season with salt and pepper to taste. Sprinkle with cilantro, if desired, and serve immediately.

SERVES 4   *Photograph pages 30–31*

Monterey
CRAB AND AVOCADO SALAD

Fresh crabmeat is delicate and expensive, so flavor it simply and don't overload it. With avocado and good mayonnaise, this combination makes a pleasant and rich first course for a special dinner.

1 lb (500 g) crabmeat
2 tablespoons lemon juice
¼ cup (½ oz/15 g) chopped parsley
½ cup (4 fl oz/125 ml) mayonnaise
salt
freshly ground black pepper or a pinch of cayenne pepper
2 large avocados
iceberg lettuce leaves
lemon wedges

❧ Pick over the crabmeat and remove any bits of shell or cartilage; no matter how carefully it was shelled, there is always some.

❧ Place in a bowl and toss with the lemon juice and 2 tablespoons of the parsley. Add the mayonnaise and toss gently to moisten the crab. Season with salt and black or cayenne pepper to taste; set aside.

❧ Halve, pit and peel the avocados. Dice neatly and add them to the crab mixture. Toss gently to combine, then mound on the lettuce leaves. Sprinkle with the remaining parsley and garnish with lemon wedges.

SERVES 6

Crab and Avocado Salad

San Francisco
CELERY VICTOR

Marinated celery salad served in this style, with a garnish of egg and tomato, was made well known by Victor Hirtzler, who was the chef at the St. Francis Hotel in San Francisco from 1904 to 1926. It is still served there today. Make it with the tender, inner heart of celery; the outside stalks are too tough.

4 heads celery
4 cups (32 fl oz/1 l) chicken stock (see glossary)
1 carrot, sliced
1 onion, quartered
6 parsley sprigs
1 bay leaf
½ cup (4 fl oz/125 ml) olive oil
3 tablespoons red wine vinegar
½ teaspoon salt
¼ teaspoon freshly ground black pepper
4 hard-boiled eggs, peeled
2 large tomatoes
anchovy fillets (optional)
2 tablespoons chopped parsley

❧ Pull off the tough outer stalks of each head of celery and set aside for another use. Neatly trim the root ends and cut off the tops, making each head about 5 in (13 cm) long. Cut in half lengthwise; set aside.
❧ In a large skillet or a Dutch oven, bring the stock to a boil with the carrot, onion, parsley sprigs and bay leaf. Cover and simmer for 5 minutes. Add the celery, placing it flat, then cover and simmer gently for about 15 to 20 minutes, until tender but not mushy. Remove from the heat and let sit, uncovered, until cool.
❧ To make the dressing, shake together the oil, vinegar and salt and pepper in a tightly capped jar.
❧ Remove the celery from the poaching liquid and drain it well. Arrange on a large serving platter. Pour the dressing over and chill for several hours, spooning the dressing over the celery occasionally.
❧ Slice the eggs and cut each tomato into 8 wedges; you will need a total of 16 nice pieces of each. Arrange 2 overlapping

Celery Victor (top) and Monte Cristo Sandwich (bottom)

slices of egg on each piece of celery and rim the platter with tomato wedges. Place an anchovy fillet over the eggs. Spoon the dressing over once again and sprinkle with parsley.

SERVES 8

San Francisco
MONTE CRISTO SANDWICH

Quite popular in the fifties, a Monte Cristo is one of those things that fell between the cracks and is rarely seen anymore. Made with good chicken and cheese on firm white bread, it is a wonderful indulgence. Though it is not actually an appetizer, the hot, lofty sandwich may be cut into pieces and served with drinks.

1 egg
½ cup (4 fl oz/125 ml) milk
salt
3 slices firm-textured white bread
softened butter
4 slices (2–3 oz/60–90 g) cooked sliced chicken breast
4 thin slices (about 2 oz/60 g) sliced Swiss (Gruyère) cheese
3 tablespoons butter

❧ In a shallow dish beat together the egg, milk and ¼ teaspoon salt; set aside.
❧ Spread each slice of bread generously on one side with softened butter and sprinkle lightly with salt. Top one slice, buttered-side up, with half the chicken and half the cheese. Top with another slice of bread and lay the remaining chicken and cheese on that. Cover with the last piece of bread, buttered-side down.
❧ Dip the sandwich in the milk-and-egg mixture, letting it sit for a moment to absorb the liquid. Heat the 3 tablespoons butter in a skillet over moderate heat. When it is melted add the sandwich and cook for about 5 minutes, until golden, gently pressing down with a spatula once or twice and turning 3 or 4 times.

MAKES 1 SANDWICH

Santa Rosa
GOAT CHEESE, OLIVE AND TOMATO SALAD

California goat cheeses come in many shapes, sizes and textures, some plain, others with herb coatings. For this recipe you will need one that is plain and fairly soft; the shape is not important. This recipe is unusual because the cheese is not simply placed on the salad, but is blended with olive oil and vinegar to make a creamy dressing.

2 oz (60 g) goat cheese, at room temperature
2 tablespoons white wine vinegar
2 tablespoons olive oil
1 tablespoon chopped fresh tarragon
salt
freshly ground black pepper
4 large tomatoes, sliced
½ cup (2 oz/60 g) sliced ripe black olives
1 tablespoon chopped parsley or additional chopped tarragon

❧ Place the cheese in a bowl and mash it with the vinegar until smooth. Whisk in the oil, then the tarragon and season with salt and pepper to taste.
❧ Arrange the sliced tomatoes on a platter and sprinkle with salt and pepper. Spoon the dressing over them and sprinkle with the olives and parsley or tarragon.

SERVES 4–6

Goat Cheese, Olive and Tomato Salad

*Cream of Olive Soup, garnished with chopped tomatoes and green onions (top),
and Fried Clam Toasts (bottom)*

Pismo Beach

FRIED CLAM TOASTS

*Unassuming seaside diners on both coasts often list clam toasts (or
clamburgers) among their offerings. They may also be made with
shrimp. These have a lightness not usually associated with fried
foods and are so puffy and appealing that most people can't stop
eating them. Serve them with cocktails or as a first course, with
lemon wedges and tartar sauce.*

½ cup (4 oz/125 g) cream cheese, at room temperature
1 garlic clove, minced (finely chopped)
1 egg, separated
1 can (6½ oz/180 g) minced (finely chopped) clams, drained
  (reserve the juice)
2 tablespoons reserved clam juice
¼ cup (2 oz/60 g) all-purpose (plain) flour
½ teaspoon salt
½ teaspoon freshly ground black pepper
strips of French bread or sandwich bread, about 1 in
  (2.5 cm) wide and ½ in (12 mm) thick
oil for frying

🦪 In a bowl beat together the cream cheese, garlic, egg yolk
and clams. Beat in the clam juice, then the flour, salt and pepper.
In a separate bowl beat the egg white until stiff, then fold it into
the cream cheese mixture.
🦪 Top each strip of bread with a thin coating of the clam
mixture, mounding it in the center. Set aside for about 1 hour
before frying.
🦪 Heat about 1½ in (4 cm) of oil to 375°F (190°C) in a skillet.
Fry a few strips at a time, clam-side down until golden, then
turn and fry the second side. Drain on absorbent paper towels
and serve hot.

SERVES 6–8

San Joaquin Valley
TOMATO ASPIC

An old-fashioned tomato aspic, topped with a spoonful of mayonnaise and a few cooked shrimp, makes a good first course. It is also a good buffet dish, to accompany cold poached salmon or chicken.

⅓ cup (3 fl oz/80 ml) dry sherry
2 envelopes (½ oz/15 g) unflavored gelatin, about 2 scant tablespoons
4 cups (32 fl oz/1 l) tomato juice
5 parsley sprigs
1 onion, thinly sliced
1 celery stalk, thinly sliced
1 teaspoon sugar
½ teaspoon salt
½ teaspoon freshly ground black pepper
6 whole cloves
¼ cup (2 fl oz/60 ml) lemon juice
2 tablespoons chopped parsley
additional parsley sprigs for garnish

❧ Stir the sherry and gelatin together in a small bowl and let the mixture stand a few minutes to soften the gelatin.

❧ Meanwhile, combine the tomato juice, 5 parsley sprigs, onion, celery, sugar, salt, pepper and cloves in a saucepan. Bring the mixture to a simmer, then cover and cook over low heat for 5 minutes. Remove from the heat and let stand for about 10 minutes more.

❧ Strain, pressing on the vegetables to extract all of the juice. Discard the vegetables and return the liquid to the pan. Add the softened gelatin, return to moderate heat, and stir for about 5 minutes without boiling, just until gelatin has dissolved. Remove from the heat, stir in the lemon juice, pour into a 4-cup (32-fl oz/1-l) mold or bowl and chill for several hours, until set. To turn out, dip the base of the mold into hot water for about 5 seconds, then invert it over a chilled platter, giving a sharp downward jerk; the aspic will fall into place. Sprinkle the top with parsley and surround with additional parsley sprigs.

SERVES 4–6

Visalia
CREAM OF OLIVE SOUP

Olives come in many styles in California, and we tend to be preoccupied with the fancy cured ones, forgetting how useful—and good—plain ripe black olives are. Chopped, they make a fine soup that will surprise you not only with its taste, but also with its simplicity. It has a smoky flavor and is not, as you might think, too salty.

3 tablespoons butter
3 tablespoons all-purpose (plain) flour
4 cups (32 fl oz/1 l) chicken stock (see glossary)
freshly ground black pepper
1 cup (4¼ oz/130 g) minced (finely chopped) ripe black olives, drained
1 cup (8 fl oz/250 ml) heavy (double) cream
salt, if needed
¼ cup (2 fl oz/60 ml) sherry
1 large green (spring) onion, minced (finely chopped)

❧ Melt the butter in a large saucepan, blend in the flour and cook over moderate heat, stirring, for about 2 minutes. Whisk in the stock, bring to a simmer and season generously with pepper. Stir in the olives and cream and bring the mixture back to a simmer. Taste, and add salt if necessary. Stir in the sherry and green onion and serve.

SERVES 4

Tomato Aspic

Fresno

PIROSHKI

Meat-filled turnovers of Russian heritage, these are usually flavored with sour cream and dill and are often sold as take-out food. As with empanadas, *you may vary the ingredients according to what you have on hand.*

1 recipe *empanada* dough (see page 38)
2 tablespoons butter
1 medium onion, chopped
⅓ lb (5 oz/155 g) ground (minced) beef or cooked,
    flaked fish
1 hard-boiled egg, chopped
2 tablespoons chopped fresh dill
½ cup (4 fl oz/125 ml) sour cream
salt
freshly ground black pepper

❧ Make the dough as directed in the recipe for *empanadas*. Roll it out on a floured surface and cut it into 3½-in (9-cm) rounds. Continue rerolling and cutting scraps until all the dough is used. Set the rounds aside; you will need 24.

❧ To make the filling, melt the butter in a skillet. Add the onion and cook gently for about 5 minutes. Scrape into a bowl.

❧ If you are using ground beef, return the pan to the heat and cook the meat until it loses its pinkness, breaking it up with a spatula as it cooks. Then, with a slotted spoon, transfer it to the bowl containing the onion. If you are using flaked fish, simply add it to the onion.

❧ Add the egg, dill and sour cream and toss gently to combine. Season with salt and pepper to taste. The mixture should be moist, but not runny.

❧ Heat the oven to 425°F (220°C). Brush the edges of each circle of dough with water and place a heaping teaspoon of filling on one side. Fold the other side over and press firmly with the tines of a fork to seal. Prick the top of each turnover twice with a fork. Place on an ungreased baking sheet and bake for about 20 minutes, until golden. Serve warm or at room temperature.

MAKES ABOUT 24 TURNOVERS

Gilroy

PARSLEY SALAD

Parsley salad has been around a long time, though you do not see it too often. Its freshness and flavor give it an affinity for fish stews, such as cioppino *(see recipe on page 68). Unlike any other salad, it feels like soft fluffy brushes in your mouth. You may, if you wish, combine curly leaf with some flat-leaf (Italian) parsley for a salad that is less "bushy."*

1 large garlic clove
⅓ cup (3 fl oz/80 ml) olive oil
2 tablespoons red wine vinegar
salt
freshly ground black pepper
4 cups (8 oz/250 g) parsley sprigs, with stems removed
⅓ to ½ cup (about 2 oz/60 g) freshly grated Parmesan cheese

❧ Combine the garlic and oil in a blender or food processor and blend until the garlic is chopped. Or mince the garlic by hand, then whisk in the oil. Blend in the vinegar and season with salt and pepper to taste. Pour the dressing over the parsley in a large bowl and toss to combine. Sprinkle with the cheese and toss again.

❧ This salad keeps, refrigerated, for a few hours, especially if you have used only curly leaf parsley.

SERVES 4

*Parsley Salad (top)
and Piroshki (bottom)*

Sacramento

ALMOND SOUP

Smooth, creamy and subtle, this soup may also be served with a handful of chopped mushrooms cooked in a little butter. Blanched almonds have the skins removed. You may purchase them this way, or do it yourself by covering them with water and bringing them to a boil. Drain well and cool for a minute, then rub off the skins between clean towels.

2 cups (10 oz/315 g) blanched, toasted almonds
4 cups (32 fl oz/1 l) chicken stock (see glossary)
1 onion, chopped
salt
freshly ground black pepper
2 tablespoons all-purpose (plain) flour
2 tablespoons butter, softened
1 cup (8 fl oz/250 ml) heavy (double) cream
2 tablespoons dry sherry
chopped chives

Pulverize the almonds in a blender or food processor. Place in a saucepan with the stock and onion, season lightly with salt and pepper, then cover and simmer for 20 minutes.

Pour the soup through a fine strainer to remove most of the onion and almond bits, pressing firmly on them to extract all the flavor you can. Return the strained soup to the pan and stir about ½ cup (2 oz/60 g) of the strained almonds back into it.

Blend the flour and butter together until smooth. Bring the soup back to a simmer and whisk in the flour-and-butter mixture. Bring just to a boil, stirring frequently, and cook until the flour has disappeared and the soup has thickened slightly. Stir in the cream and sherry and season with additional salt and pepper if necessary. Sprinkle each serving with chopped chives.

MAKES ABOUT 4 CUPS (32 FL OZ/1 L)

California

STRAWBERRY AND PEACH SOUP

Using the following recipe, you can make soup from any ripe sweet fruit. This one is slightly sweet and creamy, with a good berry flavor, and is refreshing on a hot day. Passed around in mugs, it may be sipped before you sit down at the table.

4 cups (about 2 baskets; ¾ lb/375 g) hulled (stemmed), sliced
    strawberries
¼ cup (2 oz/60 g) sugar
pinch of salt
2 tablespoons lemon juice
½ cup (4 fl oz/125 ml) yogurt
½ cup (4 fl oz/125 ml) heavy (double) cream
1½ cups (12 fl oz/375 ml) cold weak tea or water
½ cup (4 fl oz/125 ml) dry white wine
2 large peaches, peeled, pitted and finely diced

Place the strawberries in a food processor and purée until smooth, or purée them through the finest disk of a food mill. Transfer to a bowl, add the sugar, salt and lemon juice, then whisk in the yogurt, cream, tea and wine. Taste, and add more sugar if necessary, but do not make it too sweet—it should taste fresh. Stir in the peaches and chill thoroughly before serving.

MAKES ABOUT 6 CUPS (48 FL OZ/1.5 L)

Almond Soup

Strawberry and Peach Soup

THE INLAND EMPIRE AND DESERTS

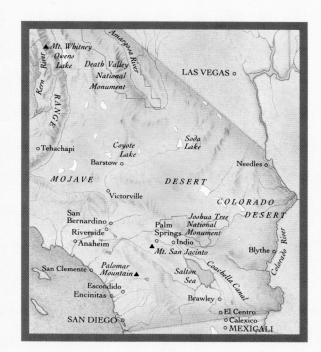

THE INLAND EMPIRE AND DESERTS

It has been said that California invented itself through water. In this region of man-made oases and wonders of irrigation, that is exactly what it did. Here, a land of milk and honey sits at the edge of the stark desert. The abrupt change in scenery unfolds south of the Central Valley, where the Tehachapi and Inyo mountains form a natural division between central and southern California. It runs along half of the Nevada border, all the way south to Arizona and Baja California. The spiny Joshua trees of the Mojave and the shifting dunes of Death Valley form the high desert in the north. The Salton Sink, a region that includes the lush Coachella and Imperial valleys, forms the lower southern Colorado Desert, where a bounty of crops grows on millions of acres of irrigated land, much of it below sea level. East of Los Angeles, just over the Santa Ana Mountains, the indentation of agricultural and recreational areas is known as the Inland Empire. It includes the cities of Riverside and San Bernardino (legendary sources of California oranges), and the mountain resorts of Big Bear and Arrowhead. Eleven wineries in nearby Temecula Valley produce a range of varietals in microclimates where cool Pacific breezes blow across the sundrenched hillsides.

Previous pages: Joshua Tree National Monument is a vast unspoiled wilderness of eerie geological formations and granite monoliths.
Left: Dates thrive in desert regions such as the Coachella Valley, where the arid climate mimics that of their Middle Eastern origins.

The Inland Empire and deserts epitomize California's climatic contrasts. Visit Palm Springs in February and you might enjoy a fresh-picked grapefruit and scones with local wildflower honey for breakfast. You could play a round of golf and then, later that same day, ride a nearby tramway straight up a mountainside to the San Jacinto wilderness, for an afternoon of skiing at 8,500 feet.

DEATH VALLEY TO DATE PALMS

Death Valley National Monument, on the state's eastern border, is the very opposite of the Inland Empire. An awe-inspiring geological wonder, it radiates magical visual effects, as the clear light accentuates dramatic points and curves. Everywhere, colors and light dance off rock formations or swirling sands. Places with names such as Artist's Palette, Dante's View and Golden Canyon con-

Joshua trees, wild relatives of the lily, are thought to have been named by Mormon pioneers who were reminded of the biblical Joshua raising his arms in prayer.

vey part of the scenic story. In some areas, only creosote bush and a few invincible desert plants can survive. In higher elevations, gnarled bristlecone pines jut from mountainsides. Deserted mining towns and ghost towns with names like Skidoo and Cold Beef Mine are sprinkled throughout. (Historians say that Cold Beef was intended to be Gold Reef, but poor penmanship perpetuated the former.) This is a hostile area, too, with summer temperatures soaring to 130 degrees Fahrenheit and bitter cold temperatures that plunge below freezing. Of course it is one of the very few areas in California without claim to some magnificent crop or culinary contribution. Only half a million people live in the entire desert area, as much of it is public land.

Here, and in the lower desert, palm and cactus fruits, *piñon* nuts, acorns, jackrabbits and other small game fed early desert Indian tribes. Along the lower Colorado River some of them caught fish with hooks made from cactus spines. But all in all, food resources were meager. Basic foods (or less) were the rule in the numerous old mining camps. Today, restaurants in Death Valley tend to serve solid, all-American food—steak, chops and fried trout. Most campers keep things as simple as possible—barbecues for hamburgers and chicken and *lots* of beer and soda in big coolers.

But as the crow flies, about 150 miles southwest of Death Valley, a miragelike oasis turns all preconceived notions of the desert upside down. In Indio, a small desert town in the Coachella Valley, just outside Palm Springs, lush groves of date palms grow "feet in the water, heads in the sun." Here, roadside stands sell rich date shakes, made with lots of vanilla ice cream. Cooks are well versed in the arts of date breads and muffins, date stuffings, fruit compotes and chutneys—as many variations as an active culinary imagination can conjure.

The exotic-looking date palms grow in harems—one male to fifty females—all of which must be hand pollinated. The most prolific variety is the familiar Deglet Noor, but Indio also grows huge Medjool dates, dark and soft, and Halawy, Zahidi and Khadrawy varieties. When the date harvest is in, the town holds a ten-day festival, complete with scenes from the Arabian Nights and an ancient market in Baghdad. And, as is traditional in agricultural communities everywhere, they crown a beauty queen to reign over the harvest.

The United States Department of Agriculture was responsible for bringing some of the best date varieties to America in 1890. The Coachella Valley was deemed the right spot because of its favorable soil and dry, warm climate. Today, the area produces ninety-five percent of the dates grown in the United States.

At one time, the Coachella and Imperial valleys formed a continuous plot of land that turned out to be ideal for growing produce once irrigation proved its value in 1901. In 1905, a monumental flood on the Colorado River left the briny, landlocked Salton Sea in its wake, separating the two valleys. Today, the Imperial Valley is the largest irrigated district in the Western hemisphere. With two complete growing seasons, it has turned out to be one of the most fertile farming regions in the world. From this land, America reaps a constant supply of tender asparagus and sweet carrots, broccoli, citrus, grapes, berries, beans, lettuce, tomatoes, melons, onions, dates and figs.

Imperial County is also one of the state's leading honey-producing areas. Because California farmers rely on millions of honey bees to pollinate crops from almonds and prunes to kiwifruit and Chinese cabbage,

The wonders of irrigation have sprouted golf courses throughout the great agricultural empire of the inland valleys. There are nearly forty courses in the Palm Springs area alone.

honey from the registered bee colonies is a natural asset. It comes in as many flavors as there are blossoms. Some are perfumed with the heady scent of oranges, others with the spiciness of wildflowers, sage, buckwheat or alfalfa—in varying degrees of intensity. Generally, the lighter the color the more delicate the flavor. Californians stir their honey in tea, drizzle it over sourdough pancakes and waffles, shake it in salad dressings and stir it in barbecue glazes. Often, in the early 1900s, strained honey was offered on menus with desserts of raisins and almonds, but is rarely seen in that simple form today.

The desert resort areas of Palm Springs, Palm Desert, La Quinta and other elaborate oases may not produce any significant crops of their own, but they simmer with good food that makes the heat bearable. Backyard chefs and sophisticated restaurateurs here often redefine European cooking styles, taking advantage of the California setting. In the irrigated desert, that might result in a honey-sweet melon sorbet, venison or quail roasted with fresh herbs, filet mignon atop an artichoke bottom, or grilled seafood with fruit *salsa*. Asparagus is often blanched, then sprinkled with an herb vinaigrette and served chilled. Salads piled high with shrimp, crab and scallops are everywhere—beside the pool and in the middle of the golf course, where rest stops are set up under canopies with outdoor air-conditioning systems.

AN ORANGE DINNER IN RIVERSIDE

Once the railroads made southern California accessible in the late 1800s, American visitors poured into the area, lured by comparisons with the Mediterranean. Some embraced the excitement of new culinary experiences. Authentic Mexican foods and oranges straight from the tree gave life to their fantasies about this place called California. Others were simply bothered by the lack of bland foods, and very few knew what to make of the Chinese way of cooking. Many visitors stayed, however, injecting their East Coast sensibilities with recipes for plum puddings and Yankee biscuits and gravy.

It was definitely a time of culinary stirring, as California was developing its own multifaceted personality. Capitalizing on the juicy symbol of the California Dream, railroad promoters invited a group of hotel executives to visit the Inland Empire city of Riverside—the "Mother Orange Colony" of California—in 1896. They promised them "a drive down the ever-famous Magnolia Avenue, where for eight miles a delightful and bewildering succession of exquisite gardens, fertile olive and orange orchards . . . meets the eye." The air, they claimed, was scented with orange blossoms, balmy breezes would caress them, the wonder of it all would make them swoon. By all accounts of this particular trip, the promoters were not exaggerating. As promised, fragrant blossoms, fertile orchards of olive trees, luscious, ripe figs and the delight of "open air barbecue" greeted the travelers, and they explored as eagerly as though they had encountered an exotic foreign land. The visitors were also pleasantly surprised at the sophistication of Riverside's early resorts and hotels.

The California cook's predilection for experimenting with the local bounty began early, as one tourist recorded on that visit. His group was served an Orange Dinner at the Casa Loma Hotel in San Bernardino, where "the shape, color and fragrance of oranges were constantly being experienced when least expected. Tiny orange biscuits were used instead of crackers, orange cider drank and orange-shaped cakes eaten . . . orange-colored this, orange-flavored that."

FISH AND SHELLFISH

A lone fishing boat trolls off the coast near Santa Cruz. Codfish along the shore and tuna further out are the main catches.

FISH AND SHELLFISH

If all the inlets, coves and bays along the winding California coastline were unraveled, they would stretch out about twelve hundred miles—quite a kettle of *cioppino*.

In fact, California is home to a comprehensive alphabet of seafood, from abalone, crab and *calamari* to salmon, sole and hundreds of other species reeled in by commercial fishing fleets up and down the coast. Inland, rivers and streams are rich with delicacies such as the fine golden trout found in the cold waters of the High Sierra. Local fish farms produce an abundance of magnificent oysters, mussels, abalone, trout, catfish, even the exotic African tilapia (bream).

Going to the fish market in California can be as overwhelming an experience as wandering the produce stalls of a farmers' market. But most of the same rules apply. Fresh is best, and the sooner it is prepared and enjoyed, the better. Your senses will guide you, as you touch to find fish that is firm, sniff for a briny or fresh aroma, look for clear eyes and bright gills and skin.

Wherever you go in California, some succulent fresh fish or shellfish will be available at any time of year. In fact it is hard to imagine a time when seafood was not prevalent in California kitchens. When early Indians and pioneers dipped their baskets and nets in bays and streams, or their cactus-needle hooks in the Colorado River, they were fishing for survival rather than for the sheer delight of fresh-caught fish. Even so, it is difficult to imagine the northern coastal Indians feeling anything but pure contentment as they cooked rich, tender salmon over an open fire under the stars. They butterflied the whole fish and skewered it on alderwood, a method *Sunset* magazine introduced to its West Coast readers in 1933.

Local seafood was not really appreciated by the newcomers until the mid- to late 1800s. Before then, Californians were meat eaters—chiefly because beef, mutton and game were so easily accessible. But when gold-rush-weary Chinese found their way to the central coast, they quickly made the best of the fruits of the sea—though most of the fish was preserved rather than cooked fresh. As the locals did not yet appreciate the delicate abalone meat the Chinese pulled from Monterey Bay (though it was appreciated at the lumber camps on the far north coast), most of it was cubed or minced, canned and exported to the Orient. A side trade also developed for abalone shells on the Atlantic coast, where, it was said, "No mantel was complete without a souvenir of fabled California in the form of a polished abalone shell."

After the mid-1800s, Italians, Portuguese, Spanish, Scandinavians, Russians and Americans all fished the coast and streams and contributed hundreds of recipes to California's fish kettle. But if any one seafood meal might be called traditional, at least in northern California, it would be one based on fresh Dungeness crab. From October to May, fishermen catch these sweet, pink-orange crustaceans along the coast from Santa Barbara north. Though fresh crab in a spicy Chinese black bean sauce is enough to make one weak with pleasure, the simplest way to enjoy Dungeness crab is really one of the best. It should be cooked, live if possible, then cleaned, cracked and presented on a platter with mayonnaise or melted butter and lemon wedges.

At the old-time fish grills in San Francisco, mahogany counters, brass rails and white tablecloths set the stage for more of the straightforward, uncomplicated seafood

Previous pages: Cioppino (recipe page 68)

preparations so characteristic of California. A couple of these grills have been serving locals since the gold rush days, when the Yugoslavian owners were the first Californians to cook fish over mesquite charcoal.

Salmon, red snapper, trout and fresh albacore are served moist and tender, with a simple herb butter or light sauce, all around the state. Other local favorites include delicate petrale sole, lightly sautéed in butter and served with a squeeze of fresh lemon and a grind of pepper. Sand dabs, small and sweet, are frequently served in the same way. You will also find seafood *enchiladas*, whole fish steamed with ginger and cilantro, sweet and sour deep-fried rock cod, spicy *seviche*, and *calamari* in coconut milk sauce. Fish may be one of the most international and versatile of all California foods.

FISH TALES

Cioppino is a universal favorite, traditionally served with a bib and plenty of chewy bread. Attributed to Italian and Portuguese fishermen with their Mediterranean roots, and memories of *bouillabaisse* in their heads, it is simply a hearty seafood stew in a tomato-flavored broth, made with the catch of the day. As to the name, some say it meant "chopped fine" in one Italian dialect. Or maybe it came from the request to "Chip in! Chip in!" as cooks with big buckets made the rounds of the local fishing boats when they arrived in the bay.

Around San Francisco, oysters have generated pages of local food lore—told and re-told on menus and in history books. Rarely do the stories match. Hangtown fry, a sort of omelet, and oyster loaf, a sandwich, were both supposedly hatched during the rough-and-tumble gold rush days in the late 1840s. One version of Hangtown fry comes from the Mother Lode town of Hangtown (later changed to Placerville) where, the story goes, a rascal was about to be hanged for some unnamed deed, but first he was allowed to order up one last meal. He requested fresh oysters—to be "fried, with scrambled eggs on top and bacon on the side." He supposedly slithered away while the cooks went searching for fresh oysters. Other, more likely versions attribute it to a restaurant cook with a good idea.

Mussels, which are farmed commercially in California, tempt buyers at Phil's Fish Market on the wharf at Moss Landing, north of Monterey.

A fly fisherman wades in the springtime waters of the Truckee River, in quest of the evasive brown trout. Like many Sierra Nevada streams, the Truckee is popular with trout fishermen from far and wide.

One look at the menus of the day, and it is easy to see why oysters generated so much print. Californians ate them by the score, in every conceivable way. First they consumed Eastern oysters, then later raised their own. Writing of the famed banquets at San Francisco's Palace Hotel in the late 1800s, the hotel chef said, "The small native California oyster (Olympia), with its characteristic faintly coppery taste, became a favorite of gourmands who first encountered it in Palace cocktails or omelets." Today, locally raised oysters still rank as a favorite, and one of the best ways to enjoy them is barbecued, preferably at one of the funky little restaurants or stands around Tomales Bay and Drake's Estero, on the northern coast. Then again, if you are an oyster lover, it's hard to beat a freshly shucked Hog Island, kissed with lemon or *mignonette* sauce and slipped directly from shell to mouth.

Whatever their preferences, once Californians discovered the treasures of fish and shellfish swimming all around them, they dipped right in. Fish inspired cooks of every persuasion to sharpen their knives, fire up their woks, light the grills, set pots to boiling and skillets to sizzling—and they have not stopped since.

Central Coast

SHRIMP TEMPURA

It is hard to find someone who does not like shrimp. They are particularly good batter-dipped and fried, their succulence sealed in with a light, crisp crust. As Helen Evans Brown described it, tempura is a Japanese version of the Italian fritto misto—a meal based on fried dishes. For a party, have two kettles of oil on the stove, one for vegetables tempura (see recipe on page 174), and another for the shrimp—and be prepared to fry while your guests eat. Salmon, snapper and cod also work well.

BATTER

1¼ cups (10 fl oz/300 ml) ice water
1 egg
2 tablespoons soy sauce
1 cup (4 oz/125 g) cake (soft-wheat) flour (see glossary)
¼ teaspoon salt
¼ teaspoon baking soda (bicarbonate of soda)

DIPPING SAUCE

⅔ cup (5 fl oz/160 ml) bottled clam juice or fish stock
   (see glossary)
¼ cup (2 fl oz/60 ml) soy sauce
¼ cup (2 fl oz/ 60 ml) dry sherry
2 tablespoons grated fresh ginger
1 tablespoon sugar

1½ lb (750 g) large shrimp (green prawns), shelled and deveined
oil for frying

🦐 To make the batter, beat together the water, egg and soy sauce. Combine the flour, salt and baking soda and add to the water mixture. Stir until barely blended; the batter should remain lumpy, with some streaks of unblended flour; set aside.

🦐 To make the dipping sauce, stir together the clam juice, soy sauce, sherry, ginger and sugar; set aside.

🦐 Pat the shrimp dry with absorbent paper towels. Heat about 2 in (5 cm) of oil in a deep kettle or Dutch oven to 360°F (185°C). A few at a time, dip the shrimp into the batter and gently slip them into the hot oil. Fry for 2 or 3 minutes, turning once or twice, until they are golden and puffy. Drain briefly on absorbent paper towels and continue frying the remaining shrimp the same way. Serve with the dipping sauce.

SERVES 6

Shrimp Tempura (top) and Teriyaki Shrimp (bottom)

ALLEN V. LOTT

Central Coast

PRAWNS AND POLENTA

This recipe is from a good cook in Cloverdale, California. Though the dish is quite substantial, it gives the illusion of being light because of its delicate taste. Flavorful prawns and creamy polenta make a stellar partnership.

3 cups (24 fl oz/750 ml) water
salt
¾ cup (3 oz/90 g) *polenta* (cornmeal/yellow maize flour)
   (see glossary)
4 tablespoons (2 oz/60 g) butter
½ cup (4 fl oz/125 ml), or more, milk or cream
12 large or jumbo shrimp (king prawns), shelled and
   deveined
2 tablespoons olive oil or vegetable oil
freshly ground black pepper
½ cup (4 fl oz/125 ml) dry white wine
2 tablespoons softened butter
2 tablespoons chopped fresh dill, tarragon, or parsley

🦐 Bring the water to a boil in a heavy saucepan with 1½ teaspoons salt. Slowly pour in the *polenta*, constantly whisking briskly so it does not form lumps. Cook over low heat, stirring frequently, for 5 to 10 minutes, until thick. Continue to cook over the lowest heat for about 10 minutes longer, stirring occasionally. Then stir in the butter and ½ cup (4 fl oz/ 125 ml) of milk or cream; it should have the consistency of hot cereal. If it is too thick, stir in more milk or cream—or even some water if you wish. Keep warm over the lowest heat while you cook the prawns.

🦐 Pat the prawns dry with paper towels. Heat the oil in a skillet until very hot. Add the prawns and cook over high heat for 2 to 3 minutes, turning and tossing almost constantly. Season with salt and pepper. Pour in the wine and boil rapidly until it is reduced to about 2 tablespoons. Add the butter, swirling the pan until it melts, then sprinkle on the herbs. Pour the *polenta* into the middle of a hot platter, arrange the prawns around it and pour the sauce over.

SERVES 4

San Francisco

TERIYAKI SHRIMP

Equally successful cooked under the broiler or over hot coals, these shrimp may be served on a bed of rice for lunch or dinner, or as an appetizer or hors d'oeuvre, with toothpicks for spearing. Marinating in a plastic bag keeps all of the shrimp submerged in the marinade and eliminates the need to turn them.

⅓ cup (3 fl oz/80 ml) soy sauce
2 tablespoons dry sherry
1 garlic clove, minced (finely chopped)
1 tablespoon grated fresh ginger
1 teaspoon sugar
16 large shrimp (green prawns), shelled and deveined

🦐 Combine the soy sauce, sherry, garlic, ginger and sugar. Place the shrimp in a plastic food-storage bag, pour in the soy sauce mixture, press out most of the air and seal the bag. Rub gently to distribute the marinade, then set the bag in a bowl and refrigerate for 2 or 3 hours, rubbing occasionally.

🦐 Remove the shrimp and place on a broiling (griller) rack; reserve the marinade. Broil 4 in (10 cm) from heat for about 2 minutes on each side, turning once and brushing two or three times with the reserved marinade.

🦐 To grill outdoors, cook over hot coals, brushing with the marinade two or three times, for 6 to 8 minutes or until the shrimp are cooked through.

SERVES 4

Placerville
HANGTOWN FRY

Hangtown, in the Sierra Nevada foothills, was so named because many people were hanged there during gold rush days, and this dish supposedly originated there. It was felt, eventually, that Placerville was a more respectable name than Hangtown (possibly the work of the first Chamber of Commerce)

16 oysters, shucked (opened), or 1 jar (4 oz/125 g) small
    oysters, drained
½ cup (2 oz/60 g) all-purpose (plain) flour
salt
freshly ground black pepper
10 eggs
1 cup (4 oz/125 g) cracker crumbs
6 tablespoons (3 oz/90 g), or more, butter

❧ Pat the oysters dry with absorbent paper towels. Stir and toss together the flour with ½ teaspoon each of salt and pepper. Beat 2 of the eggs with a sprinkling of salt and pepper.
❧ Roll each oyster in the seasoned flour, dip into the beaten egg, then roll in cracker crumbs and set aside.
❧ Beat the remaining 8 eggs with ½ teaspoon each of salt and pepper; set aside.
❧ Heat 4 tablespoons (2 oz/60 g) of butter in a large skillet over moderate heat. Add the oysters and cook for 1 minute on each side, or until lightly browned. Do not crowd them; cook them in 2 batches if necessary, adding more butter as needed. When all the oysters are cooked, discard the butter if it has burned, wipe out the pan and add 2 tablespoons fresh butter. If it has not burned, leave it in the pan.
❧ Set the pan on moderate heat, add the oysters and pour in the eggs. Cook, stirring occasionally, until the eggs are softly scrambled.

SERVES 4

San Francisco
OYSTERS KIRKPATRICK

This union of oysters on the half shell with butter, bacon, ketchup and cheese was the creation of Ernest Arbogast, who was the chef at the Palace Hotel in San Francisco around the turn of the century. They were prepared in honor of the hotel manager, Colonel John C. Kirkpatrick.

rock salt (see glossary)
12 fresh oysters, opened, on the half shell
2 tablespoons butter
4 slices bacon, cooked crisp and crumbled
¼ cup (2 fl oz/60 ml) ketchup (tomato sauce) or bottled
    chili sauce (American-style)
1 tablespoon Worcestershire sauce
3–4 tablespoons (1–1½ oz/30–45 g) grated Parmesan cheese

❧ Preheat the broiler (griller) and place a rack about 4 in (10 cm) from the heat. To keep the oysters from rocking about, spread a layer of rock salt about ½ in (12 mm) deep in a large shallow baking pan and place the oysters on it (or use a bed of crumpled foil). Top each oyster with a bit of butter and set them under the broiler for 5 minutes, just until the edges of the oysters start to curl. Remove from the broiler.
❧ Sprinkle the crumbled bacon over the oysters, dividing it evenly. Stir together the ketchup and Worcestershire sauce and place about a teaspoon of the mixture on each oyster. Sprinkle each with a scant teaspoon of grated cheese. Return the oysters to the broiler for about 3 or 4 minutes, until they are bubbling.

SERVES 4

Oysters Kirkpatrick (top) and Hangtown Fry (bottom)

Walnut Creek

CIOPPINO

This recipe is from Marion Cunningham, who has revised The Fannie Farmer Cookbook *for our generation. The trick of adding half the fish at the start of cooking and the remainder just before serving imparts more flavor to the tomato broth than does the usual method by which all the fish is tossed in at the last minute. You will be surprised by the difference.*

½ cup (4 fl oz/125 ml) olive oil
3 garlic cloves, minced (finely chopped)
2 lb (1 kg) fresh boneless fish, such as a mixture of
    scallops, shrimp (green prawns), cod, snapper or other
    firm white-fleshed fish fillets, cut into pieces
10–12 littleneck or cherrystone clams, in the shell
1 cup (8 fl oz/250 ml) dry white wine
2 cups (1 lb/500 g) fresh or canned tomatoes, peeled,
    seeded and coarsely chopped
1 teaspoon crumbled dried oregano or 2 teaspoons
    chopped fresh oregano
1 teaspoon sugar
2 bay leaves
salt
freshly ground black pepper
½ cup (1 oz/30 g) chopped parsley

❧ Pour the olive oil in a stew pot or Dutch oven and place over moderate heat. When it is hot, add the garlic and cook for 15 seconds.
❧ Add half of the fish mixture, the clams, the wine, tomatoes, oregano, sugar, bay leaves, and ½ teaspoon each salt and pepper. Turn the heat to high and bring the mixture to a simmer. Stir, and cook just below a boil for 1 minute. Lower the heat, then cover the pan and cook for 2 minutes.
❧ Add the remaining fish and cook, stirring gently, just until the rawness disappears, about 2 minutes. Stir in the parsley and serve.

SERVES 4   *Photograph pages 60–61*

San Francisco

DEVILED CRAB

In this recipe, "deviled" means that the crab is mixed with breadcrumbs, melted butter and seasonings before it is baked briefly to warm through and crisp the top. On the East Coast, deviled crab is apt to be baked in a cream sauce. The West Coast version is drier, and the flavor of crab dominates.

1 lb (500 g) crabmeat
1½ cups (6 oz/185 g) coarse dry breadcrumbs
2 celery stalks, finely chopped
2 large green (spring) onions, finely chopped
2 tablespoons chopped parsley
½ cup (4 oz/125 g) butter, melted
¼ cup (2 fl oz/60 ml) heavy (double) cream
2 teaspoons Dijon mustard
½ teaspoon salt
¼ teaspoon freshly ground black pepper

❧ Preheat the oven to 350°F (180°C). Butter six ⅓-cup (3-fl oz/80-ml) ramekins (or scallop shells) or a 4-cup (32-fl oz/1-l) baking dish.
❧ Carefully pick over the crabmeat and remove any bits of shell or cartilage. In a large bowl toss it with the breadcrumbs, celery, onion and parsley.
❧ Add the butter, cream, mustard, salt and pepper and toss to combine. Spoon into the ramekins or baking dish and bake for about 20 minutes.

SERVES 4

San Francisco

CRAB LOUIS

Like all famous dishes, this has many versions and there is little agreement about which is original. Most do have in common, however, crabmeat on shredded iceberg lettuce with a garnish of quartered or sliced hard-boiled egg, and sometimes tomato wedges and asparagus tips. The dispute lies primarily in the dressing: whether it ought to be a mayonnaise-based thousand-island type, which this is, or a lighter vinaigrette.

LOUIS DRESSING

1 cup (8 fl oz/250 ml) mayonnaise
¼ cup (2 fl oz/60 ml) heavy (double) cream, whipped
⅓ cup (3 fl oz/80 ml) chili sauce (American-style)
1 large green (spring) onion, chopped
salt
freshly ground black pepper

2 cups (1 lb/500 g) crabmeat
3 to 4 cups (½ head) shredded iceberg lettuce
8 to 12 crab legs (optional)
2 hard-boiled eggs, quartered
8 asparagus spears or tomato wedges, or both, for
    garnish (optional)

❧ Combine the mayonnaise, cream, chili sauce and green onion. Season with salt and pepper to taste; set aside.
❧ Carefully pick over the crabmeat and remove any bits of shell or cartilage; set aside.
❧ Divide the shredded lettuce among individual salad plates.
❧ Divide the crabmeat on the lettuce beds, mounding it in the center. Spoon the dressing over the crab and garnish with the crab legs and hard-boiled eggs, interspersed with asparagus spears and/or tomato wedges.

SERVES 4   *Photograph page 70*

San Francisco

CRAB SANDWICH

It is hard to beat the elegance of this open-face luxury sandwich, reminiscent of bridge luncheons and tearooms. It also makes a very good light supper dish or may be cut in strips and served as an appetizer with drinks.

2 cups (1 lb/500 g) crabmeat
1½ cups (6 oz/185 g) grated Swiss (Gruyère) cheese
¼ cup (2 fl oz/60 ml) mayonnaise
½ cup (4 fl oz/125 ml) sour cream
1 tablespoon lemon juice
1 teaspoon Worcestershire sauce
salt
freshly ground black pepper
dash of hot pepper (Tabasco) sauce
8 slices French bread, about ½ in (12 mm) thick
2 tablespoons softened butter
paprika

❧ Pick over the crabmeat to remove any bits of shell or cartilage.
❧ In a bowl toss the crab with the cheese. Stir in the mayonnaise, sour cream, lemon juice and Worcestershire sauce, then season with salt and pepper to taste and a dash of hot pepper sauce.
❧ Preheat the broiler (griller).
❧ Butter the slices of bread on one side, then spread the buttered side evenly with the crab mixture. Sprinkle lightly with paprika and broil (grill) between 3 and 4 in (7 and 10 cm) from heat for 2 or 3 minutes, or until lightly browned and bubbling.

SERVES 6

*Crab Sandwich (top)
and Deviled Crab (bottom)*

CURRIED SCALLOPS

Fish curries appear in many California cookbooks that were published in the forties and fifties, and a mild curry flavor can be just what is needed to turn leftover or bland seafood into something really interesting. Don't overdo it though; you want to complement the fish, not mask it. Serve with chutney and rice if you wish.

1½ lb (750 g) raw scallops, or 2 cups (1 lb/500 g) cooked
   fish, such as salmon or tiny shrimp (green prawns)
3 tablespoons butter
¼ cup (1 oz/30 g) all-purpose (plain) flour
2 cups (16 fl oz/500 ml) fish stock (see glossary)
1 tablespoon lemon juice
salt
freshly ground black pepper
1 small garlic clove, minced (finely chopped)
2 teaspoons curry powder

¼ cup (2 fl oz/60 ml) heavy (double) cream
2 tablespoons chopped cashew nuts

❧ If you are using scallops, pat them dry, then pull off the little tablike muscle that is sometimes attached to the side. Cut the scallops into ½-in (12-mm) pieces. If you are using cooked fish, remove any bones, then cut it, if necessary, into 1-in (2.5-cm) pieces. Leave shrimp whole.

❧ Melt the butter in a large saucepan. Add the flour and cook, stirring constantly, for 2 minutes. Add the stock, whisking until smooth, and bring to a boil. Reduce the heat and simmer for 2 minutes, then stir in the lemon juice and season with salt and pepper to taste. Add the garlic and curry powder, and raw scallops if you are using them. Simmer for 3 to 5 minutes, or until they are cooked through. If you are using cooked fish or shrimp, heat just long enough to warm through. Stir in the cream, simmer a minute, then pour into a serving bowl and sprinkle with the cashews.

SERVES 4

Crab Louis (recipe page 68)

Curried Scallops

North and South Coasts
ABALONE STEAK

Abalone is found in California coastal waters and little is sold outside the state. A large mollusk with a single, rounded shell, it attaches itself to a rock and survives on kelp. Because of its scarcity, unless you dive for it—or know someone who does—you may never know what a delicacy you are missing, for it is unlike any other fish. In his book Fading Feast, *Raymond Sokolov includes a fascinating essay on the abalone and its life, as well as instructions on how to clean it, if you happen to have a fresh one. In retail markets it is usually sold frozen, sliced, pounded and ready for cooking—and can be of excellent quality.*

4 abalone steaks, about 1 lb (500 g) total
½ cup (2 oz/60 g) all-purpose (plain) flour
1 teaspoon salt
½ teaspoon freshly ground black pepper
2 tablespoons, or more, clarified butter (see glossary)
2 tablespoons, or more, vegetable oil
tartar sauce
lemon wedges

❧ Even if you purchase the abalone ready to cook, it may need more pounding. The ideal thickness is that of a pie crust. So, if necessary, one at a time place the steaks between sheets of plastic wrap and pound away, firmly but evenly. It is difficult to overdo it; not pounded enough, abalone is inedibly tough. Combine the flour, salt and pepper. Dredge the abalone in this mixture and shake off the excess.

❧ Heat 2 tablespoons each of clarified butter and oil in a large skillet over high heat. When very hot—nearly smoking—add the abalone and cook for about 30 seconds on each side. Do not crowd the pan, and cook the fish in two batches if necessary, adding fresh butter and oil if the previous addition has burned. Serve on warm plates, with tartar sauce and lemon wedges.

SERVES 4

San Francisco
SAND DABS WITH PARSLEY BUTTER SAUCE

Sand dabs are members of the flounder family and are found in Pacific waters. Like Rex sole, they are delicate and sweet-tasting, best cooked and sauced simply with butter, lemon and parsley.

¼ cup (1 oz/30 g) all-purpose (plain) flour
1 teaspoon salt
½ teaspoon freshly ground black pepper
1½ lb (750 g) trimmed and cleaned sand dabs or
    sole or flounder
6 tablespoons (3 oz/90 g) butter
2 tablespoons lemon juice
2 tablespoons chopped parsley

❧ Toss together the flour, salt and pepper and spread on a sheet of waxed (greaseproof) paper. Dip both sides of the fish in the seasoned flour and shake off the excess.

❧ In a large skillet heat 3 tablespoons of the butter over moderate heat. Cook the floured fish for 2 minutes on each side, or until golden. Remove to a warm platter and discard any butter remaining in the pan. Return the pan to the heat and add the 3 remaining tablespoons of butter. When the butter is melted and bubbly, swirl in the lemon juice and parsley and pour it over the fish.

SERVES 4

South Coast
PAN-FRIED RED SNAPPER WITH GINGER BUTTER

Red snapper, which comes from the waters of the Gulf Coast, is firm-textured and delicate. It lends itself to grilling and pan-frying and is good with herb-flavored butter or even a mild salsa.

GINGER BUTTER

½ cup (4 oz/125 g) butter, softened
1 tablespoon Dijon mustard

Pan-fried Red Snapper with Ginger Butter (top), Abalone Steaks (center) and Sand Dabs with Parsley Butter Sauce (right)

1 tablespoon grated fresh ginger
1 garlic clove, minced (finely chopped)

2 lb (1 kg) skinless red snapper or other firm white-fleshed fish fillets
salt
freshly ground black pepper
3 tablespoons vegetable oil

❧ Beat the butter until smooth and creamy. Add the mustard, ginger and garlic, beating until blended and smooth. Scrape the mixture onto a sheet of waxed (greaseproof) paper, then push and pat it into a rough log about 4 in (10 cm) long.

❧ Wrap the paper around the log and refrigerate until firm.
❧ When you are ready to serve, pat the fish dry with absorbent paper towels, sprinkle with salt and pepper, and cut into 4 serving pieces.
❧ Heat the oil in a heavy skillet until it is almost smoking; it should be very hot, so the fish will sear and brown outside, but remain moist within. Add the fish fillets and cook for 2 minutes on each side or until they are cooked all the way through. Remove immediately to heated plates. Slice the ginger butter into 4 pieces and place one on each serving.

SERVES 4

Salmon ready for baking

ALLEN V. LOTT

Mendocino

BAKED SALMON

Salmon, because it tastes so good and holds its shape, lends itself especially well to this simple baking and braising. White wine poured around the fish keeps it moist, and fennel or dill tucked in the cavity imparts a pleasing flavor. Serve it with hollandaise sauce, boiled new potatoes and fresh peas to celebrate the Fourth of July.

3½ cups (1 bottle; 28 fl oz/750 ml) dry white wine
1 onion, thinly sliced
1 carrot, thinly sliced
1 celery stalk, thinly sliced
1 teaspoon crushed black peppercorns
salt
1 bay leaf
several sprigs of fresh dill or fennel
1 whole salmon, weighing about 6 lb (3 kg), or a center-
    cut piece from a larger fish, gutted and cleaned
freshly ground black pepper

❧ In a saucepan combine the wine, onion, carrot, celery, peppercorns, ½ teaspoon salt and the bay leaf. Bring to a boil, then simmer partially covered for 10 minutes.
❧ Preheat the oven to 325°F (165°C).
❧ Tuck the dill or fennel in the cavity of the fish and sprinkle with salt and pepper. So it is easier to remove after cooking, place the fish on a triple thickness of cheesecloth (muslin), with edges long enough to extend for several inches on both sides. Place in a large baking pan and pour on the wine and vegetables. Lay a piece of buttered waxed (greaseproof) paper over the top.
❧ Bake for 50 to 60 minutes, or until the fish is cooked through and not raw at the backbone; a thermometer inserted in the thickest part should register 140°F (60°C). Remove from the oven and let rest for 10 minutes. Using the cheesecloth as a sling, carefully lift the fish to a platter, then gently flip it over and remove the cheesecloth.

SERVES 8

San Francisco

CRAB CAKES

This is how crab cakes are made at Stars restaurant in San Francisco. A base of mashed potatoes and egg yolks makes these cakes lighter and more delicate than those made with breadcrumbs. Serve with tartar sauce.

2 cups (1 lb/500 g) crabmeat
1 tablespoon lemon juice
2 cups (1 lb/500 g) warm mashed potatoes
4 egg yolks
1 tablespoon Dijon mustard
⅛ teaspoon cayenne pepper
1 teaspoon salt
freshly ground black pepper
⅓ cup (3 fl oz/80 ml) olive oil or clarified butter (see glossary)

❧ Carefully pick over the crabmeat and remove any bits of shell or cartilage. Toss with the lemon juice and set aside.
❧ In a large bowl combine the potatoes, egg yolks, mustard, cayenne, salt and freshly ground pepper to taste. Fold in the crabmeat. Using generous ¼-cup blobs, pat and shape the mixture into 12 patties, each about ½ in (12 mm) thick.
❧ Heat 3 tablespoons of the oil or butter in a large skillet over medium-high heat. Add as many crab cakes as you can without crowding them, and cook for 3 minutes on each side, or until they are well browned. Fry the remaining cakes the same way, adding more butter or oil as necessary.

MAKES 12 CAKES, SERVING 4–6 *Photograph page 76*

SEAFOOD ENCHILADAS

This is a simple recipe that seems to result in something greater than the sum of its parts; the enchiladas are good because there is not too much in them—just crab or shrimp, well seasoned, tossed with green onion, and sauced with a fresh salsa verde. You'll find these in Mexican restaurants, but I have yet to taste any as good as homemade.

salsa verde (see recipe, page 207)
⅓ cup (3 fl oz/80 ml) vegetable oil
8 corn *tortillas*
2 cups (1 lb/500 g) cooked crabmeat or tiny shrimp
    (green prawns), or a combination
2 green (spring) onions, finely chopped
salt
freshly ground black pepper
1½ cups (6 oz/185 g) grated Monterey Jack (mild
    melting) cheese
1–2 cups (8–16 fl oz/250–500 ml) sour cream

❧ Prepare the *salsa verde* as directed in the recipe on page 207.
❧ Preheat the oven to 400°F (200°C) and grease a 9- x 13-in (23- x 33-cm) baking dish.
❧ Heat the oil in a skillet. Place each *tortilla* in the hot oil for a few seconds, until soft and pliable. Set aside in a stack as they are done.
❧ To make the filling, toss together ¼ cup (2 fl oz/60 ml) of the *salsa verde* with the crab or shrimp, green onion, and salt and pepper to taste.
❧ Place one-eighth (about ¼ cup) of the filling on each *tortilla* and roll it up loosely. Arrange seam-side down in the prepared baking pan and sprinkle with the cheese. Cover loosely with foil and bake for 15 minutes, then uncover and bake for 5 minutes longer.
❧ Spoon some of the remaining *salsa* over the top and place a small spoonful of sour cream on each *enchilada*. Pass the remaining *salsa* and sour cream at the table.

SERVES 4–6

SEVICHE

With roots south of the border, seviche is refreshing and restorative on a hot day. It is piquant and colorful and a perfect example of cooking without heat, or noncooking; the acid in the citrus juice transforms the texture of the fish, changing it from soft and translucent to firm and opaque. Almost any boneless fish will work, including sole, halibut and salmon, though scallops are traditional. In recent years the risks of contracting a food-borne illness from raw or undercooked fish have increased. To be on the safe side, it is suggested that any fish or shellfish that is to be eaten raw first be frozen at a temperature of 0°F (-18°C) or less for five days, to eradicate any parasites. Let the fish thaw in the refrigerator, then proceed with the recipe.

2 lb (1 kg) scallops or boneless fish fillets
1½ cups (12 fl oz/375 ml) fresh lime or lemon juice
salt
⅓ cup (3 fl oz/80 ml) olive oil
¼ cup (2 oz/60 g) canned green *chiles*, or 1 Anaheim
    (mild green) *chile*, seeded, peeled and finely chopped
1 large green (spring) onion, finely chopped
2 tablespoons chopped fresh cilantro
    (coriander/Chinese parsley) or 2 tablespoons chopped
    fresh dill (especially good with salmon)
2 garlic cloves, minced (finely chopped)
1 teaspoon minced (finely chopped) fresh ginger
freshly ground black pepper

❧ If using scallops, remove the tablike muscle that is sometimes attached to the side and cut them, if they are large, into halves or thirds. Cut the fish fillets into neat pieces about ½ in (12 mm) thick and 1 in (2.5 mm) square. Place in a stainless steel or glass bowl, add the lime or lemon juice and 1 teaspoon salt. Stir, then cover and refrigerate for 6 hours, or overnight if you wish.
❧ Drain thoroughly, discarding the liquid; set the fish aside.
❧ In a large bowl whisk together the olive oil, *chiles*, green onion, cilantro or dill, garlic, ginger, ¼ teaspoon freshly ground pepper and ½ teaspoon salt. Add the drained fish and toss to combine. Serve as soon as possible.

SERVES 4

Crab Cakes (recipe page 75)

ALLEN V. LOTT

Seafood Enchiladas (top)
and Seviche (bottom)

San Francisco

CRAB NEWBURG

This is an elegant dish that brings to mind California tearooms of the twenties and thirties—crabmeat, in a sherry-flavored cream sauce, served over buttered toast. It is very, very good.

2 cups (1 lb/500 g) crabmeat or crab legs
¼ cup (2 oz/60 g) butter
3 tablespoons all-purpose (plain) flour
1 cup (8 fl oz/250 ml), or more, milk
1 cup (8 fl oz/250 ml) heavy (double) cream
salt
freshly ground black pepper
pinch of ground nutmeg
2 egg yolks
¼ cup (2 fl oz/60 ml) dry sherry
4 slices hot buttered toast, cut crosswise into triangles
chopped parsley for garnish

❦ Carefully pick over the crabmeat and discard any shell or cartilage; set aside.
❦ Melt the butter in a medium saucepan. Add the flour and cook over medium heat, stirring constantly, for 2 minutes. Add 1 cup milk, whisking until smooth, then whisk in the cream. Bring the mixture to a boil, stirring constantly, then season to taste with salt, pepper and nutmeg.
❦ Blend a little of the hot cream mixture into the egg yolks, then pour them into the saucepan. Add the crabmeat and simmer for a moment, until heated through. Then stir in the sherry. If it seems thick add another tablespoon or two of milk. Spoon over hot buttered toast and sprinkle with parsley.

SERVES 4

Sierra Nevada

GRILLED TROUT

Trout is a perfect fish for a single serving. Wrapping it in corn husks is an Indian trick for keeping the flesh moist and preventing the delicate skin from tearing.

4 large ears (cobs) of corn, in their husks
4 trout, 8–10 oz (250–315 g) each, cleaned
4 tablespoons (2 oz/60 g) softened butter
salt
freshly ground black pepper
⅓ cup (3 fl oz/80 ml) melted butter
lemon wedges

❦ Remove the husks from the corn, taking care not to tear them. Remove the silk also.
❦ Pat the fish dry with absorbent paper towels and spread the cavity of each fish with a tablespoon of softened butter. Sprinkle them inside and out with salt and pepper.
❦ Spread 3 large corn husks out on a flat surface, overlapping them slightly. Place a fish on top and cover it with 3 more husks. Tie a piece of string about 12 in (30 cm) long around the middle of the husk-covered fish. Make 2 more ties, around the tail and head; set aside. Wrap the remaining fish.
❦ Prepare a barbecue fire and position the grilling rack between 4 and 6 in (10 and 15 cm) from the heat.
❦ Brush the ears of corn with melted butter and sprinkle them with salt and pepper.
❦ Place the wrapped fish over hot coals and cook for about 15 minutes, turning frequently. Place the corn on the grill for about the last 7 minutes. Turn them several times and brush once or twice more with melted butter. Remove fish and corn to warm plates or a platter and garnish with lemon wedges.

SERVES 4   *Photograph page 4*

Crab Newburg

Grilled Albacore with Cilantro Butter (left)
and Grilled Salmon (right)

GRILLED ALBACORE WITH CILANTRO BUTTER

Albacore is white-fleshed tuna and is caught by both commercial and game (sport) fishermen from Washington to California. Much of it goes to canneries, but more is becoming available fresh. The meat is firm and rich, making it ideal for grilling because it does not dry out.

CILANTRO BUTTER

½ cup (4 oz/125 g) butter, at room temperature
2 tablespoons chopped fresh cilantro
   (coriander/Chinese parsley)
1 tablespoon finely grated lemon zest
1 tablespoon lemon juice
¼ teaspoon salt
¼ teaspoon freshly ground black pepper

FISH

2 lb (1 kg) albacore steaks, each about 1 in (2.5 cm) thick
olive oil
salt
freshly ground black pepper

🐟 To prepare the cilantro butter, combine the butter with the cilantro, lemon zest, lemon juice, salt and pepper. Beat until completely smooth and blended. Scrape the butter onto waxed (greaseproof) paper or plastic wrap, then push and pat it into a log shape about 4 in (10 cm) long. Wrap tightly and refrigerate until firm. Just before cooking the fish, cut the log into 6 pieces.

🐟 Prepare a barbecue fire and adjust the grilling rack between 4 and 6 in (10 and 15 cm) from the heat.

🐟 Use a sharp knife to trim any skin from the fish. Rub with olive oil and then sprinkle with salt and pepper. Grill for about 6 minutes on each side, or until cooked through. If you have any doubts, cut into it and check. Remove from the grill to warm plates and place a slice of cilantro butter on each serving.

SERVES 6

GRILLED SALMON

Salmon is simplicity itself to grill: it cooks quickly, and no sauce is needed, just a squeeze of lemon and a pat of butter. If you are grilling fillets with skin on, you can easily remove the skin midway through the cooking.

6 salmon steaks or boneless fillets, each about 1 in (2.5 cm)
   thick
olive oil
salt
freshly ground black pepper
6 tablespoons (3 oz/90 g) softened butter
lemon wedges

🐟 Prepare a barbecue fire and position the grilling rack between 4 and 6 in (10 and 15 cm) from the heat.

🐟 Rub the fish lightly with oil and sprinkle with salt and pepper. Cook (skin-side down, if applicable) for 5 minutes.

🐟 Turn with a wide spatula and cook for about 5 minutes longer—during which time you may peel the skin from the top. Remove to a platter, browned side up, and top each steak with a tablespoon of butter.

🐟 Garnish with lemon wedges.

SERVES 6

Tomales Bay

BARBECUED GLAZED OYSTERS

Plump oysters skewered with mushrooms and swathed in a tangy, sweet mustard glaze may be served as a first course or appetizer, or a main course on a bed of rice.

⅓ cup (3 fl oz/80 ml) Dijon mustard
¼ cup (2 fl oz/60 ml) dry white wine
¼ cup (2 fl oz/60 ml) honey
2 tablespoons soy sauce
1 tablespoon vegetable oil
3 to 5 drops hot *chile* oil (see glossary)
24 mushroom caps
24 oysters, shucked (opened)

❧ To make the glaze, in a small saucepan whisk together the mustard, wine, honey, soy sauce and oils. (The amount of *chile* oil used depends on how spicy you want the glaze. Remember it is very hot, and too much can be lethal!) Bring to a boil, then reduce the heat and simmer for 5 minutes; set aside.
❧ Blanch the mushrooms for 2 minutes in a pan of boiling, salted water to soften them; drain well and pat dry.
❧ Prepare a barbecue fire and position the grilling rack between 4 and 6 inches (10 and 15 cm) above the heat.
❧ Pat the oysters dry with paper towels. On skewers, thread the oysters alternately with the mushrooms, lay the skewers across a platter and brush them lightly with the glaze. Let them stand for 10 minutes and brush again.
❧ Grill over hot coals for about 10 minutes, turning frequently and brushing once or twice more with the glaze.

SERVES 4

Barbecued Glazed Oysters

ALLEN V. LOTT

San Francisco

OYSTER LOAF

James Beard writes in his book American Cookery *that oyster loaves were once called "peacemakers": wayward husbands who had stayed out too late often took one home as a gesture of reconciliation. The goodness of oyster loaf lies in its simplicity: a crunchy shell of French bread, generously buttered and filled with fried oysters. It was popular in early San Francisco and, with the comeback of oysters since the seventies, is a frequent visitor to tables again today. Pass lemon wedges and ketchup at the table if you wish.*

1 loaf French bread, either round or long
⅓ cup (3 fl oz/80 ml) melted butter
24 oysters, shucked (opened), or 1 jar (16 oz/500 g) oysters, drained
1½ cups (6 oz/185 g) fine dry breadcrumbs
3 eggs, well beaten
vegetable oil for frying

❧ Preheat the oven to 350°F (180°C). Slice off the top third of the French bread and set it aside to be used as a lid. Scoop out the insides from the bottom section, leaving a shell ½ in (12 mm) thick. Brush the interior of the shell and the cut side of the top generously with melted butter.
❧ Place in the oven for 10 to 15 minutes, until lightly toasted.
❧ While the bread toasts, pat the oysters dry with absorbent paper towels. Roll them in the breadcrumbs, dip into the beaten egg, then roll again in breadcrumbs to coat.
❧ Heat about ¼ in (6 mm) of oil in a large skillet over moderately high heat. Add the oysters and fry them, without crowding, for 2 minutes on each side, or until golden; do this in two batches if necessary. Drain briefly on absorbent paper towels and sprinkle lightly with salt.
❧ Fill the toasted bread with the hot oysters and replace the top. To serve, cut into large slices with a sharp knife.

SERVES 6

Monterey

CLAM CAKES

Clam cakes are coastal diner food, where they might be put in small buns and called clamburgers. This can be a real treat with the usual hamburger condiments of lettuce and tomato, but tartar sauce rather than mayonnaise. They are also good on their own, for Sunday breakfast or supper.

2 cups (18 oz/560 g) minced fresh clams, or 4 cans (6½ oz/200 g each) minced clams, drained
4 eggs
1 cup (2 oz/60 g) fresh white breadcrumbs
2 tablespoons melted butter
1 tablespoon lemon juice
½ teaspoon salt
dash hot pepper (Tabasco) sauce
vegetable oil for frying
lemon wedges
tartar sauce

❧ In a bowl, stir together the clams, eggs, breadcrumbs, butter, lemon juice, salt and hot pepper sauce.
❧ Film a large skillet with about ¼ in (6 mm) of oil and set over moderate heat. When it is quite hot, drop in heaping tablespoons of clam batter—they will flatten out—cooking only as many as you can without crowding. Fry the cakes for 2 to 3 minutes on each side, pressing down gently with a spatula, then drain them briefly on absorbent paper towels. Serve with lemon wedges and tartar sauce.

MAKES ABOUT 24 CAKES, SERVING 6

*Oyster Loaf (top)
and Clam Cakes (bottom)*

THE CENTRAL COAST

THE CENTRAL COAST

The central coast is cool mist and fog, layered with days of sunshine. Its famous profile is carved by breathtaking cliffs that drop to the sea, creating one of the most gorgeous coastlines in the world.

It is artichokes and garlic, and the gritty, wonderful tales of John Steinbeck's novel *Cannery Row*. The opulence of Hearst Castle and the simplicity of the Spanish missions coexist in this strip of land that runs between the sea and the man-made north-south artery called Interstate 5. On the coast side, it begins around Point Conception and stretches north to Santa Cruz. Its landmarks are cypress trees sculpted and stretched by the wind, and lush groves of California redwoods. In the fertile inland valleys, farms and orchards meet the peaks of the Coast Range, which marks the dividing line from the great Central Valley on the other side.

The list of crops found along the central coast and inland is enough to send any cook into a contented reverie. Garlic, onions, mushrooms, artichokes, lettuce, broccoli, cauliflower, peppers, strawberries and apples all flourish. Add some spot prawns and Monterey Jack cheese, and life is more than good.

Although the Central Valley is more widely known as the heartland of California's agriculture, the Salinas Valley, just east of Monterey, is another of the most prolific farming regions in the world. The tons of lettuce that grow here uphold Salinas' claim as the "salad bowl" of America. Here also, over thirty thousand acres of grapes grow in the warm, dry climate—many of them to be

Previous pages: Oblivious to the view of one of the world's most spectacular coastlines, cattle graze in pastures along the Big Sur coast. Left: Mission San Carlos Borromeo del Rio Carmelo in Carmel is a classic example of California's Spanish heritage—an influence felt in architecture, language and cuisine since the 1770s.

transformed into fine California wines. Near San Luis Obispo, to the south, the vines of Paso Robles and the Edna Valley are also making wine drinkers very happy.

Strawberries proliferate on thousands of acres, with the heaviest concentration around Watsonville and Salinas. Plump, juicy and brilliantly red, they have long inspired old-fashioned strawberry shortcakes—rich, homemade biscuits slathered with ripe berries and cream—as well as garnet-colored jams and jellies.

ARTICHOKE COUNTRY

Castroville, just north of Salinas, has a famous arched sign over its main street, proclaiming the town to be the "Artichoke Capital of the World." And, thanks to the Italians who introduced the delicious thistle, it is. Artichoke soup, deep-fried artichoke hearts and steamed artichokes with dipping sauces are regular "fast-food" fare. All the frozen or marinated artichoke hearts sold under American labels pass through the town's single processing plant.

Californians are happily familiar with artichokes, but outside the state, some people still find the green globes slightly intimidating. They are really very easy to cook, however, and in the simplest preparation require only a knife and a deep pot. First, select artichokes that are heavy for their size, compact and firm. Growers say that the globes are somewhat flared and conical in the summer and fall, and more tight and rounded in the winter and spring. When you're ready to cook, trim the stem, remove the tiny outer, lower leaves (they snap off) and trim off the prickly points of the leaves. Add a squeeze of fresh lemon to enough water to cover the artichokes and boil them gently until the base is tender (test with a fork). Artichokes are meant to be eaten with the hands, enjoyed leaf by leaf. You eat just the tender tip (each one dipped in melted butter or mayonnaise) and discard the rest of the leaf, peeling and eating down to the heart, or artichoke bottom. Once the fine chokes are revealed, cut or scoop them out and enjoy the sweet, nutty heart.

GARLIC IN GILROY

To most northern Californians, the central coast town of Gilroy means garlic—bushels and braids of it. The annual Gilroy Garlic Festival, originally inspired by the garlic fest in Arleux, France, draws thousands of visitors and hundreds of cooks to this fragrant town every summer to celebrate the earthy, pungent bulb of culinary legend. Prize-winning recipes at the festival swing from different versions of forty-clove chicken and garlic soup to the inevitable garlic ice cream and brownies.

Depending on the amount used and whether it is cooked or raw, garlic adds varying nuances of flavor to countless recipes. In California, it has a place in every ethnic cuisine, as it can be subtle or bold, hot or sweet. When chopped raw and blended in classic *aïoli* (the garlic mayonnaise of Provence), it tastes hot and strong, making *aïoli* a brilliant counterpoint to crisp raw vegetables or boiled seafood. But when roasted slowly, whole heads of garlic (usually about ten or twelve cloves) become mellow and soft, as the flavor turns sweet and nutty. When

Fishing boats dock at the wharf in Moss Landing, north of Monterey. Unlike many other central coast towns, Moss Landing still retains the salty flavor of a fishing village.

cooked in this manner, the cloves may be gently pulled apart, squeezed and smeared on fresh hearty bread or served as a garnish for roasted meats.

When nearby onion and tomato harvests and processing coincide with Gilroy's garlic harvest, locals say that the air smells like one giant pot of Italian pasta sauce bubbling away. Heading south to Morro Bay, you could forage for clams to add to that Gilroy pasta sauce. Morro Bay, known for its salt-water taffy, smoked fish and clams, is one of the few active fishing villages on the West Coast. Here (and at nearby Pismo Beach), people dig for clams while sandpipers and curlews, great blue herons, cormorants and California murres soar or scurry about the area that was designated an official bird sanctuary twenty years ago.

To the south, Big Sur and Monterey, two of the most well-known sites in all of California, are almost intoxicating in their natural beauty. Redwood forests, crashing waves, verdant green hills and windswept landscapes all have enticed writers, photographers and artists for generations. But the magic is best experienced firsthand.

When chill fog dampens nearby coastal forests, cooks there are inspired to ladle out hearty soups or bowls of steaming pasta tossed with local clams and mussels. And when the fog burns off, people emerge onto sunny decks perched above ocean views. They dig into big green salads of chilled prawns and artichoke hearts, or maybe just hamburgers and plenty of California Chardonnay (much of it produced in the central coast area).

Beaches around Big Sur and Monterey are more suited to walking and poking around tidepools than to swimming, and lots of people go just for that reason. The richness of marine life in the area is unique in the world, in part because of the rich mineral foods found in Monterey Bay. At Point Lobos State Reserve, the bay is filled with the bobbing heads of whiskered sea otters, playing or just lolling about in the water—a sight worth the trip.

Monterey has looked to the sea from its beginnings. The city's wharf originally served as the pier where trading schooners from around Cape Horn unloaded their cargo, bringing coffee, vanilla, exotic spices and iron cooking pots along with silks, hand-tooled boots and belts to the missions. During the Spanish-Mexican era (before California officially became an American state in 1850), Monterey was the capital as well as the social center of the area. Being a hub for the hide and tallow trade, rancho life here was a round of hard riding and wheeling and dealing. With cooks working day in and day out, the rancheros delighted in putting on their share of celebrations and barbecues with the plentiful beef. The discovery of abundant seafood was yet to come, as the rancheros were definitely land-bound, rarely leaving their horses.

SAMPANS TO CANNERY ROW

Monterey's history as a fishing center began in the 1850s, when Chinese workers began moving south from the gold country. Around the same time, entire families sailed directly from China, establishing villages at Point Lobos and nearby Pescadero Point. Except for the early coastal Indians, the Chinese were the first to tap the rich vein of seafood in the Monterey Bay. In addition to eating the fresh fish in soups and stews, they split and salted halibut, flounder, cod, yellowtail and several other varieties and dried them in the sun on acres of wooden racks. Most of the dried fish was exported—to San Francisco, to gold and silver miners throughout the state and to China. The

Seals frolic in a rich bed of seaweed off the Carmel coast.

Chinese were also the first to take advantage of the now-prized abalone supply. Later, Japanese divers who had developed diving expertise at home came and really pulled in the abalone, which was highly underrated by the locals.

Europeans arriving from the gold country and elsewhere soon discovered Monterey for themselves and took an aggressive lead in the fishing business, leaving only the squid to the Chinese. Today, the "Feast of the Lanterns" in Pacific Grove replays the scene of Chinese sampans sitting out on the moonless night water, burning pitchwood fires to attract the squid and scoop them up in their nets. Squid, or *calamari*, is still a central coast specialty, served in a delicious variety of ways, all of which depend on keeping the flesh tender and maintaining that distinctive squid flavor. Most cooks, however, would rather order squid in a restaurant than deal with the messy preparation. India Joze, a popular Santa Cruz eatery, specializes in the little mollusks—even to the point of hanging paper cutouts of squid from the ceiling. In the scheme of India Joze's unusual decor, the squid-mobiles dancing mid-air over diners' heads seem quite appropriate.

Once the fishing industry was underway, Monterey was far better known for Cannery Row, where sixteen sardine canneries could barely keep up with the supply of fish from 1921 until the late 1940s, when the sardine population mysteriously dwindled. Before the sardine boom, salmon was the most important variety of fish in Monterey Bay and plentiful enough to inspire the building of the first local cannery.

MEAT, POULTRY AND GAME

Cattle graze before the surrealistic facade of the Sierra Nevada near Marysville. In the 19th century, huge rancheros stretched for miles across the state's inland valleys.

MEAT, POULTRY AND GAME

At one time, meat meant *beef* to Californians. The lucrative hide and tallow trade kept cattle on the California ranges well into the 1860s, and beef was king. It was dried for jerky, ground or shredded for *carne con chile* and *enchiladas*, marinated or rubbed with garlic and roasted. Sauced, stewed, stir-fried or, in the fine hotels, topped with béarnaise sauce, it was consumed with relish (both literally and figuratively) in every way, shape and form. Today, Californians still like their beef, and the industry is the second largest agricultural business in the state.

Game and game birds were also abundant and, until the cattle trade flourished and after it was felled by drought in 1863, game was a mainstay throughout California. Missionaries, pioneers and gold miners also trapped bear and hunted venison, antelope, elk, rabbits, ducks, quail, geese and grouse. According to Helen Brown's *West Coast Cookbook* (a treasury of California cooking and history published in 1952), "The butcher shops in the Gold Country . . . were more apt to have deer and bear meat than they were mutton or beef. The earliest restaurants served game because there was little else, and early cook books had recipes using pheasant for 'chicken salad,' deer for 'meat loaf,' and sage hen for 'fricasy.'"

Menus in California between the late 1800s and the early 1900s enticed diners with a variety of meat and game. Poultry was generally found only on ranches where it was raised or in Chinatowns. Saddle of venison, antelope and grizzly bear steaks, elk steaks in Spanish sauce and the now-abandoned delicacy of calf's head in oil or brain sauce were more common fare.

Today, most game, such as boar, geese, quail and Muscovy duck from the Alexander Valley, is raised privately. One farm in Petaluma, a major poultry center north of San Francisco, raises fancy white ducks that, they say, are descended from the White Pekins of China. These succulent grain-fed ducks are found in local markets and served by home and restaurant chefs who add flourishes of local fruits and herbs and sometimes a reduction of a good California Pinot Noir. In Chinese markets in Los Angeles and San Francisco, storefront windows reveal hundreds of spit-roasted ducks gleaming with mahogany-colored glaze, ready to be taken home and eaten with plum sauce. In most California kitchens you will find a variety of other meats—lamb, veal and pork—from chops and loins to sausages. Go to North Beach in San Francisco and someone is sure to be turning out a delicate veal *scaloppine* or a version of Joe's Special, a ground beef or sausage, spinach and egg scramble. In San Francisco's Mission district or in Los Angeles, heavenly pork *chile verde* simmers in home and restaurant pots, while on the foggy Mendocino coast, lamb chops might be marinating in balsamic vinegar, olive oil and rosemary. And, despite the impression that most Californians are obsessed with diets, their love of big, juicy hamburgers is evident everywhere. Grilling is the preferred way to cook them, and avocados, melted Monterey Jack cheese, sautéed mushrooms and *salsa* are all popular toppings.

Chop suey, which many people associate with meat and believe to have a Chinese origin, is a wild card. Chinese restaurant owners in California really concocted it to please the occidental palate, creating as many versions as there were ingredients available (the name translates loosely as "odds and ends"). In 1916, a menu from San Francisco listed seventeen variations, from chicken giblets or roast pork to boneless chicken and, simply, meat chop suey.

Previous pages: Turkey with Prune Stuffing (recipe page 106)

POULTRY

Poultry has been a standard in every kitchen since the 1930s, when commercial production was stepped up, making it plentiful and affordable. Roasted, smoked, grilled, stir-fried, baked in a clay pot or skewered as a kabob, it is definitely an everyday food throughout the state. Chicken farms abound and range from those that sell organic, free-range birds to those that epitomize the world of mass-production. Thousands of turkeys are also raised on farms in the Central Valley.

Ranch chicken is a wonderful example of poultry prepared in the robust and inventive ranch style of northern California and the Central Valley, where traditional Spanish sauces take on a California twist. The recipe incorporates local almonds and olives in a robust red chili powder sauce redolent with herbs, spices and wine—a list of ingredients that might confound some cooks. But when the cornmeal-coated chicken is simmered to tender perfection with the sauce, it becomes a dish to savor and, suddenly, all the ingredients make perfect sense.

In the wine country, you might find chicken breasts in a reduced champagne sauce, or a whole chicken, skewered and herb-roasted, Tuscan style. Chicken pie with mushrooms might come from a homey Central Valley country kitchen, where plentiful fruit is also paired with poultry, as in a prune stuffing or grilled chicken salad with melon and avocado.

OUTDOOR COOKERY

Trends may come and go, but the unmistakable aroma of the backyard barbecue has long characterized informal, straightforward dining in California. In the state that almost invented sliding glass doors to open onto patios and decks, it is a way of life and perhaps the most popular means of cooking meat, game and poultry. Many meats, such as flank steak, were once thought to be exclusive candidates for slow braising. But as backyard grilling took

An edible curtain of cooked ducks is one of the many exotic sights and flavors to be discovered in San Francisco's Chinatown.

A plucky rooster proclaims his deep dislike of barbecued chicken, chicken *enchiladas, teriyaki chicken and other fowl recipes.*

off in the 1950s, these meats acquired a new status when marinated and seared on the grill. In fact, it is not unusual to have an entire meal prepared on the grill, with produce, such as fresh pineapple, bell peppers, eggplant, zucchini and perhaps garlic bread or *polenta*, grilled along with a main course.

To Americans visiting California in the early railroad days, barbecue was a wonderful revelation, recorded at one event as "a genuine old-time California affair, in a rough-and-tumble, help-yourself, happy-go-lucky style." In those raucous days, the guests gathered, armed with skewers, around large outdoor pits and ate chunks of meat cut from whole sides of beef. As one East Coast visitor described it: "The meats were barbecued in first-class style. Beef and mutton were done to a turn, and many, after having had a liberal supply, like Oliver Twist, called for 'more.'"

Today, grilling equipment runs the gamut from portable kettle-style barbecues for grilling or smoking to more elaborate and costly gas grills. *Hibachis*, small and sturdy, are favorites for tiny city decks or rooftops; at campgrounds, built-in stone pits are standard.

Experienced cooks offer these tips for outdoor cooking: Bring large pieces of meat to room temperature before cooking. Use most basting sauces only during the last ten or fifteen minutes of cooking, as they usually contain sugar or oil, which will burn and flare up. Disregard the prohibition against turning steaks and burgers more than once on the grill. They actually retain juices better if they are turned four or five times.

JOE'S SPECIAL

This dish supposedly originated in San Francisco at a popular restaurant called Little Joe's, where it is still prepared by dexterous line cooks. It is fun to sit at the counter and watch them. The ingredients may be varied somewhat to suit what you have on hand, but all versions seem to include beef, spinach, eggs and onion. Some cooks like to add half a pound or so of cooked mushrooms.

3 tablespoons vegetable oil
1 onion, chopped
1 lb (500 g) ground (minced) beef
salt
freshly ground black pepper
1 lb (500 g) fresh spinach, chopped and cooked to yield
   1 cup (8 oz/250 g)
4 eggs, beaten
1 tablespoon chopped fresh basil or 1 teaspoon dried basil
¼ cup (1 oz/30 g) grated Parmesan cheese

❦ Heat the oil in a skillet. Add the onion and cook gently, stirring, for about 5 minutes. Scrape the onion into a bowl and return the skillet to heat. Add the beef, season with salt and pepper and cook, breaking it up with a fork or spatula, until it is no longer pink. Spoon any accumulated fat from the pan.
❦ Return the onions to the beef, then add the spinach and mix well. Season to taste with salt and pepper and cook, stirring, for about 3 minutes. Pour in the eggs, sprinkle with basil, then cook and stir just until the eggs are set. Sprinkle with the cheese and serve immediately.

SERVES 4

Beef Sauté with Artichokes and Mushrooms (top)
and Joe's Special (bottom)

BEEF SAUTÉ WITH ARTICHOKES AND MUSHROOMS

Old-fashioned recipes often called for a steak to be "smothered" after cooking—sometimes with mushrooms or onions, as in a dish offered at the Brown Derby restaurant in Hollywood. Artichokes have a texture and flavor that goes particularly well with beef, and together they make a dressy dish that is good for a small, fancy dinner. Once the artichoke bottoms are done, the final cooking takes only minutes, and despite the long list of ingredients, this recipe is really quite simple.

¼ cup (1 oz/30 g) all-purpose (plain) flour
4 cups (32 fl oz/1 l) water
3 tablespoons lemon juice
3 large artichokes
2 tablespoons butter
2 tablespoons minced (finely chopped) shallots or
   green (spring) onions
¼ lb (125 g) small mushroom caps, or larger
   mushrooms, halved
salt
freshly ground black pepper
2 tablespoons olive oil or vegetable oil
1 lb (500 g) beef tenderloin (fillet), cut into 1-in (2.5-cm) cubes
¼ cup (2 fl oz/60 ml) beef stock (see glossary)
¼ cup (2 fl oz/60 ml) heavy (double) cream
2 tablespoons chopped parsley

❦ Place the flour in a saucepan, whisk in the water and lemon juice, and bring to a boil over medium heat. Cook the artichokes, following the instructions in the recipe for Palace Court salad on page 44. Cut the prepared artichoke bottoms into quarters and set aside in a bowl.
❦ Heat the butter in a skillet over moderate heat. Add the shallots and cook for 1 minute, then add the mushroom caps, season with salt and pepper, and cook for about 5 minutes more, stirring frequently, until tender. Scrape into the bowl with the artichokes.
❦ Return the skillet to high heat and add the oil. When it is almost smoking, carefully slide the beef cubes in and cook them, tossing and stirring almost constantly, until lightly browned on all sides, about 2 or 3 minutes—the meat should remain very rare.
❦ Pour in the stock and cream, return the vegetables to the pan, along with any juices they have rendered, and boil rapidly until the liquid has reduced by about half and thickened slightly. Season with salt and pepper, toss with the parsley and serve immediately.

SERVES 4

SUKIYAKI

Sukiyaki is a Japanese dish, similar to Chinese chop suey, but lighter, and prepared in a more orderly, ritualistic fashion, from ingredients previously and neatly sliced or chopped and arranged on a platter at your side. You can cook it beside the table in the dining room if you like, or in the kitchen, in an electric skillet or wok. Whatever the heat source, it must be very hot.

1 lb (500 g) beef tenderloin (fillet) or sirloin tip
2 large green (spring) onions, thinly sliced diagonally
2 cups (8 oz/250 g) thinly sliced mushrooms

Sukiyaki

½ cup (4 oz/125 g) bamboo shoots
½ cup (2 oz/60 g) shredded Chinese (napa or celery) cabbage
3 tablespoons soy sauce
½ cup (4 fl oz/125 ml) beef stock (see glossary)
1 teaspoon sugar
3 tablespoons vegetable oil
¼ lb (125 g) soybean cake or soybean curd (*tofu*; see
  glossary), cut into small cubes
½ cup (2 oz/60 g) watercress leaves

🍴 Cut the beef into thin strips about ⅛ in (3 mm) thick and 2 in (5 cm) long; set aside. Have the prepared onions, mushrooms, bamboo shoots and cabbage at hand, either in separate small bowls or in small piles on a platter. Stir together the soy sauce, stock and sugar and set aside.
🍴 Heat the vegetable oil in a very large, heavy skillet. (If you

have a medium-sized skillet, divide the ingredients in half and cook the *sukiyaki* in 2 smaller skillets.) Add the beef, then stir and toss for about 3 minutes. Push the meat to one side, then add the onions and cook for about 2 minutes, keeping them somewhat separate. Push them aside with the beef, then add the mushrooms, bamboo shoots and Chinese cabbage, keeping them also somewhat separate, and stir and cook for about 3 minutes more. During these last 3 minutes, gradually add the soy sauce mixture (adding it all at once would make the dish watery), letting each previous addition evaporate slightly before pouring in more.
🍴 Push the meat back into the center of the skillet, leaving the vegetables around the outside, and toss it with the soybean curd. Sprinkle with the watercress and serve immediately.

SERVES 4

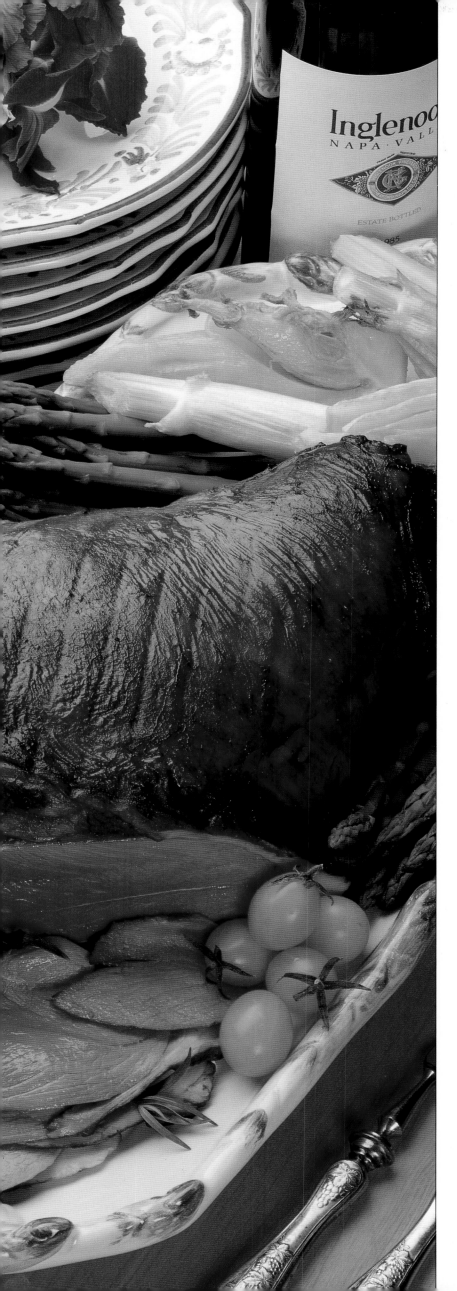

California

HERBED AND GLAZED HAM

Marinades need not always be made of liquids. For this recipe, a fresh ham is first rubbed with a salty dry marinade that accentuates its natural flavor, then is brushed with a mixture of honey and ginger during cooking to make a dark, sweet glaze.

1 tablespoon salt
2 teaspoons coarsely ground black pepper
2 tablespoons chopped fresh thyme or 2 teaspoons dried thyme
1 tablespoon chopped fresh sage or 1 teaspoon dried sage
2 garlic cloves, minced (finely chopped)
2 tablespoons vegetable oil
1 leg of pork, 6–8 lb (3–4 kg)
½ cup (4 fl oz/125 ml) honey
2 tablespoons dry mustard
2 tablespoons Worcestershire sauce
1 tablespoon ground ginger

🍂 Combine the salt, pepper, thyme, sage and garlic. Rub the oil over the pork, then coat the meat evenly with the salt mixture. Refrigerate, covered, for several hours or overnight.
🍂 In a small bowl blend together the honey, mustard, Worcestershire sauce and ginger.
🍂 Prepare a barbecue fire for indirect cooking (see glossary) and place the grilling rack about 5 in (12 cm) from heat.
🍂 Set the meat on the rack, then cover the barbecue and open the vents halfway. Cook for about 2½ hours, turning the meat once and adding more coals about every 45 minutes to maintain a constant temperature. During the last hour, brush the pork with the honey mixture every 15 minutes. Pork is done when it has reached an internal temperature of 160°F (71°C). Let the meat rest for about 15 minutes before carving it.

SERVES 10

Napa Valley

NAPA VALLEY LEG OF LAMB

I first had this at the Robert Mondavi Winery, where it was prepared for a visiting chef. It is a good and simple way to cook a whole leg of lamb in a covered-kettle barbecue and results in a roast that is well browned and juicy with a subtle, smoky flavor.

1 bottle, about 3½ cups (28 fl oz/750 ml) dry red wine
½ cup (4 fl oz/125 ml) olive oil
3 large garlic cloves, mashed
2 tablespoons chopped fresh tarragon
1 teaspoon salt
½ teaspoon freshly ground black pepper
1 leg of lamb, 6–7 lb (3–3.5 kg), trimmed of outside fat

🍂 Whisk together the wine, olive oil, garlic, tarragon, salt and pepper. Place the lamb in a shallow nonaluminum roasting pan. Pour in the wine mixture, rubbing it into the meat. Cover and refrigerate for at least 8 hours, turning the lamb occasionally and rubbing it with the marinade.
🍂 Prepare a barbecue fire for indirect cooking (see glossary) and place the grilling rack about 5 in (12 cm) from the heat.
🍂 Remove the lamb from the marinade and place it on the grill. Cover the barbecue and open the vents about halfway. Cook for 45 minutes on each side, adding more coals to the fire if necessary to maintain a constant temperature. Brush occasionally with the reserved marinade. The meat is done when it has reached an internal temperature of 130°F (55°C) for rare, or 145°F (65°C) for medium. Let it rest for 10 minutes, then carve across the grain into thin slices and arrange on a warm platter.

SERVES 8

Herbed and Glazed Ham (left) and
Napa Valley Leg of Lamb (right)

BEEF AND BROCCOLI STIR-FRY

The Chinese have a knack for doing the most with the fewest and simplest ingredients. By cutting tender beef into small pieces and stir-frying it with vegetables, they can make a little meat seem to be much more. This dish is also fast, colorful and very good for a small, quick dinner. Serve with rice.

¾ lb (375 kg) beef tenderloin (fillet)
½ cup (4 fl oz/125 ml) beef stock (see glossary)
1 tablespoon cornstarch (cornflour)
1 tablespoon soy sauce
1 tablespoon dry sherry
4 tablespoons (2 fl oz/60 ml) olive oil or peanut oil
1 lb (500 g) broccoli florets
pinch of red pepper flakes
salt

❦ Cut the beef into strips about 1 in (2.5 cm) long, ¼ in (6 mm) thick and ½ in (12 mm) wide. Set aside.

❦ In a small cup or bowl, stir together the stock, cornstarch, soy sauce and sherry; set aside.

❦ In a wok or a large heavy skillet, heat 2 tablespoons of the oil until very hot. Add the broccoli, then toss and stir it for 2 minutes. Cover and cook for 2 minutes more, tossing once or twice. Taste a piece; it should be crisp, but not raw. Cook for a minute or two longer if necessary. Remove to a side dish.

❦ Return the skillet to high heat, add the remaining 2 tablespoons of oil and heat just until it is smoking hot. Add the strips of beef and stir and toss them rapidly for about 2 minutes, until they are brown outside but still pink inside. Stir up the stock and cornstarch mixture and add it to the skillet.

❦ Add the broccoli and red pepper flakes, salt to taste, then stir and toss rapidly for about 1 minute, until the liquid has thickened and broccoli is heated through. Serve immediately.

SERVES 4

CHOP SUEY

There was a time when kitchenettes all over San Francisco's Chinatown had in their windows neon signs that glowed with the word chopsuey. *It is a very good and quickly made stir-fried dish of meat—pork, veal, beef or chicken—and crisply cooked vegetables, served over rice. Chow mein, made similarly, is served over crisp noodles. You rarely see chop suey any more, which is a shame; it is so easy and good for you, too.*

2 tablespoons vegetable oil
4 celery stalks, diagonally sliced
1 onion, thinly sliced
½ lb (250 g) pork or other meat, cut across the grain into small, thin strips
1 cup (3 oz/90 g) thinly sliced mushrooms
1 green or red bell pepper (capsicum), seeded and thinly sliced
1 cup (3 oz/ 90 g) bean sprouts
1 cup (8 fl oz/250 ml) beef stock (see glossary)
1 tablespoon cornstarch (cornflour)
2 tablespoons soy sauce
2 large green (spring) onions, diagonally sliced
salt
freshly ground black pepper

❦ In a large, heavy skillet, preferably of cast iron, or in a wok, heat the oil over high heat until it is smoking hot. Do not leave the pan unattended for even a minute; hot oil can ignite. Add the celery and onion and cook briskly, stirring and tossing furiously, for about 2 minutes.

❦ Add the pork, mushrooms and pepper and continue cooking over high heat, tossing and stirring all the while, for about 3 minutes more, until the meat is cooked through. Add the bean sprouts and cook, tossing, for 1 minute.

❦ Quickly stir the broth, cornstarch and soy sauce together until blended. Add to the other ingredients along with the green onion, and cook for 1 minute more, until thickened. Season with salt and pepper to taste, and serve over rice.

SERVES 4

EGG ROLLS

Egg rolls are fried Chinese pastries, usually with a filling of meat and vegetables, enclosed in an egg dough wrapper (the store-bought ones are very good). They are crispy and crunchy outside and moist and succulent inside.

1 cup (4 oz/125 g) finely chopped cabbage
salt
½ lb (250 g) ground (minced) pork
¼ lb (125 g) mushrooms, finely chopped
freshly ground black pepper
2 tablespoons soy sauce
2 tablespoons dry sherry
1 tablespoon cornstarch (cornflour)
2 teaspoons sesame oil (see glossary)
3 tablespoons vegetable oil
1 cup (3 oz/90 g) bean sprouts
2 medium carrots, finely grated
2 medium green (spring) onions, chopped
1 package (1 lb/500 g) egg-roll wrappers (about 24)
1 egg, beaten with 2 tablespoons water
oil for frying

❦ Toss the cabbage with 1 teaspoon salt and let stand at least 30 minutes, while you continue.

❦ In a skillet, cook the pork until it loses its pinkness, breaking it up with a fork or spatula. Remove the pork with a slotted spoon and transfer it to a large bowl. Remove all but 2 tablespoons of fat from the pan and return it to moderate heat.

❦ Add the mushrooms, season with salt and pepper and stir and toss for several minutes, until they are tender and any liquid has evaporated. Add them to the bowl with the pork.

❦ Whisk together the soy sauce, sherry, cornstarch, sesame oil, ½ teaspoon salt and ¼ teaspoon pepper; set aside.

❦ Wipe out the skillet with absorbent paper towels and return it to high heat. Pour in the vegetable oil and, when it is almost smoking, add the bean sprouts, carrots and green onion. Season lightly with salt and pepper, and stir and toss vigorously for about 1 or 2 minutes. Add the soy sauce mixture and toss for a minute or so longer, until slightly thickened. Add to the bowl with the pork and mushrooms. Rinse the salted cabbage and pat it dry, then add it to the bowl also. Combine thoroughly, then let cool to room temperature, tossing occasionally.

❦ To fill the egg rolls, place a wrapper on your work surface and, in the center about 1 in (2.5 cm) from the bottom, place a heaping tablespoon of filling. Paint all the edges of the wrapper with beaten egg. Bring the bottom of the wrapper up and over the filling, fold the sides over the middle and then roll them up, so that you have a tubular shape. Let the rolls rest, covered with a damp kitchen towel, for about 15 minutes before frying them.

❦ Heat about 1½ in (4 cm) of oil in a heavy pan to 360°F (185°C). Place about 5 egg rolls in the hot oil, seam-side down.

❦ Fry them for about 3 minutes total, until golden, turning them once. Drain on absorbent paper towels and, if necessary, keep them warm in a 225°F (100°C) oven until you have enough to start serving. Serve as soon as possible.

MAKES 24 ROLLS

Beef and Broccoli Stir-Fry (top), Egg Rolls (top left and center) and Chop Suey (bottom)

Los Angeles

CHICKEN ENCHILADAS

These are lighter and less rich than the beef enchiladas on page 102 and they are easier to make, as the sauce, which is fresh, green and lively, is not cooked, but simply whirled in a food processor.

½ cup (4 fl oz/125 ml) vegetable oil
about 16 corn *tortillas*

FILLING

4 cups (1½ lb/750 g) shredded cooked chicken breast meat
2 cups (8 oz/250 g) grated Monterey Jack (mild melting) or
    Cheddar cheese
2 large green (spring) onions, finely chopped
½ cup (4 oz/125 g) canned diced mild green *chiles*
½ cup (4 fl oz/125 ml) heavy (double) cream
salt
freshly ground black pepper

salsa verde (see recipe, page 207)
2 cups (16 fl oz/500 ml) sour cream

🐾 Oil a 10- x 15-in (25- x 38-cm) baking pan, or two smaller pans. Preheat the oven to 350°F (180°C).
🐾 Heat the oil in a skillet. Lower each *tortilla* into the hot oil for just a few seconds, until it is pliable, then set it aside in a stack as it is done.
🐾 To make the filling, toss together the chicken, cheese, onion and *chiles*. Moisten with the cream and season with salt and pepper to taste. Place about ¼ cup of filling in each *tortilla*

Chili Size topped with Chili Con Carne

and roll it up loosely. Place, seam-side down, in the prepared baking pan or pans. Cover snugly with foil.
🐾 Bake the filled *tortillas* for 25 minutes, then remove the foil and bake for 5 minutes longer. Spoon some of the *salsa verde* over the top and place a small spoonful of sour cream on each *enchilada*. Pass the remaining *salsa* and sour cream at the table.

SERVES 6

Los Angeles

CHILI SIZE

A "size" is really a chiliburger—a meat patty on a toasted bun, topped with chili con carne, *grated cheese and onions if you wish.*

1 lb (500 g) ground (minced) beef
1 teaspoon salt
½ teaspoon freshly ground black pepper
vegetable oil, if needed
2 hamburger buns, split and toasted
2 cups *chili con carne* (see recipe below), heated
½ cup (2 oz/60 g) grated Cheddar cheese
1 medium red (Spanish) onion, finely chopped

🐾 Season the beef with salt and pepper and form it into 4 patties, each 3 in (7.5 cm) across. If you wish to barbecue them, grill about 4 in (10 cm) from hot coals until done to your liking. If you are cooking indoors, film a skillet with oil and cook the patties over moderately high heat until done.
🐾 Place half a toasted bun, flat-side up, on each plate. Top with a meat patty, then spoon ½ cup chili over the meat. Sprinkle with cheese and onions, and serve immediately.

SERVES 4

San Diego

CHILI CON CARNE

Though chili is a Texas dish, it is certainly a part of California cookery. There is little agreement about what makes a proper chili, whether cubed meat or ground should be used, whether beans should be included or not. Here is a good recipe that has chunks of meat for character, but no beans. It is robust, though not too spicy for timid palates, and wonderful with a platter of sliced tomatoes, and the red beans and rice on page 167.

¼ cup (2 fl oz/60 ml), or more, vegetable oil or shortening
    (vegetable lard)
2 lb (1 kg) stewing beef, cut into 1-in (2.5-cm) cubes
¼ cup (1 oz/30 g) all-purpose (plain) flour
2 onions, chopped
1½ cups (one 28-oz/875-g can) chopped, drained tomatoes
1½ cups (one 12-oz/375-ml can) beer
3 tablespoons chili powder
salt
freshly ground black pepper
water, or additional beer, if needed

🐾 Heat ¼ cup oil or shortening in a large heavy pan or Dutch oven. Toss the beef cubes in the flour, dust off the excess, and brown them lightly on all sides in the hot oil. Don't crowd the pan; cook the beef in two batches if necessary, adding more oil or shortening as needed.
🐾 Return all the meat to the pan and add the onions. Cook, stirring and tossing frequently, for about 5 minutes. Add the tomatoes and beer, then stir in the chili powder and season with salt and pepper to taste. Cover partially and simmer for about 2 hours, until the meat is very tender, adding more water or beer if needed to keep the meat covered.

SERVES 6

Tacos (top) and Chicken Enchiladas (bottom)

Los Angeles

TACOS

A taco is made from a folded corn tortilla that is fried until crisp and filled with meat, shredded lettuce, grated cheese and chopped tomato and onion. Tacos are of Mexican origin—and you find them everywhere from street fairs to fast-food joints. You can vary the meat and vegetables to suit what you have on hand; cooked shredded chicken and pork are good instead of beef, and diced avocado and shredded radishes make nice additions.

oil for frying
8 to 10 corn *tortillas*
1 lb (500 g) ground (minced) beef
1 onion, chopped
1 tablespoon chili powder
salt
freshly ground black pepper
¼ cup (2 fl oz/60 ml) tomato sauce or tomato purée
about 2 cups (4 oz/125 g) shredded iceberg lettuce
1½ cups (6 oz/185 g) finely shredded Cheddar cheese
1 large fresh tomato, chopped
2 large green (spring) onions, chopped
salsa verde (see recipe, page 207) or bottled taco sauce

🦐 To make the *taco* shells, heat about ⅓ to ½ in (8 to 12 mm) oil in a skillet to about 375°F (190°C). One at a time, lower a *tortilla* into the hot oil. After a couple seconds, use a spatula or pair of tongs to fold it in half, forming a semicircle. Fry for about one minute, until golden, then turn and cook the other side. Remove from the oil and open the *tortilla* slightly—so the filling will be easy to insert later—and let it cool, curved-side down, like a rocking horse, on absorbent paper towels.

🦐 Place the ground beef and onion in another skillet and cook, breaking the meat apart with a fork or spatula, until it loses all its pinkness.

🦐 Drain off any fat in the pan. Add the chili powder and season generously with salt and pepper. Stir in the tomato sauce; the mixture should be moist, but not runny.

🦐 Spoon some of the filling into each *taco* shell. Top with some lettuce, cheese, tomato and chopped onion. Do not fill the shells too full, or they will be difficult to eat; a proper *taco* should fit into your mouth. Pass the *salsa* or *taco* sauce at the table. For a buffet, set the meat-filled shells out, along with the other filling ingredients in individual bowls, and let guests assemble their own.

SERVES 6

Central Coast

CARNE SECA

Carne seca—dried beef or beef jerky—was a staple for early California explorers because it provided nourishment and kept indefinitely without refrigeration. Its chewy, salty quality still appeals to some people and it makes a good nibble with cold beer.

2 lb (1 kg) flank steak
1 cup (8 fl oz/250 ml) dry red wine
½ cup (4 fl oz/125 ml) soy sauce
1 cup (8 fl oz/250 ml) Worcestershire sauce
½ cup (4 fl oz/125 ml) red wine vinegar
1 tablespoon crushed black peppercorns
4 garlic cloves, mashed

❧ Place the flank steak in the freezer for an hour or so, until it is very firm—but not frozen—to make slicing easier. With a long, sharp knife, cut the meat into diagonal slices less than ¼ in (6 mm) thick. Lay the slices flat in a large glass or enamel baking dish.

❧ Combine the red wine, soy sauce, Worcestershire sauce, vinegar, peppercorns and garlic. Pour over the meat, cover, and marinate in the refrigerator for about 4 hours, turning the slices occasionally.

❧ Remove the meat from the marinade and pat it dry with absorbent paper towels. Arrange the slices in a single layer on wire racks (such as those used for cooling cakes and cookies) and set the racks on foil-covered baking sheets. Place in a 175°F (80°C) oven for about 2 or 3 hours, until dry and dark brown, but still pliable. Watch it closely; during the last half hour or so the meat can burn quickly. Let cool completely, then store airtight.

MAKES ABOUT 30 STRIPS

Los Angeles

CHICKEN MOLE

Moles are Mexican in origin and vary from long-simmered and complicated sauces, combining various types of chiles and spices as well as chocolate, to simpler sauces such as this, that are lighter, easier and good with chicken or turkey.

½ lb (250 g) *tomatillos* (see glossary)
1 can (4 oz/125 g) diced mild green *chiles*
2 garlic cloves, minced (finely chopped)
1 onion, chopped
1 tomato, peeled and seeded
1 cup (8 fl oz/250 ml) chicken stock (see glossary)
3–4 lb (1.5–2 kg) chicken pieces
¼ cup (2 fl oz/60 ml) olive oil
salt
freshly ground black pepper
½ cup (3 oz/90 g) pumpkin seeds or sunflower seeds
¼ cup (1 oz/30 g) coarsely chopped blanched almonds

❧ Remove the papery husks from the *tomatillos* and chop them coarsely. Combine them in a food processor with the *chiles*, garlic, onion and tomato. Process briefly, until the ingredients are coarsely chopped, but not puréed. Stir in the chicken stock and set aside.

❧ Pat the chicken pieces dry with absorbent paper towels. Heat the oil in a large skillet. Add the chicken pieces and brown them for about 5 minutes on each side, sprinkling them with salt and pepper as they cook. Remove from the pan, discard the fat and wipe out the pan.

❧ Return the pan to the heat and pour in the *tomatillo*-and-stock mixture. Add the browned chicken pieces, pumpkin seeds and blanched almonds, then cover and simmer for about 20 minutes, until the chicken is cooked through. If the sauce

seems too thin, uncover the pan and boil the sauce rapidly to thicken it slightly. Then arrange the chicken on a platter and pour the sauce over.

SERVES 4

Los Angeles

BEEF ENCHILADAS

Of Mexican influence, enchiladas are filled and rolled tortillas. They are easy to make in quantity for a party or buffet and can be prepared with meat, poultry, cheese or vegetables inside. These are stuffed with beef and served with a spicy tomato sauce. The chicken enchiladas with salsa verde (see recipe on page 100) are completely different in taste and some of the ingredients are not as common. Both are good with guacamole (page 34) or sour cream.

FILLING

3 tablespoons vegetable oil or shortening (vegetable lard)
2 onions, chopped
2 garlic cloves, minced (finely chopped)
1 lb (500 g) ground (minced) beef
2 cups (8 oz/250 g) grated Cheddar cheese
2 hard-boiled eggs, chopped
½ cup (2 oz/60 g) chopped ripe black olives
1 tablespoon chili powder
salt
freshly ground black pepper

SAUCE

3 tablespoons vegetable oil or shortening (vegetable lard)
1 onion, chopped
2 cups (16 fl oz/500 ml) tomato purée or tomato sauce
1 cup (8 fl oz/250 ml) beef stock (see glossary)
1 tablespoon chili powder
2 teaspoons ground cumin
salt
freshly ground black pepper
2 tablespoons wine vinegar
drops of hot pepper (Tabasco) sauce

about 16 flour *tortillas*
1 cup (4 oz/125 g) grated Cheddar cheese

❧ To make the filling, heat the vegetable oil or shortening in a skillet over moderate heat. Add the onion and cook gently for about 10 minutes, until soft. Stir in the garlic and scrape the mixture into a bowl.

❧ Return the skillet to the heat, add the ground beef and cook, breaking it up with a fork or spatula, until the meat loses its redness. Discard the fat, season the meat with salt and pepper, and add it to the bowl with the onions. Add the cheese, eggs, olives and chili powder and toss to combine. Season with salt and pepper to taste. Set aside.

❧ To make the sauce, heat the oil or shortening in a saucepan over moderate heat. Add the onion and cook gently for about 10 minutes.

❧ Add the tomato purée, stock, chili powder and cumin. Season with salt, pepper, vinegar and hot pepper sauce; it should be spicy, but not too acid. Simmer uncovered for about 10 minutes, then set aside.

❧ Preheat the oven to 325°F (165°C) and oil 2 baking dishes, about 9- x 13-in (23- x 33-cm) each.

❧ To form the *enchiladas*, place two heaping tablespoons of filling in the center of each *tortilla*. Roll them up loosely and place, seam-side down, in the prepared baking dishes; it does not matter if they touch. Spoon the sauce on top, covering each *tortilla* completely. Sprinkle with the cheese and bake for about 25 minutes, until the cheese is melted and the sauce bubbles.

SERVES 8

*Beef Enchiladas (top), Chicken Mole (left)
and Carne Seca (right)*

Corn Dogs

Santa Cruz
CORN DOGS

Sunshine, sand, salt-water taffy and cornbread-coated franks are synonymous with California's beaches in the summer. Wooden popsicle sticks, perfect for skewering the hot dogs, are available in craft stores and many supermarkets. For a snack-sized dog, or corn puppy, cut the sausages in half before skewering.

1 cup (4 oz/125 g) cornmeal (yellow maize flour)
1 cup (4 oz/125 g) all-purpose (plain) flour
1 tablespoon sugar
1 tablespoon baking powder
1 teaspoon salt
1 teaspoon chili powder
1 cup (8 fl oz/250 ml) milk
2 eggs
¼ cup (2 fl oz/60 ml) vegetable oil
oil for frying
10 frankfurters
mustard

❧ In a bowl stir and toss together the cornmeal, flour, sugar, baking powder, salt and chili powder. In a separate bowl, beat together the milk, eggs and oil. Add the liquid to the dry ingredients and stir until smooth and blended. In a heavy skillet, heat about 1½ in (4 cm) of oil to 360°F (185°C).
❧ Pat each frankfurter dry with absorbent paper towels and impale it on a popsicle stick. Two or 3 at a time, dip them in the cornmeal batter. The batter is quite thick, so you may need to use a knife to spread it evenly after dipping. Let the excess drip back into the bowl.
❧ Fry in the hot fat until the corn dogs are golden all over, turning them several times, for about 3 minutes. Drain briefly on absorbent paper towels and serve hot, with mustard.

MAKES 10 CORN DOGS

San Jose
PORK AND PRUNE SKEWERS

The sweetness of a puréed onion really highlights the taste of pork, and a long marinade helps keep the small cubes from drying out during cooking. This is an old-fashioned combination that works well on the barbecue.

1 onion, peeled and cut in pieces
⅔ cup (5 fl oz/160 ml) orange juice
2 tablespoons soy sauce
2 tablespoons vegetable oil
2 lb (1 kg) pork tenderloin (fillet), cut into 1½-in
    (4-cm) cubes
24 pitted prunes

❧ Purée the onion in a food processor and then combine it in a bowl with the orange juice, soy sauce and oil. Add the pork and prunes and toss to coat. Cover and refrigerate for several hours, or all day, tossing occasionally.
❧ Prepare a barbecue fire and place the grilling rack between 4 and 6 in (10 and 15 cm) from the heat.
❧ Remove the pork and prunes from the marinade and pat them dry with absorbent paper towels. Thread them onto long metal skewers, pushing them snugly together and alternating 1 or 2 cubes of pork with each prune. Grill for about 20 minutes, turning frequently, until well browned and the meat is no longer pink in the center.

SERVES 6   *Photograph page 106*

Pork and Prune Skewers (top, recipe page 105) and Smothered Chicken (bottom)

Central Valley

TURKEY WITH PRUNE STUFFING

Both turkeys and prunes are produced in California's Central Valley, and this pairing of ingredients is a natural—and very successful—union. Do not use dried fruit that is old and hard—sometimes not even long cooking will soften it. Nor would I recommend your using packaged dry bread cubes. To my taste, freshly cut cubes made from firm-textured sandwich bread make a much better stuffing, without any flavor of stale bread.

1 cup (6 oz/185 g) moist dried prunes
6 cups (12 oz/375 g) fresh bread cubes
2 teaspoons dried sage
½ teaspoon ground cinnamon
¼ cup (2 oz/60 g) butter
1 onion, chopped
4 celery stalks, diced
½ cup (4 fl oz/125 ml), or more, chicken or turkey stock
   (see glossary)
salt
freshly ground black pepper

1 turkey, about 10 lb (5 kg)
¼ cup (2 oz/60 g) softened butter

🐾 Cover the prunes with boiling water and let them stand for 5 minutes. Drain well and chop coarsely, then set aside.

🐾 In a large bowl, toss the bread cubes with the sage and cinnamon. Melt the butter in a skillet, add the onion and celery and cook for 10 minutes, until softened. Add this mixture to the bread and toss lightly. Add the stock and prunes and toss until mixed; handle the mixture gently, so that it remains light and the bread does not break apart too much. If you like a very moist stuffing, add a little more stock, but do not make it soggy. Keep in mind that it will absorb some moisture inside the bird. Season to taste with salt and pepper.

🐾 Preheat the oven to 325°F (165°C).

🐾 Place the stuffing in the turkey, filling the cavity loosely. Truss the turkey and rub it with the softened butter. Sprinkle with salt and pepper and place it breast-up on a rack in a roasting pan. Cook for approximately 15 minutes per pound.

🐾 After it has been in the oven for 45 minutes, start basting the turkey every 20 minutes or so with the accumulated juices from the pan. Remove the bird from the oven and let it rest for about 15 minutes before carving it.

SERVES 10   *Photograph pages 90–91*

Central Coast

SMOTHERED CHICKEN

Recipes for this old-fashioned chicken stew appear in many turn-of-the-century California cookbooks and they all combine chicken, onions, mushrooms and cream in various proportions.

¼ cup (2 fl oz/60 ml) olive oil or butter
1 chicken, about 3 lb (1.5 kg), cut up
salt
freshly ground black pepper
1 large onion, chopped
¼ cup (1 oz/30 g) all-purpose (plain) flour
2 cups (16 fl oz/500 ml) chicken stock (see glossary)
1 lb (500 g) mushrooms, sliced
¼ cup (2 fl oz/60 ml) heavy (double) cream
2 tablespoons chopped parsley

❦ Heat the oil or butter in a large heavy skillet over moderate heat. Add the chicken pieces, sprinkle with salt and pepper and cook for about 5 minutes, until lightly browned. Turn, sprinkle again with salt and pepper and brown the other side for about 5 minutes more. Remove the chicken to a side dish.

❦ Add the onion to the fat remaining in the pan, and cook gently for about 5 minutes, until soft. Add the flour and cook, stirring, for about 2 minutes. Whisk in the chicken stock and bring to a boil, then season lightly with salt and pepper. Reduce the heat and simmer for about 2 minutes, then return the chicken pieces to the pan. Cover and cook over low heat, so the sauce is just simmering, for 10 minutes.

❦ Add the mushrooms and simmer, covered, for another 10 minutes. Stir in the cream and parsley and serve.

SERVES 4

Fresno

LAMB KABOBS

Fresno and the surrounding area have a considerable Armenian population, and among that group lamb is a popular meat. This is traditionally served with rice pilaf. Use only tender cubes cut from the meaty part of the leg; other cuts of lamb are too tough.

½ cup (4 fl oz/125 ml) dry red wine
¼ cup (2 fl oz/60 ml) olive oil
1 onion, finely chopped
2 teaspoons chopped fresh rosemary or 1 teaspoon
    dried rosemary
½ teaspoon salt
½ teaspoon freshly ground black pepper
2 lb (1 kg) lean boneless lamb, cut in 1½-into (4-cm) cubes

❦ In a large bowl combine the wine, oil, onion, rosemary, salt, pepper and lamb. Toss to combine, then cover and refrigerate for several hours, or all day, tossing 3 or 4 times.

❦ Prepare a barbecue fire and place the grilling rack between 4 and 6 in (10 and 15 cm) from the heat.

❦ Remove the lamb from the marinade and pat it dry with absorbent paper towels. Thread the meat onto long metal skewers, pushing the pieces together snugly.

❦ Grill for 8 to 10 minutes, turning frequently, until lightly browned.

SERVES 4–6

Lamb Kabobs

Petaluma

CHICKEN PIE WITH MUSHROOMS

Nearly every part of the country has a version of chicken pie. In the Midwest, the crust is apt to be made of biscuit dough; in the Pennsylvania Dutch country, the chicken is stewed in a broth with huge squares of homemade egg noodles and there is no top crust at all. Most often in California, cubes of chicken meat are combined with a creamy sauce, then covered with a flaky pie dough and baked long enough to brown the crust.

CRUST

1½ cups (6 oz/185 g) all-purpose (plain) flour
1 teaspoon salt
½ cup (4 oz/125 g) vegetable shortening (vegetable lard)
5 tablespoons (2½ fl oz/75 ml) water

FILLING

14 tablespoons (7 oz/220 g) butter
½ lb (250 g) mushrooms, quartered
1 cup (4 oz/125 g) all-purpose (plain) flour
5 cups (40 fl oz/1.25 l) chicken stock (see glossary)
½ cup (4 fl oz/125 ml) heavy (double) cream
salt
freshly ground black pepper
¼ cup (½ oz/15 g) chopped parsley
2 tablespoons chopped fresh tarragon or 1 teaspoon dried tarragon
4 cups (1½ lb/750 g) diced cooked chicken
2 tablespoons lemon juice

❧ Preheat the oven to 425°F (220°C). Butter a baking dish of about 6-cup (48-fl oz/1-l) capacity and a top diameter of about 10 in (25 cm).

❧ To make the dough, combine the flour and salt in a bowl. Drop in the shortening and, using your fingertips or a pastry blender, cut the fat into the dry ingredients until the mixture resembles coarse crumbs. Add the water, a tablespoon at a time, stirring well with a fork after each addition; add only enough to make the dough cohesive, but not sticky.

❧ On a lightly floured surface, roll out the pastry dough so that it is a little larger than the top of the baking dish and about ⅛ in (3 mm) thick; set aside.

❧ Melt 2 tablespoons (1 oz/30 g) of the butter in a skillet and cook the mushrooms in it for about 10 minutes, stirring frequently; set aside.

❧ Melt the remaining 12 tablespoons (6 oz/185 g) in a large saucepan. Add the flour and cook, stirring, for about 2 minutes. Whisk in the chicken stock and bring to a boil. Add the cream, season with salt and pepper to taste, and simmer for about 5 minutes, stirring frequently. Stir in the cooked mushrooms, the parsley, tarragon, chicken and lemon juice. Season with additional salt and pepper if necessary.

❧ Pour the mixture into the prepared baking dish. Cover with the dough and crimp the edges. Cut a few vents in the top for steam to escape. Bake for about 30 minutes, until the pastry is golden brown and the sauce is bubbling.

SERVES 4–6

Tamales

Los Angeles

TAMALES

More than just about anything else I can think of, tamales should be made with helping hands and plenty of time; it is quite daunting to face them alone. There are corn husks to be soaked, masa harina *(the cornmeal lining) to be beaten, and* chili con carne *to be simmered. Just spreading the filling on the corn husks seems to require three hands. But* tamales *are definitely worth the effort. You can make them any size you want. These are quite large, similar to those you would see in most Mexican restaurants in California.* Tamales *made in Mexico are much smaller—I have seen some that are no more than a bite.*

chili con carne (see recipe, page 100)
5 oz (155 g) dried corn husks (see glossary)
3½ cups (12 oz/375 g) *masa harina* (see glossary)
2 cups (16 fl oz/5000 ml) warm beef stock (see glossary) or water
¾ cup (6 oz/185 g) lard or vegetable shortening (vegetable lard)
2 teaspoons salt
20 to 30 pitted ripe black olives

❧ Prepare the *chili con carne* and set it aside to cool to room temperature. Or cook it a day or two ahead and refrigerate it.
❧ Pick over the corn husks, removing any imperfect ones. Pour boiling water over them and allow them to soak for at least an hour. Drain and pat dry, then cover with a moist towel until you are ready to use them.
❧ Combine the *masa harina* with the warm stock or water. Place the lard or shortening in a bowl and beat it vigorously (an electric mixer is useful here). Gradually add the *masa* mixture, then the salt, beating all the while. Continue beating for 10 minutes, until a small blob of the mixture will float when dropped in water. Cover with a damp cloth and set aside.
❧ To form a *tamale*, place a large husk on your work surface. The husk should be about 5 in (13 cm) wide and just a little longer. Overlap a couple husks if necessary—but a husk in 1 piece is easier to work with. Place a scant ¼ cup of the *masa* mixture on the husk, then press it out with your fingers, spreading it almost to the edges. Place about 2 heaping tablespoons of *chili con carne* in the middle and top that with 2 ripe olives. Fold the edges of the husk over the filling—do not roll it—just fold it. Spread a narrow piece of husk, just about 2 in (5 cm) wide, with about a tablespoon of the *masa*.
❧ Lay that over the seam, *masa*-side down. Then roll the *tamale* very gently between your hands and the work surface, so that it forms a cylinder. Do not be too rough with it; the filling should remain in the middle. Twist the ends slightly and tie each with a piece of string or a long, thin piece of husk used like string. With a pair of scissors, clip the ends of the husks so they are neat. Fill and form the remaining *tamales* the same way.
❧ To cook them, arrange the *tamales* on a rack over boiling water in a large kettle. Cover and steam for 1 hour.

MAKES ABOUT 16 TAMALES, SERVING 8

San Francisco

CHICKEN TETRAZZINI

Steamtable food has contributed to the diminished reputation of this comforting blend of chicken, cream sauce and spaghetti. Despite the fact that it dries out quickly after cooking, it is frequently kept warm for much too long. The dish is named after Luisa Tetrazzini, a rather stout opera singer and gourmand who was popular in the early part of this century. She loved performing—and eating—in San Francisco.

Chicken Pie with Mushrooms (top) and Chicken Tetrazzini (bottom)

½ lb (250 g) spaghetti
3 tablespoons butter
¼ cup (1 oz/30 g) all-purpose (plain) flour
1½ cups (12 fl oz/375 ml) chicken broth (see glossary)
½ cup (4 fl oz/125 ml) heavy cream
salt
freshly ground black pepper
¼ lb (125 g) mushrooms, thinly sliced
¼ cup (2 fl oz/60 ml) dry sherry
pinch of ground nutmeg
3 cups (1 lb/500 g) diced cooked chicken, preferably white meat
¼ cup (1 oz/30 g) breadcrumbs
¼ cup (1 oz/30 g) grated Parmesan cheese

❧ Preheat the oven to 400°F (200°C) and butter a baking dish of about 8-cup (64-fl oz/2-l) capacity.
❧ Cook the spaghetti in plenty of boiling salted water until done, then drain it well. While it cooks, prepare the sauce. Melt the butter in a saucepan, add the flour, and cook together for about 2 minutes. Whisk in the stock and bring to a boil. Add the cream, blend well, then simmer for about 5 minutes, stirring frequently. Season to taste with salt and pepper. Add the mushrooms and simmer, covered, for about 5 minutes more. Stir in the sherry and nutmeg, then fold in the chicken.
❧ Place the spaghetti in the baking dish, then spoon the chicken and sauce on top. Spread with the breadcrumbs and cheese and bake for about 20 minutes.

SERVES 4–6

CITRUS-GRILLED CHICKEN

This fat-free dish of chicken breasts marinated in citrus juice and grilled over coals is right in keeping with the trend toward lighter eating that seems especially prevalent in health-conscious California.

¾ cup (6 fl oz/180 ml) fresh orange juice
¼ cup (2 fl oz/60 ml) fresh lemon juice
¼ cup (2 fl oz/60 ml) fresh lime juice
1 tablespoon grated lemon zest
3 garlic cloves, minced (finely chopped)
1 tablespoon chopped fresh tarragon or 1 teaspoon
 dried tarragon
½ teaspoon salt
¼ teaspoon freshly ground black pepper
6 large chicken breast halves, skinned

❦ In a bowl blend together the juices, lemon zest, garlic, tarragon, salt and pepper. Place the chicken in a large, heavy plastic food-storage bag and pour in the juice mixture. Press out the air and seal the bag. Squeeze gently, rubbing the marinade into the chicken. Set the bag in a large bowl and refrigerate for 2 to 4 hours, turning and rubbing occasionally.

❦ Prepare a barbecue fire and position the grilling rack between 4 and 6 in (10 and 15 cm) from the heat.

❦ Remove the chicken from the marinade and grill it for about 25 minutes, turning frequently, until it is well browned on both sides and cooked through.

SERVES 6

Citrus-grilled Chicken (left) and
Skewered Chicken Livers (right, recipe page 113)

TERIYAKI CHICKEN

Teriyaki was brought to the West Coast by travelers from Hawaii. It produces chicken pieces that are moist, with a shiny dark glaze. The oriental soy and ginger marinade is also good for beef, pork and firm-textured fish, such as tuna.

⅔ cup (5 fl oz/160 ml) soy sauce
½ cup (4 fl oz/125 ml) dry sherry
⅓ cup (3 fl oz/80 ml) vegetable oil
1 tablespoon sugar
2 garlic cloves, minced (finely chopped)
2 tablespoons grated fresh ginger or 2 teaspoons
 ground ginger
1 tablespoon grated orange zest
2 chickens, about 2½ lb (1.25 kg) each, split in half

❦ To make the marinade, whisk together the soy sauce, sherry, oil, sugar, garlic, ginger and orange zest. Let the mixture stand for about an hour, so that the flavors blend.

❦ Place the chicken in a heavy plastic food-storage bag and slip that bag inside another (to protect against leaks). Pour the marinade into the bag with the chicken and seal both bags well. Rub gently to distribute the marinade and place the bags in a bowl. Refrigerate for between 1 and 8 hours; the longer the chicken marinates, the more pronounced the teriyaki flavor will be.

❦ Remove the chicken from the bags, reserving the marinade. Broil about 6 in (15 cm) from the heat, for about 10 or 12 minutes on each side, brushing occasionally with some of the reserved marinade for about the first 15 minutes. The chicken should be well browned, with no tinge of pink when cut at a joint.

SERVES 4–6

ALLEN V. LOTT

Teriyaki Chicken

Merced
RANCH CHICKEN

According to the late James Beard, this spicy recipe of chicken pieces in a sauce of chili powder, almonds and olives from the San Joaquin Valley is an excellent example of California ranch cookery at the beginning of the century. Serve it with an orange and red onion salad and beer.

1 chicken, about 4 lb (2 kg), cut up
cornmeal (yellow maize flour)
¼ cup (2 fl oz/60 ml) olive oil
salt
freshly ground black pepper
1 onion, finely chopped
3 garlic cloves, minced (finely chopped)
½ teaspoon ground nutmeg
1 teaspoon ground cumin
1 teaspoon ground coriander seed
1 cup (8 fl oz/250 ml) red wine
1 cup (8 fl oz/250 ml) chicken stock (see glossary) or water
3 tablespoons chili powder
½ cup (2 oz/60 g) blanched slivered almonds
½ cup (2 oz/60 g) pitted green olives, halved
sprigs of fresh cilantro (coriander/Chinese parsley) or
   chopped parsley

🦃 Roll the chicken pieces in cornmeal to coat them completely. Heat the oil in a large skillet or Dutch oven and brown the chicken pieces on all sides, sprinkling them with salt and pepper as they cook. This will take about 10 minutes.
🦃 When the chicken is well browned, add the onion, garlic, nutmeg, cumin and coriander seed. Blend in the wine and stock or water, then cover and simmer for 20 to 30 minutes, until the chicken is cooked through.
🦃 Add the chili powder and simmer a few minutes more. Remove the chicken to a hot platter and add the almonds and olives to the sauce, seasoning with salt and pepper to taste. Spoon the sauce over the chicken and sprinkle with sprigs of cilantro or chopped parsley.

SERVES 4 OR 5

Petaluma
SKEWERED CHICKEN LIVERS

There is little wavering about chicken livers: you either like them or you don't. For those who love them, these are a treat—brown and crisp outside, moist and succulent inside, with overtones of a soy sauce and herb marinade. Serve them on a bed of rice for a main course, or as an appetizer with an aïoli (garlic mayonnaise) for dipping.

3 tablespoons olive oil
2 tablespoons soy sauce
1 large green (spring) onion, chopped
½ teaspoon dried thyme
¼ teaspoon freshly ground black pepper
1 lb (500 g) chicken livers, trimmed and halved
¼ cup (2 fl oz/60 ml) melted butter or additional olive oil

🦃 In a bowl combine the 3 tablespoons olive oil, the soy sauce, green onion, thyme and pepper. Add the chicken livers and toss to coat. Marinate for about an hour, tossing once or twice.
🦃 Prepare a barbecue fire and place the grilling rack between 4 and 6 in (10 and 15 cm) from the heat. Thread the marinated livers snugly onto 4 skewers and brush with melted butter or additional olive oil. Grill for about 10 minutes, turning occasionally and brushing lightly with the remaining butter or oil. The livers are done when they are no longer pink inside.

SERVES 4   *Photograph page 110*

Ranch Chicken

ROAST WILD DUCK

Mr. Prentis C. Hale of San Francisco and Cloverdale, California, has decades of hunting experience, and this is how he likes his wild duck—very rare and accompanied by homemade grape jelly and lemon wedges, along with a generous serving of wild rice, and lots of paper napkins. Lacking homemade grape jelly, you can substitute currant jelly. Wild duck roasted this way is also good cold, with a spicy mustard. Be forewarned; this will smoke and splatter in the oven.

1 wild duck per person
grape or currant jelly
lemon wedges

❧ Preheat the oven to 500°F (260°C) and line a roasting pan with foil to make cleaning up easier.
❧ Roast the duck for 18 minutes for very rare meat. (Add 2 or 3 minutes to the roasting time if you like your meat medium.) Serve immediately, with the jelly and lemon wedges.

SERVES 1

BUTTERFLIED GRILLED SQUAB

Not long ago we ate game birds only if there were a hunter in the family. Nowadays pen-raised birds, such as quail and squab, are sold in many markets year round. Because they survive on a diet of wild things, the wild ones do have a gamier flavor that many people find appealing. However they are raised, these birds are best cooked simply and served with a tart accompaniment, such as grape or currant jelly, or unsweetened applesauce, and buttered wild rice or wild rice with walnuts and dates (see recipe on page 136). In the Napa Valley, these might be grilled over grapevine wood or roots. At home, coals work just fine.

1½ cups (12 fl oz/375 ml) dry red wine
⅓ cup (3 fl oz/80 ml) olive oil
1 teaspoon fennel seeds
1 teaspoon juniper berries
½ teaspoon salt
¼ teaspoon freshly ground black pepper
2 teaspoons chopped fresh rosemary or 1 teaspoon
    dried rosemary, crumbled
4 squab (pigeon), butterflied (sliced lengthwise and
    opened out)

❧ Whisk together the wine, olive oil, fennel seeds, juniper berries, salt, pepper and rosemary. Place the squab in a large heavy plastic food-storage bag and pour in the wine mixture.
❧ Press out the air and seal the bag. Squeeze gently, rubbing the marinade into the squab.
❧ Set the bag in a bowl and refrigerate for at least 4 hours, turning and rubbing it occasionally.
❧ Prepare a barbecue fire and place the grilling rack between 4 and 6 in (10 and 15 cm) from the heat. Remove the squab from the marinade, reserving the marinade, and pat the birds dry with absorbent paper towels.
❧ Grill over hot coals for 15 to 20 minutes, turning and brushing with the reserved marinade 3 or 4 times. They are done when well browned and the breast meat is slightly pink when slashed at the thickest part.

SERVES 4 *Photograph page 116*

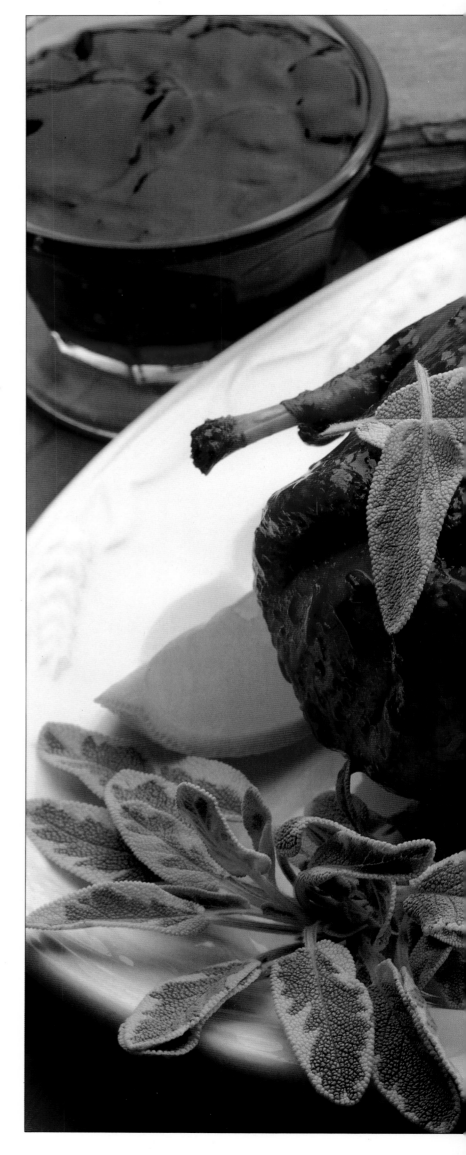

Roast Wild Duck

Butterflied Grilled Squab (recipe page 114)

Berkeley

DUCK BREAST SALAD ON GREENS

This salad, of rare duck breast (or squab or quail) on a bed of small, tender garden lettuces or field greens with a light vinaigrette, is typical of those that became popular at Chez Panisse in Berkeley, where Alice Waters' style of cooking heralded a completely new attitude toward restaurant food and cooking in the seventies. This dish makes a chic first course or luncheon dish and is quite suitable for a home cook too; all of the elements can be made ready ahead of time.

2 skinless, boneless duck breast halves, about 6 oz (185 g) total
2 tablespoons olive oil
salt
2 tablespoons chopped shallots or green (spring) onions
¼ cup (2 fl oz/60 ml) brandy
½ cup (4 fl oz/125 ml) duck stock or chicken stock
   (see glossary)
1 tablespoon dry sherry

VINAIGRETTE

2 tablespoons minced (finely chopped) shallots or green
   (spring) onions
⅓ cup (3 fl oz/80 ml) olive oil
2 tablespoons red wine vinegar or sherry vinegar
the reserved duck cooking juices

salt
freshly ground black pepper
½ pound (250 g), more or less, mixed baby or garden
   lettuces, or field greens (see glossary), washed and dried
1 tablespoon chopped parsley or a handful of chervil sprigs

🦆 To prepare the duck breasts, pat them dry with absorbent paper towels. Heat the olive oil until almost smoking in a heavy skillet, preferably one with a nonstick surface. Add the duck breasts and brown them for about 2 or 3 minutes on each side, sprinkling them lightly with salt as they cook. They should remain pink, but not raw, in the center. Remove them to a dish to cool while you continue.

🦆 Return the pan to heat and add the shallots. Cook for about 2 minutes, then add the brandy, stock and sherry. Scrape the bottom of the pan with a spatula to remove any browned bits, then raise the heat to high and boil until the liquid is reduced to about ¼ cup. Strain into a small bowl.

🦆 To prepare the vinaigrette, whisk together the shallots with the oil, vinegar and the reserved duck cooking juices. Season to taste with salt and pepper.

🦆 To assemble the salad, cut the duck breast into diagonal slices about ¼ in (6 mm) thick. Stir any juices from the slicing into the vinaigrette. Toss the lettuces with enough of the vinaigrette to make them glisten and arrange on a large platter or individual plates.

🦆 Arrange the slice of duck breast on top and drizzle them with vinaigrette. Sprinkle with parsley or chervil.

SERVES 4

Duck Breast Salad on Greens

THE CENTRAL VALLEY

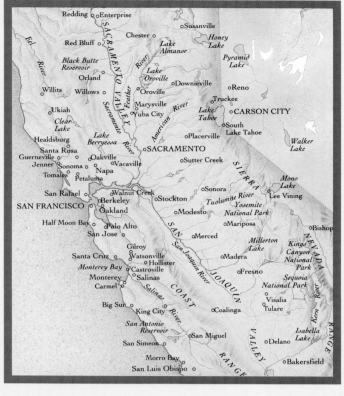

THE CENTRAL VALLEY

Millions of almond, walnut, pistachio, peach, plum, pear, nectarine, apricot and cherry trees stand in uniform rows on hundreds of thousands of acres throughout the great Central Valley. Beyond the sweet perfume of fruit and nut orchards, the valley is laden with a dizzying array of produce. Where the crops end, cattle and poultry ranches begin. Fields of lush green broccoli, flooded squares of rice, patchworks of feathery-topped carrots and asparagus, hillsides covered with gnarled grapevines and vast cottonfields yield just some of the crops grown in this region.

Long and flat, the Central Valley sweeps through the heart of the state. From the east-west passes of the Tehachapi Mountains beyond Bakersfield, it runs almost five hundred miles north to Redding. This larger-than-life farmland, cradled by coastal mountains to the west and the Sierra Nevada and the gold country to the east, actually encompasses two major valleys: the Sacramento in the north and the San Joaquin in the south. Rice, wheat, stone fruit, nuts and olives thrive in the central and northern counties. The southern end of the Central Valley is somewhat warmer, with a longer growing season more suited to crops such as cotton, oranges, tomatoes, cherries, sugar beets and raisins—though these crops are not necessarily limited to north or south.

Previous pages: Endless varieties of fruits and vegetables grow in every corner of the long, flat Central Valley that sweeps five hundred miles throught the heart of the state. Left: The California Aqueduct carries its precious fluid from the lakes of the distant north to the checkered fields of the Central Valley.

Migrant farm workers bring crates of green beans to be weighed after a day of backbreaking work. Strongly unionized since 1975, migrant workers harvest a large percentage of the state's fresh produce.

Both valleys are fed by melting snows from the slopes of the Sierras, which flow into the Sacramento and San Joaquin rivers. As most of that runoff flows naturally to the northern counties, the precious commodity is diverted to the thirsty south by one of the most sophisticated irrigation systems in the United States.

The Sacramento Delta area is a rich agricultural complex in its own right. A web of dammed and leveed waterways, it marks the confluence of the Sacramento, Mokelumne and San Joaquin rivers. The entire delta is alive with shad and salmon, sturgeon, catfish and bass—all quite delicious when grilled and served up with the local bounty, as they are in local restaurants and backyards. With crushed almonds to coat the fish, asparagus to steam and serve with locally grown wild rice, it is easy to see how beautifully simple, often unintentionally healthy, California menus have become. Marketplace cuisine is at its height here.

Throughout the Central Valley, winters are cool and moist, summers hot, clear and dry, giving rise to meals based on plenty of salads, fruit soups, informal barbecues and an abundance of fresh fruit pies. A typical menu from a local magazine published in the 1940s called for "biscuits with fig jam, three kinds of salads and boysenberry ice cream"—California regional fare based on fresh, wholesome foods. And it still holds true in the 1990s. Much of the valley is farm country, where, for after-school snacks, kids might sip on mugs of apricot nectar and eat oatmeal-raisin cookies. Cooks here are adept at canning, preserving and pickling.

Chico, at the far north end of the Central Valley, is a perfect example of small-town California with exotic produce in its backyard. The area is rich with almond orchards, and yards are dotted with loquats, pomegranates, persimmons and even kiwifruit. Kiwifruit—now identified as much with California as with New Zealand—was first planted in the Chico area in 1937. It remained a novelty for some time. But slowly, the fuzzy brown fruit with its glistening green flesh and tiny black seeds worked its way into salads, tarts, jams and muffins and daiquiris. Growers say that kiwifruit was first served to the public at Trader Vic's famous restaurant in San Francisco in 1961. Today, thanks to an innovative West Coast developer of specialty produce, the Central Valley now grows about sixty-three million pounds of kiwifruit a year—ninety-five percent of that grown in the United States—and it has become an everyday fruit. (Kiwifruit is harvested in the late fall. As California's seasons are just the opposite of New Zealand's, the two countries can enjoy each other's crops.)

Pistachios were introduced to the Central Valley in the 1920s, but it took forty years of research to perfect the variety that is grown commercially. The tender nuts grow suspended in grapelike clusters on female trees and, when the nut is ripe, the shell splits. Most of these nuts are sold in their natural tan skins, pure California style. Before the Californian growers established themselves, pistachios—dyed an improbable reddish-brown—were imported, principally from Iran. When politics halted the trade, Californians found that they had a better market for undyed pistachios.

The black Mission fig, actually an Adriatic fig, was first planted in California missions in the 1760s. Over a century later, the Calimyrna fig was introduced by a horticulturist in Fresno. Actually, it is a Smyrna fig, with a "Cali" attached to its name. The warm, dry climate of the Central Valley is kind to figs that require those conditions to develop the best flavor, high sugar content and thin skins. Smyrnas are prized for the syrupy sweetness and a nutty flavor that comes from kernels in the seeds, making fresh Calimyrnas in cream one of the most tempting desserts ever created, with an incomparably luscious flavor and richness. On menus, this combination was popular all over California around the turn of the century. Also common were figs stewed with citrus peel and cinnamon or poached in liqueur. Today, 99.9 percent of all the figs grown in the United States come from California's Central Valley.

Olives, originally grown for oil in the Spanish missions, emerged as a sought-after condiment once large-scale curing methods were developed around the 1890s. Offered as "California olives" by any hotel or railroad dining service that could procure a supply, they were at first considered a delicacy. Over the years, and especially after 1910, when it was discovered that olives could be canned, mild ripe or "black" olives became a cooking staple. The *California Farmer* magazine called them "poor man's mushrooms" and indeed, Californians tossed them in *tamale* pie, in salads with oranges and red onions, spaghetti sauce, chicken pot pie, and savory breads—from Italian types to Mexican *chile* corn bread. Today, the town of Lindsay at the southern end of the Central Valley is the olive-growing and processing center of the state. Olives are also grown throughout the region by several smaller, specialty growers who produce dry-cured or spicy versions of olives stuffed with anchovies, almonds, mushrooms, garlic or *jalapeño* peppers.

THE MELTING POT

Beginning around the mid-1800s in this region, each newly arrived family brought a distinctive style of cooking to the pot. Most came from the lands in which California's crops originated. Italians rejoiced in being able to grow peppery arugula and mild bell peppers, deep purple eggplant, oniony chives and crisp broccoli in California's Mediterranean climate. Armenians, who found the soil in Fresno to be similar to that of their homeland, grew figs, melons and pistachios and became some of the most productive raisin growers in the state. Well known in the Middle East, raisins in California are said to have been first produced as a result of a natural disaster. In 1873, a devastating heat wave in the southern valley withered plantings of Egyptian Muscat grapes, turning them into shrivelled, dried husks—or raisins. One grower took his raisins to San Francisco and found a

A vast grid of citrus groves stretches east from Bakersfield.

grocer who was willing to sell them as a "Persian delicacy." Of course they sold out and, from that point on, it seems, raisins were served at California tables in every course—rolled in grape leaves, stuffed in turkey and chicken, sprinkled in salads and listed as a dessert on hundreds of turn-of-the-century restaurant menus. California raisins today are grown from the delicate-skinned Thompson seedless grapes—another major crop in the Central Valley.

Greek, German, French, Basque, Chinese and Japanese farmers also contributed crops to the Central Valley bounty and, with them, recipes that remain part of the California heritage: *baklava* made with honey and walnuts, prunes soaked in port, apple strudel, creamy flan, vegetables stir-fried with hot peppers, *sukiyaki*. It is a heritage that offers anyone in California an opportunity to taste the foods of the world in his or her own backyard, if not at a local charity bazaar or potluck meal.

Potatoes, vegetables that prefer moderate weather, are harvested along the cooler eastern edges of the Central Valley.

EGGS, CHEESE AND GRAINS

California produces cheeses of all types—Italian, Swiss, Greek, Mexican and English—and the right cheese for every occasion can be found in shops like this one in the Napa Valley.

EGGS, CHEESE AND GRAINS

Three staples—eggs, cheese and grains—form the basis of an infinite variety of California favorites, from *huevos rancheros* to sourdough bread.

Tortillas, of course, were the staff of life in the Spanish mission days, when early recipes called for a "pair of stout wrists, patience and perseverance." Those strong wrists were essential to push the stone *metate* and *mano* (mortar and pestle) together to grind wheat or corn flour. They were needed to form the soft dough, then roll and pat it

The classic coupling of fresh pastries and coffee attracts crowds to this bright Danish bakery.

Previous pages: Ripe Olive Bread (top, recipe page 144) and Avocado and Teleme Omelet (bottom, recipe page 144)

into the stacks of thin, round *tortillas*—cooked on a copper or iron plate over an open fire — that were eaten with every meal. *Tortillas* are now an everyday grocery item, as common as bagels in New York or corn bread in Texas, and factories large and small turn them out by the millions for Californians of every persuasion.

Along with *tortillas*, the Spanish missionaries introduced cheese-making to California. Their first California cheese was soft, creamy and light and became known as *queso del país*, cheese of the land, or *queso blanco*, white cheese. After the gold rush, when a Scotsman named David Jacks came along, California's only native cheese was given its American name. Jacks, though unlucky in the mines, became a wealthy landowner in Monterey and Big Sur on the central coast. On his land, he operated dairy ranches in partnerships with Swiss and Portuguese dairymen. The milk surplus from his many dairies was transformed into the same type of soft and nearly spreadable cheese that the missionaries made. But because Jacks was a shrewd merchandiser, the cheese became forever known as Monterey Jack. The cheeses now sold under this name bear little resemblance to the original, however. The flavor is still mild and mellow, but the cheese is now firm and easy to slice. It melts to a nice, creamy texture—good for omelets and *chiles rellenos*, the classic Mexican-inspired dish of mild *chiles* stuffed with cheese, dipped in a beaten egg batter and fried. The egg transforms the *chiles* into golden, fluffy morsels to be baked and topped with *enchilada* sauce.

With characteristic melting-pot fervor, California today produces French, Italian, Swiss, Greek, Mexican and English cheeses of all types—soft and semisoft, naturally ripened, unripened and processed. As with most agricultural products, the industry includes major cooperatives and small family-owned farmsteads. The Marin French Cheese Company has been producing Camembert and Brie near Petaluma (known for chicken and eggs, too) since 1865. Made from the milk of Jersey cows that graze on clover-filled pastures nearby, the Marin cheeses have a distinctive flavor and are less runny than their European counterparts. Goat cheese, though not produced in large quantities, has become a California specialty, produced mainly on small farms. With its tart edge and soft texture, it lends itself to every course. Often, it is served as an appetizer, spread on olive-oil-brushed toast rounds with sun-dried tomatoes and fresh basil, or sprinkled over thin-crusted pizza.

Of all the grains grown in California, rice is by far the most significant to cooks. Since 1910, when the dense, swampy soils around Sacramento proved hospitable to Japanese short-grain rice, the crops have grown—and the state now produces tons of short- and medium-grain white rice.

Wild rice (which is technically a grass, but is cooked and eaten like a grain) is now a treasured California crop as well. In fact, California is the only state outside Minnesota growing the aquatic grasses that yield the seeds of this dark delicacy. Processing, which involves cleaning, drying, steaming and shelling, transforms the originally green seeds into nutty-tasting, coffee-colored kernels. Rather than harvesting in the time-honored way—paddling out in canoes and flailing ripened kernels into the boat—California growers harvest their wild rice mechanically and dry it in large rotating drums. The end product is delicious, with slender, dark kernels that but-

Pasta salads are among the tempting dishes offered for sale at the Oakville Grocery in the Napa Valley.

terfly during cooking to reveal a soft, cream-colored interior. To cook, wild rice requires more liquid and time than does regular white rice; generally, three parts liquid to one part wild rice and between thirty-five and fifty minutes, in a covered pot.

Although wheat once dominated California crops, it is much less significant today. California is second only to Arkansas in the production of rice, and does not produce much else in the way of grains (for people, anyway). But the grain-based foods created and consumed in California are sweeping in their scope and variety and include breads and noodles native to the homelands of its immigrants from virtually every country in the world.

Pizza-by-the-slice makes a perfect snack for strolling or rolling on Venice Beach. Californians tend to add artichoke hearts, olives and other local goods to the standard New York–style slice.

Northern California

BACON AND HERB FRITTATA

A frittata is a large omelet left unfolded. You can vary the filling (or topping, actually) with any cooked meat, ham or vegetables. Happily, a frittata is equally good warm or cold, making it perfect for a picnic, too.

¼ cup (2 fl oz/60 ml) olive oil
½ lb (250 g) mushrooms, sliced
8 eggs
1 teaspoon salt
½ teaspoon freshly ground black pepper
½ lb (250 g) bacon, crisply cooked and crumbled
2 teaspoons chopped fresh thyme or winter savory
1 cup (4 oz/125 g) grated Monterey Jack (mild melting) cheese

❦ Preheat the broiler (griller). Heat the oil in a 9- or 10-in (23- or 25-cm) skillet, preferably one with a nonstick surface. Add the mushrooms and cook for about 10 minutes, until they are soft, and any liquid they exude has evaporated. Remove from heat.

❦ In a bowl beat the eggs with the salt and pepper. Return the skillet to low heat, spread the mushrooms evenly over the bottom and pour in the eggs. Sprinkle with the bacon and herbs, then cover and cook for about 3 minutes. Uncover, sprinkle with the cheese, then place under a hot broiler (griller)

for a minute or two, until the cheese has melted and is very lightly browned. To serve, cut into wedges.

SERVES 4

Central Coast

CHEESE AND MUSHROOM PIE

A California version of quiche, combining eggs, Monterey Jack or Teleme cheese and mushrooms, is a favorite along the central coast. With roast beef for dinner, or a green salad for a light lunch, it never fails to please. Wild mushrooms, such as chanterelles, would be very good here; if you lack those, the cultivated ones are fine.

½ recipe basic pie dough (see *empanadas*, page 38) rolled out and used to line a 9-in (23-cm) pie dish, unbaked
3 tablespoons butter
½ lb (250 g) mushrooms, thinly sliced
salt
freshly ground black pepper
1 cup (4 oz/125 g) grated Teleme or Monterey Jack (mild melting) cheese
3 eggs
½ cup (4 fl oz/125 ml) heavy (double) cream or milk
pinch of ground nutmeg

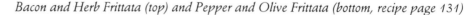

Bacon and Herb Frittata (top) and Pepper and Olive Frittata (bottom, recipe page 131)

Cheese and Mushroom Pie

🦋 Preheat the oven to 425°F (220°C). Line the inside of the pie shell with a sheet of heavy-duty foil or a double thickness of regular foil, pressing it in. Bake for about 8 minutes, until the edges are set, then remove the foil and continue baking for about 4 minutes more, until the pastry is pale brown. Let cool before filling. Reduce the oven temperature to 350°F (180°C).

🦋 Melt 2 tablespoons of the butter in a skillet over medium heat. Add the mushrooms, season with salt and pepper to taste and cook, stirring frequently, for 10 minutes, or until tender. If necessary, raise the heat to high during the last

couple of minutes to evaporate any juices. Spread the mushrooms over the bottom of the pie shell and sprinkle with the cheese.

🦋 Beat together the eggs, cream or milk, ½ teaspoon salt, ¼ teaspoon pepper and the nutmeg. Pour the mixture into the pie shell and dot with the remaining butter. Bake for 30 to 35 minutes, until browned on top and a knife inserted just off center comes out clean. Remove and let the pie stand a few minutes before serving.

SERVES 4–6

Penne with Goat Cheese

PENNE WITH GOAT CHEESE

Laura Chenel has been making goat cheese by hand in Santa Rosa for over ten years, and I first had this dish made with one of her California chèvre *cheeses. It blends well with the pasta, melting slowly into a smooth, thick sauce that is particularly good with* penne, *because it gets inside the quills, spreading its tangy flavor throughout. Serve as a first course before roast chicken or beef, or as a luncheon dish with a salad.*

1 lb (500 g) *penne* (see glossary)
1 cup (8 fl oz/250 ml) heavy (double) cream
½ cup (4 oz/125 g) butter
½ lb (250 g) soft goat cheese, cut into pieces
salt
freshly ground black pepper
½ cup (2 oz/60 g) toasted walnuts, finely chopped

❧ Drop the *penne* into a large pot of boiling salted water. While it cooks, make the sauce: pour the cream into a skillet and bring it to a boil. Boil gently for several minutes, until it has thickened and reduced by about half. Add the butter and let it melt slowly into the cream, stirring frequently. Keep warm over lowest heat.
❧ Drain the *penne* when it is done. Immediately add the cheese to the cream mixture, stirring until it is partially melted. In a large bowl—or the pan in which you cooked the pasta—toss the *penne* with the sauce, season with salt and pepper to taste, toss in the walnuts and serve.

SERVES 4

PEPPER AND OLIVE FRITTATA

With a salad, bread and chilled white wine, this open-faced omelet with Mediterranean overtones is a most successful and colorful blending of ingredients. Basque sheepherders in northern California and Nevada often made omelets in this style, to be eaten hot or cold. Large basil leaves, used as a garnish, remain greener if they are torn into pieces, not chopped.

2 green bell peppers (capsicums)
2 red bell peppers (capsicums), or two more green ones
8 eggs
1 teaspoon salt
½ teaspoon freshly ground black pepper
3 tablespoons olive oil
½ cup (2 oz/60 g) sliced ripe black olives
½ cup (4 oz/125 g) crumbled goat cheese
2 tablespoons small basil leaves, or large leaves, torn into pieces

❧ Place the peppers on a rack about 4 in (10 cm) from a hot broiler (griller) and broil them, turning frequently, for 15 minutes, or until they are blistered on all sides. Place in a paper bag, close the bag, and let the peppers stand for 15 minutes.
❧ Carefully peel off the skins, using a knife point to help you with any stubborn spots. Remove the stems, open the peppers and scrape out the seeds. Cut the peppers into ½-in (12-mm) strips and set aside.
❧ In a bowl, beat the eggs with the salt and pepper. Heat the oil in a 9- or 10-in (23- or 25-cm) skillet, preferably one with a nonstick surface. Add the peppers and spread them evenly over the bottom. Sprinkle with the olives. Pour in the eggs, then cover and cook over low heat for about 3 minutes. While the eggs cook, preheat the broiler (griller).
❧ Uncover the *frittata* and sprinkle with the cheese. Slip under a hot broiler for about 2 minutes, until lightly browned.
❧ Scatter the basil leaves on top and serve. If you plan to serve the *frittata* cold, sprinkle with basil just before serving.

SERVES 4   *Photograph page 128*

PASTA SALAD WITH PEPPERS

A perfect pasta salad looks good, tastes good and is satisfying to eat. In these days of boxed mixes and concoctions from the delicatessen, you will find that homemade pasta salad bears no resemblance to what you can buy when out and about. The technique of tossing the hot pasta with oil and then letting it cool to room temperature so that each strand is separate and glistening comes from the restaurateur Jeremiah Tower. Serve the salad as soon as possible and remember that, once refrigerated, pasta never regains its fresh-cooked taste or texture.

3 red bell peppers (capsicums)
3 green or yellow bell peppers (capsicums), or a combination
1 lb (500 g) spaghetti, *spaghettini* or other pasta
¾ cup (6 fl oz/180 ml) olive oil
salt
freshly ground black pepper
⅓ cup (¾ oz/25g) chopped Italian or flat-leaf parsley
2 medium green (spring) onions, chopped
1 garlic clove, minced (finely chopped)
¼ cup (2 fl oz/60 ml) white wine vinegar
⅓ cup (¾ oz/25 g) chopped fresh basil or small basil leaves

🐚 Place all the peppers on a rack about 4 in (10 cm) from a hot broiler (griller) and broil them, turning frequently, for about 15 minutes, until they are blackened and blistered on all sides. Place them in a paper bag, close the bag and let it stand for about 15 minutes.
🐚 Carefully peel off the skins, using the point of a small sharp knife to remove any stubborn spots. Open the peppers and scrape out the seeds. Cut into ½-in (12-mm) strips and set aside.
🐚 Cook the pasta in plenty of boiling salted water until done.
🐚 Drain thoroughly, then toss in a large baking pan with ½ cup (4 fl oz/125 ml) of the olive oil. (Spread in a baking pan, rather than mounded in a bowl; it cools faster.) Season generously with salt and pepper. Let the pasta cool until tepid, tossing frequently.
🐚 In a large bowl stir together the remaining ¼ cup olive oil with the peeled peppers, parsley, green onions and garlic. Stir in the vinegar and season with salt and pepper to taste. Add

the pasta and toss to combine. Taste, adding more salt and pepper if necessary. Just before serving, toss with the basil.

SERVES 6

NOODLES WITH ARTICHOKE HEARTS

Frozen artichoke hearts are among the most useful vegetables I know. In this recipe, they marry so well with the noodles that it really is not worth the effort of trimming and cooking fresh artichokes. They also put this dish well within the reach of the cook in a hurry; you can have it ready in just a few minutes.

2 packages (9 oz/280 g each) frozen artichoke hearts
½ cup (4 oz/125 ml) water
12 oz (375 g) wide noodles
½ cup (4 fl oz/125 ml) olive oil
salt
freshly ground black pepper
2 large green (spring) onions, thinly sliced
2 tablespoons chopped parsley
1 tablespoon chopped fresh oregano or 1 teaspoon crumbled dried oregano
freshly grated Parmesan cheese

🐚 Place the artichoke hearts and water in a saucepan, put the lid on the pan and bring to a boil. Reduce the heat and simmer them for 6 to 8 minutes, or until tender when pierced. Drain thoroughly and set aside.
🐚 Cook the noodles in a large pot of boiling salted water. While the noodles cook, heat the olive oil in a skillet. Add the artichoke bottoms, season with salt and pepper, and keep warm over low heat.
🐚 When the noodles are done, drain and toss them in a large bowl with the warmed oil and artichokes, green onion, parsley and oregano. Pass Parmesan cheese at the table.

SERVES 4–6

Noodles with Artichoke Hearts

Pasta Salad with Peppers

San Francisco

SPICY THAI NOODLES

Thai food is wonderful and, like Chinese food, allows one to do so much with very little. But it is not as easy to prepare at home as are some other ethnic cuisines, simply because the ingredients are harder to come by—unless you are near a specialty market. Here is an unorthodox version of a classic Thai dish—noodles with spicy peanut sauce flecked with green onion and cilantro—made with plain old linguini.

½ cup (4 oz/125 g) smooth peanut butter
2 tablespoons lemon or lime juice
¼ cup (2 fl oz/60 ml) soy sauce
1 teaspoon red pepper flakes
3 tablespoons sesame oil (see glossary)
10 drops hot *chile* oil (see glossary)
1 lb (500 g) *spaghettini, linguini* or other thin pasta
¾ cup (6 fl oz/180 ml) olive oil
8 green (spring) onions, washed, trimmed and cut
    diagonally into ½-in (12-mm) pieces
⅓ cup (¾ oz/25 g) chopped cilantro (coriander/Chinese
    parsley)
a few cilantro (coriander/Chinese parsley) sprigs
2 tablespoons chopped peanuts

To make the sauce, whisk together until smooth the peanut butter, lemon juice and soy sauce, then blend in the red pepper flakes, sesame oil and hot *chile* oil; set aside.

Cook the pasta in plenty of boiling salted water until done.

Drain it thoroughly, then toss with the olive oil. Let it sit until cooled to room temperature, tossing frequently.

Pour the peanut mixture over the noodles and toss to coat.

Add the green onions and cilantro leaves and toss to combine. Mound the noodles in a bowl, or spread them on a platter, and garnish with chopped cilantro sprigs and chopped peanuts.

SERVES 6–8

Sacramento Valley

HERBED RICE SALAD

Like pasta salads, rice salads are best made fresh and carefully seasoned. The secret of getting taste into the rice is to toss it with olive oil, salt and pepper while it is still warm, so that it marries with these flavors as it cools. Do not overload this recipe with too many ingredients; it is best kept simple.

4 cups (about 17 oz/520 g) cooked warm rice
½ cup (4 fl oz/125 ml) olive oil
salt
freshly ground black pepper
⅓ cup (¾ oz/25 g) chopped parsley
1 large green (spring) onion, chopped
2 tablespoons chopped fresh mint
1 tomato, peeled, seeded and chopped
¼ cup (1 oz/30 g) sliced green or ripe black olives
3 to 4 tablespoons (1½–2 fl oz/45–60 ml) white wine vinegar

In a large bowl toss the warm rice with the olive oil. Season generously with salt and pepper and let cool to room temperature, tossing occasionally.

Add the parsley, green onion, mint, tomato and olives and toss to mix. Add the vinegar and toss to blend. Taste, and add more salt, pepper or vinegar if necessary; the salad should be flavorful and pleasantly acid, but not tart.

SERVES 6   *Photograph page 137*

Spicy Thai Noodles

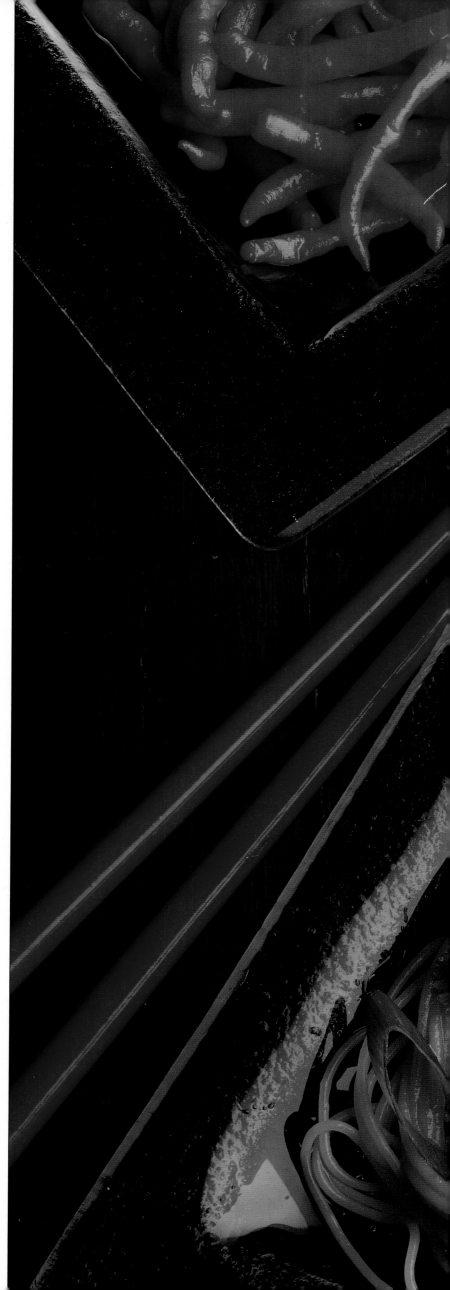

Wild Rice with Walnuts and Dates (top) and Bulgur Pilaf (bottom)

WILD RICE WITH WALNUTS AND DATES

Thanks to increased production in California, wild rice is less expensive and more accessible than ever. Because of its nuttiness, it is especially compatible with sweet dried fruit, such as prunes, apricots and raisins. Serve this with poultry, game, pork or any smoked meat.

4 tablespoons (2 oz/60 g) butter
1 onion, chopped
4 celery stalks, diced
1 cup (5 oz/155 g) wild rice (see glossary)
3 cups (24 fl oz/750 ml) chicken or beef stock (see glossary)

1 teaspoon salt
½ cup (2 oz/60 g) chopped toasted walnuts
½ cup (2½ oz/75 g) finely cut dates

❧ Heat the butter in a heavy saucepan. Add the onion and celery and cook gently for 10 minutes. Add the rice and continue to cook and stir for 3 minutes more. Add the stock and salt and bring to a boil. Reduce the heat, cover the pan and simmer for about 1 hour. Taste the rice; the grains should be firm but not crunchy. Cover and cook for a few minutes longer if necessary.

❧ Add the walnuts and dates and toss to combine, then set aside off the heat for 5 minutes before serving, to allow the dates to soften a little.

SERVES 6

136

Gilroy
GARLIC CUSTARDS

This dish may not appeal to you, unless you know that long-simmered garlic becomes smooth, mild and almost buttery. These individual custards are good served with roast or grilled lamb or as a first course, on a bed of lightly dressed field greens.

6 heads garlic
¼ cup (2 oz/60 g) crumbled goat cheese
2 tablespoons sun-dried tomato purée*
3 eggs
¼ cup (1 oz/30 g) fresh breadcrumbs
1½ cups (12 fl oz/375 ml) milk
½ cup (4 fl oz/125 ml) heavy (double) cream
½ teaspoon salt
¼ teaspoon freshly ground black pepper

❧ Separate the garlic heads into cloves, leaving them in their papery skins. Simmer the garlic in salted water to cover for between 30 and 40 minutes, or until very soft. Drain thoroughly, then purée them through a food mill or sieve to separate the pulp from skins.
❧ Preheat the oven to 325°F (165°C) and butter six ⅓-cup (3-fl oz/80-ml) ramekins or custard cups.
❧ Beat together the goat cheese and tomato purée until smooth, then beat in the eggs and the garlic purée. Warm the milk and cream in a small saucepan until hot, then whisk into the garlic mixture. Season with salt and pepper.
❧ Divide the custard among the prepared ramekins and place them in a baking pan. Pour boiling water into the baking pan to come halfway up the ramekins.

Garlic Custard, garnished with additional sun-dried tomato purée (left) and Herbed Rice Salad (right, recipe page 134)

❧ Bake for about 50 minutes, or until set. Remove from the water and let the custards sit 5 minutes before unmolding.

*Oil-packed, sun-dried tomatoes (see glossary), finely chopped and then puréed in a food processor or forced through a sieve.

SERVES 6

California
BULGUR PILAF

Bulgur is made from whole wheat grains and has a chewy texture and nutty flavor similar to brown rice. Though it has Middle Eastern origins, it is increasingly popular here as a side dish instead of rice or potatoes and is also used in many substantial salads.

3 tablespoons butter or olive oil
1 onion, chopped
1 cup (5 oz/155 g) bulgur (see glossary)
2 cups (16 fl oz/500 ml) chicken stock (see glossary)
salt
freshly ground black pepper
1 cup (8 oz/250 g) cooked peas
¼ cup (1 oz/30 g) chopped toasted almonds

❧ Heat the butter or olive oil in a large saucepan. Add the onion and cook gently for 5 minutes, until soft. Add the bulgur and cook, stirring, for 2 minutes more. Pour in the stock, season with salt and pepper to taste and bring to a boil. Cover and cook over low heat for 15 minutes, or until it is tender.
❧ Remove the bulgur from heat, add the peas and almonds and toss to combine.

SERVES 4–6

SOURDOUGH BAKING

*Though sourdough has been romanticized, there is no secret to its
success. It depends on capturing rogue or wild yeasts, which are
present in the atmosphere, in a mixture of grain and liquid that is
allowed to ferment. It is no surprise that many starters are unreli-
able, though I have had consistent success with the following
system. It was developed by Jerry DiVecchio of Sunset magazine,
who worked for two years with Dr. George York, a food chemist*
*at the University of California at Davis, to develop the technique.
Using the system, you really can trap your own wild yeast from
the air and bake a chewy, crusty sourdough loaf with its unmistakable tang and sourness—and no commercial yeast added.
Sourdough baking begins with a starter.*

SOURDOUGH STARTER

1 cup (8 fl oz/250 ml) nonfat milk
3 tablespoons low-fat yogurt
1 cup (4 oz/125 g) all-purpose (plain) flour

liquid rises to the surface, stir it back in. If the liquid has turned light pink in color, it has started to spoil; discard that batch and begin again.

❧ After the curd has formed, add the flour and stir until the mixture is smooth.

❧ Cover tightly and set in a warm place again. Let the starter stand for between 2 and 5 days, until the mixture is full of bubbles and has a good sour smell. The starter is now ready to use as directed.

❧ So that you will always have an ample supply, replenish the starter each time you use it by adding equal amounts of warm milk and flour. For example, if you used 1 cup starter, warm 1 cup (8 fl oz/250 ml) skim milk and add it to the starter with 1 cup (4 oz/125 g) flour. Stir until smooth, then cover tightly and let the mixture stand in a warm place for a few hours or overnight—until bubbly—then cover and store in the refrigerator.

❧ If you bake infrequently, discard about half the starter every 3 or 4 weeks, and replenish it with warm milk and flour. You may also freeze it for a month or two, which will slow its action, though it will still work. If the starter was frozen, let it stand in a warm place for about 24 hours, or until it is bubbly, before using.

San Francisco

SOURDOUGH BREAD

This bread has a thick, crisp crust and a moist, springy, sour interior.

1½ cups (12 fl oz/375 ml) warm water
1 cup (8 fl oz/250 ml) sourdough starter (preceding recipe)
5 cups (1¼ lb/625 g), more or less, all-purpose (plain) flour
1 tablespoon salt
2 tablespoons cornmeal (yellow maize flour)

❧ In a large bowl, combine the water, starter and 2½ cups (10 oz/315 g) of the flour. Beat until smooth, cover with plastic wrap and let stand in a warm place (in a gas oven with the pilot light on or in an electric oven with the interior light on or on top of the water heater) for 6 to 8 hours or overnight, until thick, full of bubbles and spongy looking.

❧ Add the salt and enough remaining flour to make a fairly stiff but manageable dough. Turn out onto a lightly floured surface and knead for a minute or two, then let the dough rest for 10 minutes.

❧ Knead again for about 10 minutes, or until the dough is smooth and elastic, adding just enough flour to keep it from being too sticky. Place in a greased bowl, cover and let rise until double in bulk.

❧ Punch the dough down and divide it in half. Plump each piece into a round, then draw your hands down the sides, stretching the dough toward the bottom and turning it as you work. Continue stretching and turning until the round is perfectly smooth. Pinch the bottom of the loaves firmly where the seams come together. Sprinkle a large baking sheet with the cornmeal and place the formed loaves on it, pinched-side down. Cover loosely and let them rise until double in bulk.

❧ Preheat the oven to 375°F (190°C).

❧ With a razor blade or a sharp knife, slash a ½-in (12-mm) deep X across the top of each risen loaf, then spray or brush them with cold water.

❧ Bake for 10 minutes, then spray or brush with cold water again. Bake for 10 minutes more and brush or spray again. Bake for 40 minutes more (the total baking time is 1 hour), then transfer the loaves to racks to cool.

MAKES 2 MEDIUM-SIZED ROUND LOAVES

Sourdough Bread (top), Sourdough Pancakes (left, recipe page 142) and Sourdough Starter (right)

❧ Heat the milk to between 90°F and 100°F (32° and 38°C). Remove from the heat and stir in the yogurt. Pour into a warmed container and cover tightly. Place in a warm spot (between 80°F and 100°F/27°C and 38°C, but not above 110°F/43°C). Good places are the top of a water heater, in a gas oven with only the pilot light, or an electric oven with the interior light on. After 6 to 8 hours, the mixture will clabber, forming a soft curd that does not flow readily when the container is tilted slightly. Check periodically and, if a clear

Watsonville

CHILE EGG PUFF

This dish goes together with a flick of the whisk. It has a good dairy flavor and is the kind of cheese and egg dish that is often made for breakfast parties in California. And it is perfect to make ahead and take along to a potluck because it can be reheated and is always a hit with guests. Serve it with ham, bacon or sausages.

10 eggs
½ cup (2 oz/60 g) all-purpose (plain) flour, sifted
1 teaspoon baking powder
1 teaspoon salt
2 cups (16 fl oz/500 ml) small curd cottage cheese
1 lb (500 g) Monterey Jack (mild melting) cheese, grated
½ cup (4 fl oz/125 ml) melted butter
1 can (7 oz/220 g) diced mild green *chiles*

❧ Preheat the oven to 350°F (180°C). Butter a 9- x 13-in (23- x 33-cm) baking dish.
❧ Crack the eggs into a large bowl and beat thoroughly. Stir and toss together the flour, baking powder and salt, sift them over the eggs and beat until blended. Beat in the cottage cheese, grated Monterey Jack cheese, butter and *chiles*. Pour the mixture into the prepared pan and bake for 35 to 45 minutes, or until puffy and set, and a knife inserted slightly off center comes out clean.

SERVES 10

Fresh Apple Muffins (top) and Fried Camembert (bottom, recipe page 144)

Imperial Valley

FIG MUFFINS

Nearly all of the fig supply in the United States is produced in California, and the padres grew them quite successfully in the early mission gardens—hence the name Mission figs, by which they are still called today. These moist muffins use dried figs, which is often the only way you find this fragile fruit outside California.

1½ cups (12 fl oz/375 ml) boiling water
1 cup (6 oz/185 g) dried Mission (black) figs
2 eggs, beaten
¾ cup (6 oz/185 g) sugar
⅓ cup (3 fl oz/80 ml) melted butter
2 tablespoons grated orange zest
½ teaspoon almond extract (essence)
2 cups (8 oz/250 g) all-purpose (plain) flour
2 teaspoons baking powder
¼ teaspoon baking soda (bicarbonate of soda)
½ teaspoon salt
½ cup (2 oz/60 g) chopped toasted almonds or walnuts

❧ Preheat the oven to 400°F (200°C). Grease muffin tins or line them with paper baking cups (paper cases).
❧ Pour the boiling water over the figs and let them stand for 15 minutes. Drain thoroughly, reserving ½ cup (4 fl oz/125 ml) of the liquid. With a pair of scissors or a sharp knife, cut the figs into ½-in (12-mm) bits, discarding the stems; set aside.
❧ In a bowl, combine the reserved fig-soaking liquid with the eggs, sugar, butter, orange zest and almond extract and beat until smooth. In another bowl, stir and toss together the flour, baking powder, baking soda and salt. Add to the egg mixture, beating just until the batter is blended. Stir in the figs and nuts.
❧ Spoon into the prepared muffin tins, filling them about three-quarters full. Bake for 15 to 18 minutes, or until a toothpick inserted in a muffin comes out clean. Remove from the oven and serve warm.

MAKES ABOUT 12 MUFFINS

Pajaro Valley

FRESH APPLE MUFFINS

As popular as muffins are, it is hard to find good ones that are pebbly-textured and slightly crumbly and neither too sweet nor too dense. These are spicy and very moist, with the crunch of apples and nuts. Have them for dinner, with roast pork or chicken. The optional glaze makes a sweeter muffin, the sort you might want to bake for a special breakfast.

2 cups (8 oz/250 g) all-purpose (plain) flour
2 teaspoons baking powder
1 teaspoon baking soda (bicarbonate of soda)
1½ teaspoons ground cinnamon
½ teaspoon salt
3 eggs
¾ cup (6 fl oz/180 ml) milk
½ cup (3 oz/90 g) firmly packed brown sugar
½ cup (4 fl oz/125 ml) melted butter or vegetable oil
2 medium apples, peeled, cored and finely diced
1 cup (4 oz/125 g) chopped walnuts
½ cup (3 oz/90 g) raisins or currants

GLAZE

2 tablespoons butter
2 tablespoons heavy (double) cream
¼ cup (1½ oz/45 g) brown sugar
½ teaspoon ground cinnamon

Fig Muffins (top right) and Chile Egg Puff (bottom)

🦋 Preheat the oven to 400°F (200°C) and generously butter muffin tins.

🦋 In a large bowl, stir and toss together the flour, baking powder, baking soda, cinnamon and salt. In another bowl, beat together the eggs, milk, sugar and butter or oil. Stir in the apple, nuts and raisins or currants. Add to the combined dry ingredients and beat with a wooden spoon just until the batter is blended.

🦋 Spoon into the prepared muffin tins, filling them two-thirds full. Bake for about 20 minutes, or until a toothpick inserted into a muffin comes out clean.

🦋 Make the glaze while the muffins bake: combine the butter, cream, sugar and cinnamon in a small pan, bring to a boil and boil for 1 minute. Set aside, kept warm.

🦋 Remove the muffins from the oven and, if you have made the glaze, poke each muffin a few times with the tines of a fork, then drizzle each with a generous teaspoonful of the glaze. Let the muffins cool in the pans for about 3 minutes, then turn out onto racks. Serve warm.

MAKES ABOUT 16 MUFFINS

141

Solvang
EBLESKIVER

Ebleskiver are sweet Danish dumplings that look like round puffy pillows and are similar in flavor and style to a pancake. They are baked on top of the stove, in a special pan with rounded wells, and are often served with applesauce. With a dusting of powdered sugar, they will remind you of cake doughnuts. You are likely to find ebleskiver in Solvang, where there is a large Danish population.

1 cup (8 fl oz/250 ml) sour cream
⅔ cup (5 fl oz/160 ml) milk
3 eggs, separated
¼ cup (2 fl oz/60 ml) melted butter
¼ cup (2 oz/60 g) sugar
2 cups (8 oz/250 g) all-purpose (plain) flour
1 teaspoon baking soda (bicarbonate of soda)
1 teaspoon salt
1 teaspoon ground nutmeg
powdered (icing) sugar

🌿 In a bowl combine the sour cream, milk, egg yolks, melted butter and sugar and beat to blend. In another bowl, stir and toss together the flour, baking soda, salt and nutmeg. Add to the sour cream mixture and stir briefly just until barely combined.

🌿 Beat the egg whites until they stand in soft peaks. Stir one-third of the whites into the batter to lighten it, then scoop the batter on top of the remaining whites and fold them together.

🌿 Set the *ebleskiver* pan over medium heat. It is hot enough when drops of water flicked into the wells dance and sputter before evaporating. Grease the wells generously with vegetable shortening or butter. Pour in the batter, filling each cup one-half to two-thirds full. Cook for 3 or 4 minutes, until browned and puffy, then turn the dumplings carefully—a pair of knitting needles, chopsticks or teaspoons are useful in nudging them over—and brown the other side for a minute or two. Sprinkle with powdered sugar and serve. Bake the remaining batter the same way.

MAKES ABOUT 24 DUMPLINGS

Sierra Nevada
SOURDOUGH PANCAKES

Sourdough pancakes would be a little tough if you did not add some baking soda. Remember, if you want griddlecakes for breakfast, you will have to start the night before.

1 cup (8 fl oz/250 ml) sourdough starter (see recipe, page 138)
1 cup (8 fl oz/250 ml) warm water
1 cup (4 oz/125 g) all-purpose (plain) flour
2 tablespoons sugar
½ teaspoon salt
¼ teaspoon baking soda (bicarbonate of soda)
1 egg, beaten
2 tablespoons melted butter

🌿 Stir together the starter, water and flour. Beat until smooth, then cover with plastic wrap and let the mixture stand in a warm place 6 to 8 hours or overnight, until bubbly and sour-smelling.

🌿 Combine the sugar, salt and soda in a small cup, then stir into the starter mixture. Add the egg and butter and stir with a fork until blended.

🌿 Grease a griddle or frying pan and set it over moderate heat until a few drops of water sprinkled on the surface sputter and move about before evaporating. Drop a scant ¼ cup of batter onto the pan for each griddlecake and bake until the top is full of bubbles and the bottom lightly browned. Flip with a spatula and cook the other side until golden. Keep warm on a platter in a 200°F (95°C) oven until you have enough to serve—though the sooner they are eaten, the more tender they will be.

MAKES ABOUT 15 PANCAKES   *Photograph pages 138–139*

Ebleskiver

Petaluma

AVOCADO AND TELEME OMELET

These compatible ingredients from the Petaluma area fall together in a most meltingly tender way. An omelet takes only a few seconds to cook, so have the filling at hand when you begin.

3 eggs
¼ teaspoon salt
pinch freshly ground black pepper
1 tablespoon butter
¼ cup (2 oz/60 g) finely diced avocado
¼ cup (1¼ oz/40 g) finely grated Teleme cheese
1 teaspoon chopped fresh tarragon or parsley

❧ Crack the eggs into a small bowl, add the salt and pepper and whisk with a fork for 10 seconds—just to blend the yolks and whites.

❧ Put a skillet that has a bottom diameter of about 8 in (20 cm) and, preferably, a nonstick surface over high heat and drop in the butter. As it melts, swirl the pan to coat the bottom and sides. In about 2 minutes, when the butter is quite hot and is on the verge of browning but has not actually browned, pour in the eggs. Let them cook for about 10 seconds, then grab the handle and swirl the pan around rather vigorously for about 10 more seconds. Stop swirling and, with a spatula, lift some of the cooked egg at the edges, tilting the pan so the raw egg from the center flows underneath. When the eggs are mostly set but still creamy, scatter the avocado, cheese and herb on one side. With a spatula, fold the other half of the omelet over the filling, then leave the pan over high heat for just a few seconds more. Rapidly turn the pan upside down over a warm plate, so that the omelet falls out, bottom up. Push it into shape with a fork if necessary.

SERVES 1   *Photograph pages 124–125*

Sonoma

POLENTA WITH CHEESE AND SAUSAGE

If you can make hot cereal, you can make polenta, *a savory cornmeal porridge of northern Italian extraction. Every cook should master it, because it is delicious and makes a good last-minute dish for a quick dinner or unexpected company. It also blends so wonderfully with additions and variations.*

3 cups (24 fl oz/750 ml) water
salt
¾ cup (3 oz/90 g) *polenta* (cornmeal/yellow maize flour)
4 tablespoons (2 oz/60 g) butter
½ cup (4 fl oz/125 ml), or more, milk or cream
½ lb (250 g) cooked link sausage, such as *kielbasa* (boiling sausage) or Italian sausage
1 tablespoon vegetable oil
1½ cups (about 8 oz/250 g) diced Monterey Jack (mild melting) or Teleme cheese
freshly ground black pepper

❧ Bring the water to a boil in a large, heavy saucepan with 1 teaspoon salt. Slowly pour in the *polenta*, whisking constantly, then cook over low heat, stirring frequently, for 5 minutes or until thick. Continue to cook over the lowest heat for 10 minutes more, stirring occasionally; it will become very thick. Stir in the butter and ½ cup of milk or cream.

❧ While the *polenta* cooks, prepare the sausages. Halve them lengthwise, then cut crosswise into ½-in (12-mm) pieces. Heat the oil in a skillet and cook the sausage pieces for 5 or 10 minutes, until lightly browned. Drain briefly on absorbent

paper towels, then stir into the *polenta* along with the cheese. The cheese should not melt entirely; let a few small, soft bits remain. Season with salt, if necessary, and pepper to taste. If the mixture is stiff rather than creamy, stir in a little bit more milk or cream.

SERVES 4–6

Visalia

RIPE OLIVE BREAD

The late Helen Evans Brown was a frequent contributor to Sunset *magazine and a specialist in West Coast cookery in the forties and fifties. She wrote many books, including the* West Coast Cookbook, *published in 1952, from which this recipe is adapted. It is moist and slightly salty and good thinly sliced to serve with meats and cheese.*

2 eggs
1 tablespoon sugar
½ teaspoon salt
¼ cup (2 fl oz/60 ml) olive oil
½ cup (4 fl oz/125 ml) milk
1 cup (4¼ oz/130 g) chopped ripe black olives, drained
1 cup (4 oz/125 g) all-purpose (plain) flour
2 teaspoons baking powder

❧ Preheat the oven to 350°F (180°C). Grease and flour an 8½- x 4½- x 2½-in (22- x 11- x 6-cm) loaf pan.

❧ In a large bowl beat the eggs with the sugar, salt, oil, milk and olives.

❧ Stir and toss together the flour and baking powder. Add to the combined ingredients and stir just until blended; do not overbeat. Pour into the prepared pan and bake for about 1 hour, or until a wooden skewer or broom straw inserted in the loaf comes out clean. Let cool in the pan for 10 minutes, then turn out onto a rack to cool completely.

MAKES 1 LOAF   *Photograph pages 124–125*

Petaluma

FRIED CAMEMBERT

The California Camembert and Brie cheeses made by the Marin French Cheese Company and sold under the Rouge et Noir label work perfectly for this—a warm, creamy mixture of softly melted cheese with crunchy breadcrumbs and toasted almonds. Similar in style to old-fashioned fried cheese balls, this is a substantial spread to serve with wine or drinks, accompanied by crisp crackers or sliced French bread.

2 Camembert cheeses, 8 oz (250 g) each
1 egg, well beaten
1 cup (1½ oz/45 g) fresh white breadcrumbs
4 tablespoons (2 fl oz/60 ml) olive oil
1 tablespoon butter
¼ cup (1 oz/30 g) sliced almonds
salt

❧ Dip each cheese—rind and all—in the beaten egg, then roll it in the breadcrumbs to coat completely. Heat 3 tablespoons of the olive oil in a skillet over moderately high heat. When the oil is hot, add the cheeses and brown them well, for about 4 minutes on each side. Remove to a warm platter.

❧ Wipe out the skillet and return it to the heat. Add the butter and the remaining tablespoon of oil. When the butter has melted, add the almonds and salt. Stir and toss for a minute or two, until lightly browned, then spread them over the tops of the cheeses.

SERVES 6–8   *Photograph page 140*

Polenta with Cheese and Sausage

Flour Tortillas (top left) and Huevos Rancheros (bottom)

Los Angeles

FLOUR TORTILLAS

Soft, plain and simple, these are delicious warmed and buttered, or used for quesadillas (see recipe on page 34).

2 cups (8oz/250 g) all-purpose (plain) flour
1 teaspoon salt
¼ cup (2 oz/60 g) vegetable shortening (vegetable lard) or lard
½ cup (4 fl oz/125 ml), more or less, warm water

❧ In a large bowl, stir and toss together the flour and salt. Drop in the lard or shortening and blend it into the dry ingredients just as if you were making a pie crust. Add ⅓ cup (3 fl oz/80 ml) warm water and stir to blend. Add more warm water by tablespoons, stirring after each addition, until you have a stiff dough. Turn onto a lightly floured surface and knead for a minute or two, until smooth.
❧ Divide the dough into 8 fairly equal pieces and roll each between your palms into a round ball. Cover with a towel and let them stand for 20 minutes.

🐦 Preheat a griddle or skillet—do not use one with a nonstick surface—to 475°F (245°C).

🐦 On a floured surface, roll each ball into a circle about 6 in (15 cm) across. Bake each *tortilla* on the hot griddle for between 1 and 1½ minutes on each side, until barely browned and beginning to blister. Serve as soon as possible.

MAKES ABOUT 8 TORTILLAS

Monterey
GRILLED CHEESE AND BREAD SKEWERS

I first came across these morsels served at a backyard barbecue, to be enjoyed with a big platter of grilled new potatoes and tiny zucchini—and that was it. The cheese and bread offered so much heft that nobody missed meat. Since these kabobs do not need a terribly hot fire, they may be cooked over the embers that remain when the main course is removed from the grill.

10 sun-dried tomato halves in oil (see glossary)
½ cup (4 fl oz/125 ml) olive oil
1 garlic clove, minced (finely chopped)
¼ teaspoon salt
½ lb (250 g) French bread (half a large loaf), cut into 1-in (2.5-cm) cubes
¾ lb (375 g) Monterey Jack (mild melting) cheese, cut into ½-in (12-mm) cubes

🐦 Prepare a barbecue fire, or use an existing fire, and place the grilling rack between 4 and 6 in (10 and 15 cm) from the heat.

🐦 Drain 2 tablespoons of oil from the jar of sun-dried tomatoes into a large bowl. Pat the tomato halves dry with paper towels and cut them into quarters; set aside.

🐦 Stir the olive oil, garlic and salt into the tomato oil. Toss the bread cubes in the oil mixture until coated. On skewers, alternately thread bread cubes, cheese cubes and pieces of tomato.

🐦 Grill over coals for just about 5 minutes, turning frequently, or until the bread is lightly toasted and the cheese *starts* to melt. Serve immediately.

SERVES 4–6

San Diego
HUEVOS RANCHEROS

"Rancher's eggs" are an example of early California ranch cookery. They were prepared a little differently everywhere, though most were made with a poached or fried egg on a fried tortilla, *topped with a spicy* chile *sauce or salsa and some cheese. These are light, because the* tortillas *are merely heated in a skillet, not fried, and the sauce is tame enough not to jolt you first thing in the morning.*

SAUCE

2 tablespoons vegetable oil
1 onion, chopped
1 can (28 oz/875 ml) tomatoes, drained (reserve the juice) and chopped
2 teaspoons chili powder
¼ teaspoon red pepper flakes
½ cup (4 fl oz/125 ml) tomato juice (reserved from the drained tomatoes)
½ teaspoon salt

1 tablespoon red wine vinegar
1 garlic clove, minced (finely chopped)

4 flour *tortillas* (see recipe, page 146)
4 tablespoons (2 oz/60 g) butter
8 eggs
1 cup (4 oz/125 g) grated Monterey Jack (mild melting) or Cheddar cheese
fresh cilantro (coriander/Chinese parsley) sprigs

🐦 To make the sauce, heat the oil in a large saucepan. Add the onion and cook gently for 5 minutes. Add the tomatoes, chili powder, pepper flakes, tomato juice and salt. Bring to a boil, then simmer, uncovered, over low heat for about 30 minutes, until slightly thickened. Remove from the heat and stir in the vinegar and garlic.

🐦 In an ungreased cast-iron skillet or griddle (do *not* use a nonstick pan), cook the *tortillas* over high heat for several seconds on each side, until brown and blistered a little. Place on individual ovenproof plates or a large platter.

🐦 Preheat the broiler (griller) and set a rack 4 in (10 cm) from the heat. Melt the butter in a skillet over moderate heat, then fry the eggs until they are done to your liking. Spoon a couple of tablespoons of sauce on each *tortilla* and top with 2 fried eggs. Spoon the remaining sauce over the *tortillas* and around the eggs and sprinkle with cheese. Place under the broiler for just about 1 minute, until the cheese is melted. Garnish with cilantro sprigs.

SERVES 4

Grilled Cheese and Bread Skewers

ALLEN V. LOTT

147

Southern California

CORN TORTILLAS

Every nation has a flat round bread that can vary from pita to pancakes. To Mexicans and many Californians, tortillas are the bread of life. And for purists, corn tortillas made with masa harina (corn flour, milled from dried corn kernels that have been treated with lye) are the only real thing. They are firmer, coarser and more flavorful than those made with white flour. Most are machine-made now, but occasionally it is fun to try making tortillas at home. Handmade, they have a rough-hewn look that you just will not find in the automated world.

2½ cups (10 oz/315 g) *masa harina* (see glossary)
1 teaspoon salt
2 cups (16 fl oz/500 ml) warm water, and more if needed

🌿 Combine the *masa harina* and salt in a bowl. Add 2 cups of water and stir until the dough forms a rough ball; if it is too dry to hold together, add a little more water.

🌿 Between your palms, roll chunks of dough into roundish balls 1½ to 2 in (4 to 5 cm) across—you should have about 15. Keep the pieces you are not working on loosely covered with plastic wrap so that they do not dry out. One at a time, place the balls between 2 sheets of plastic wrap, then press, pat and roll the dough into a circle approximately 6 in (15 cm) across. Peel away the wrap.

🌿 Preheat an ungreased griddle or heavy skillet—do not use one with a nonstick surface—to 475°F (245°C) and cook the *tortillas*, one or two at a time. Place them on the hot griddle for 1 minute, then turn and cook for 30 seconds more. They should remain soft. As they are done, stack them and serve as soon as possible.

MAKES ABOUT 15 TORTILLAS

Southern California

SPANISH RICE

This dish bears no resemblance to the anemic mixture that often passes for Spanish rice in Mexican restaurants. It is fragrant, well flavored with tomato and bacon, and can stand on its own as a main course.

½ lb (250 g) bacon
½ lb (250 g) mushrooms, thinly sliced
1 onion, chopped
2 celery stalks, thinly sliced
1 garlic clove, minced (finely chopped)
1 cup (5 oz/155 g) long-grain rice
1 teaspoon chili powder
1 cup (8 fl oz/250 ml) tomato sauce or tomato purée
1 cup (8 fl oz/250 ml) water
2 cups (16 fl oz/500 ml) stewed tomatoes
½ teaspoon salt
½ teaspoon freshly ground black pepper
1 teaspoon dried basil

🌿 Cut the bacon into 1-in (2.5-cm) pieces. Fry until crisp in a large skillet or Dutch oven, then drain on absorbent paper towels. Remove all but 4 tablespoons of fat from the pan.

🌿 Return the pan to medium heat and add the mushrooms, onion, celery and garlic. Cook, stirring frequently, for 10 to 15 minutes, until the vegetables are softened. Add the rice and chili powder, then cook and stir for 3 minutes longer.

🌿 Add the tomato sauce, water, stewed tomatoes, salt, pepper, basil and reserved bacon. Stir to combine, then cover and simmer gently for about 20 to 25 minutes, until the rice is cooked and the liquid is absorbed.

SERVES 4

Spanish Rice (top left), Corn Tortillas (top right) and Chiles Rellenos (bottom, recipe page 150)

Central California

EGGS FOO YUNG

These oriental egg-and-vegetable pancakes were probably introduced by the many Chinese chefs who cooked for logging camps around the turn of the century. They are good with fried rice (see recipe below) and also make a nice, light luncheon dish. You may vary the meat and vegetables to suit what you have.

SAUCE

1 cup (8 fl oz/250 ml) chicken stock (see glossary), at
   room temperature
1 tablespoon cornstarch (cornflour)
1 tablespoon soy sauce
1 tablespoon vinegar
1 teaspoon sugar

2 tablespoons vegetable oil or peanut oil
½ cup (3 oz/ 90 g) finely chopped green beans
1 large carrot, finely grated
½ cup (4 oz/125 g) chopped water chestnuts, fresh or canned
2 large green (spring) onions, chopped
½ cup (1½ oz/45 g) bean sprouts
½ cup (4 oz/125 g) cooked tiny shrimp (green prawns)
6 eggs
½ teaspoon salt
¼ teaspoon freshly ground black pepper
vegetable or peanut oil for sautéing

🍂 To make the sauce, stir the chicken stock and cornstarch together in a small saucepan. Add the soy sauce, vinegar and sugar and cook, stirring frequently, until the sauce boils and thickens; set aside.
🍂 Heat the oil in a large skillet over high heat. Add the green beans and carrot and cook for about 2 minutes, tossing and stirring. Remove from heat and add the water chestnuts, green onion, bean sprouts and shrimp. Stir and toss to combine.
🍂 In a large bowl beat together the eggs, salt and pepper. Stir in the vegetable mixture.
🍂 Film the bottom of a large skillet with about ⅛ in (3 mm) of oil and set over moderate heat. Set the pan with the sauce in it over low heat, so that the sauce will be warm for serving. When the oil is quite hot, gently drop the egg mixture into the pan in ¼-cup blobs—they will spread to a thickness of about ½ in (12 mm). Cook for about 2 minutes on each side, until well browned. Continue frying the remaining egg mixture the same way, adding more oil to the pan as needed. Keep warm on a platter in a 200°F (95°C) oven if necessary until you have enough to start serving, then pour the sauce over them.

MAKES ABOUT 10 PATTIES, SERVING 5

Monterey

CHILES RELLENOS

Anaheim chiles are not fiery—they are long, mild and perfect for filling with whatever you fancy. Rellenos are stuffed with Monterey Jack cheese, coated with egg batter and fried until golden, then covered with spicy tomato sauce. This may sound involved but, except for the final baking just to warm them through, everything may be done ahead. Like huevos rancheros, chiles rellenos were popular in early California and have remained a favorite.

enchilada sauce (see recipe, page 102)
12 long Anaheim (mild green) chiles
¾ lb (375 g) Monterey Jack (mild melting) cheese, in one piece
6 eggs, separated
3 tablespoons milk
1 teaspoon salt

⅓ cup (1½ oz/45 g) all-purpose (plain) flour
oil for frying
1 cup (4 oz/125 g) grated Monterey Jack (mild melting) cheese

🍂 Prepare the *enchilada* sauce as directed; set aside.
🍂 Place the *chiles* on a rack 4 in (10 cm) from a hot broiler (griller) and broil, turning frequently, for about 10 minutes, until they are blistered on all sides. Place in a paper bag, close the bag and let it stand for 15 minutes.
🍂 Carefully peel off the skins, taking care not to break the *chiles*. Make a lengthwise slit in each *chile* and gently pick out the seeds. Set the *chiles* aside. Cut the Monterey Jack cheese into strips about ½ in (12 mm) wide and 2 in (5 cm) long; place a piece of cheese inside each *chile*.
🍂 In a large bowl, beat the egg yolks and milk, then add the salt and flour and beat until smooth. In another large bowl, beat the egg whites until stiff. Stir a large spoonful of the beaten whites into the yolk mixture, then fold in the remaining whites.
🍂 Preheat the oven to 350°F (180°C); grease a large baking pan.
🍂 In a large skillet or Dutch oven, heat about 1½ in (4 cm) of oil to 360°F (185°C). One at a time, dip the cheese-filled *chiles* into the egg batter, then carefully slide them into the hot oil.
🍂 Fry only 3 or 4 at a time; they puff and need room to expand.
🍂 Cook for 2 minutes on each side, or until golden. Drain on absorbent paper towels, then place in a single layer in the prepared baking pan. Spoon the *enchilada* sauce over and sprinkle with the grated cheese. Bake for about 20 minutes.

SERVES 6   *Photograph pages 148–149*

San Francisco

FRIED RICE

The fried rice that we know is probably made to please the occidental rather than the oriental palate. By itself, fried rice may be served as a luncheon or light dinner dish. It takes well to additions, such as small cooked shrimp or bits of leftover diced pork or chicken, or even a handful of raisins or a diced banana.

¼ cup (2 fl oz/60 ml) vegetable oil
4 cups (about 17 oz/520 g) cooked rice
2 large green (spring) onions, chopped
2 tablespoons soy sauce
2 eggs, beaten
freshly ground black pepper

🍂 Heat the oil in a large, heavy skillet until almost smoking. Add the rice, stirring and tossing almost constantly for 3 minutes, until heated through. Add the green onions and soy sauce and toss to combine. Push the rice to one side, then pour the eggs into the other side of the pan. Stir them briskly for a moment, until scrambled, then toss with the rice so that the bits of egg are scattered throughout. Season with pepper.

SERVES 4

Fresno

ARAM SANDWICHES

These are pinwheel sandwiches made from lavosh, *or Armenian cracker bread, softened and rolled up with a filling of ham, cheese and vegetables. Sandwiches for all seasons—good for cocktail parties, buffets, barbecues and picnics.*

1 12-in (30-cm) round of *lavosh* (see recipe, page 152)
6 oz (185 g) cream cheese
6 oz (185 g) goat cheese
3 tablespoons heavy (double) cream
1 garlic clove, minced (finely chopped)

Fried Rice (top) and Eggs Foo Yung (bottom)

1 tablespoon lemon juice
1 tablespoon chopped fresh oregano or 1 teaspoon
   dried oregano
½ teaspoon salt
8 oz (250 g) thinly sliced cooked ham
8 oz (250 g) thinly sliced Swiss cheese
1 small red (Spanish) onion, thinly sliced
1 head (about 8 oz/250 g) shredded butter lettuce

🦐 Gently rinse the *lavosh* under cold running water for about 10 seconds on each side. Place on a clean, damp towel and cover with another damp towel. Let stand for 1 hour to soften.
🦐 Meanwhile, blend together the cream cheese, goat cheese and cream, then beat in the garlic, lemon juice, oregano and salt.

🦐 Remove the lavosh from the towels and place on a sheet of plastic wrap. Spread with about half the cheese mixture and top with a layer of ham. Follow with a layer of Swiss cheese, then spread all but 2 tablespoons of the remaining cheese mixture over that. Scatter the onion and lettuce on top. Using the plastic wrap to lift the edge of the bread, carefully roll the sandwich up tightly.
🦐 Spread the remaining cheese mixture along the length of the seam and press to seal. Cover with plastic wrap and refrigerate for up to two days before serving. To serve, cut into 1-in (2.5-cm) slices.

SERVES 4–6   *Photograph page 152*

151

California
CALIFORNIA PIZZA

Pizza is casual food, perfect for eating out of hand and for topping in imaginative ways—and you can really use your imagination. In such restaurants as Wolfgang Puck's Spago in Los Angeles and Postrio in San Francisco, potato slices and smoked salmon are likely to turn up on pizza as frequently as mushrooms and cheese are. You can bake pizza on a conventional round pan, but a heavy black baking sheet, placed on the lowest shelf of an electric oven, or right on the floor of a gas oven, will give your pizza a crisper bottom.

DOUGH

1 package (¼ oz/7 g) dry yeast, about 2½ teaspoons
1⅓ cups (11 fl oz/330 ml) warm water
4 cups (1 lb/500 g), more or less, all-purpose (plain) flour
2 teaspoons salt
¼ cup (2 fl oz/60 ml) olive oil

TOPPING

½ lb (250 g) mushrooms, thinly sliced
2 tablespoons olive oil
2 cups (16 fl oz/500 ml) tomato sauce or tomato purée
1 cup (8 fl oz/250 ml) fresh tomato pulp (from 3 medium
    tomatoes peeled, seeded, juiced and diced)
½ lb (250 g) fresh mozzarella cheese, thinly sliced
6 oz (185 g) goat cheese, diced or broken in bits
2 tablespoons chopped fresh marjoram or oregano
¼ cup (½ oz/15 g) chopped fresh basil, or small basil leaves

Lavosh (top) and Aram Sandwiches (bottom, recipe page 150)

ALLEN V. LOTT

❧ To make the dough, sprinkle the yeast over the warm water in a large bowl, stir and let it stand for several minutes to dissolve. Add 3 cups (12 oz/375 g) of flour, the salt and oil, and beat until smooth. Add about 1 cup more flour, or enough to make a manageable dough. Turn out onto a lightly floured surface and knead for 10 minutes, sprinkling on additional flour as necessary to keep the dough from being too sticky. Put into a greased bowl, cover and let rise until double in bulk, about 1½ hours.

❧ Punch the dough down and divide in half. Let rest for about 10 minutes.

❧ Preheat the oven to 450°F (230°C).

❧ Patiently push, pat, roll and stretch the dough until you have two circles, each between 12 and 14 in (30 and 35 cm) across. Place them on cookie sheets or pizza pans. Fold the outside edges of the dough in slightly, to make a small rim around the perimeter. Prick the dough several times with a fork.

❧ To make the topping, toss the mushrooms with the olive oil and set aside. On each circle of dough, spread 1 cup of tomato sauce, then dot each with ½ cup of tomato pulp. Divide the mushrooms evenly over the pizzas, then the cheeses. Sprinkle with the marjoram or oregano.

❧ Bake for about 20 minutes, either on the lowest shelf of an electric oven or the floor of a gas oven, until the pizzas are golden around the edges and bubbly. Remove from the oven and sprinkle with the basil. Serve hot, cut into wedges.

MAKES TWO 12- TO 14-INCH PIZZAS

Fresno
LAVOSH

A Middle Eastern bread, thin, crisp and brittle, lavosh *is also known as Armenian cracker bread. It is baked in thin, plate-sized rounds and used for Aram sandwiches, a popular item in many delicatessens (see recipe on page 150), or as an accompaniment for cheeses, dips and smoked meats.*

1 package (¼ oz/7 g) dry yeast, about 2½ teaspoons
1½ cups (12 fl oz/375 ml) warm water
2 teaspoons salt
3½–4 cups (14–16 oz/450–500 g) all-purpose (plain) flour
3 tablespoons poppy seeds or toasted sesame seeds

❧ Sprinkle the yeast over the warm water in a large bowl, then stir and let it stand for a few minutes to dissolve. Add the salt and 2 cups (8 oz/250 g) of the flour and beat until blended.   Add enough of the remaining flour to make a manageable dough. Turn out onto a lightly floured surface and knead for about 10 minutes, or until smooth and elastic, sprinkling on a little more flour if necessary to keep the dough from being too sticky.

❧ Place in a greased bowl, cover and let the dough rise until double in size. Punch down, then cover and let it rise again until double.

❧ Divide into 8 fairly equal pieces and, between your palms, roll each into a round ball. Cover with a towel and let the balls rest for 20 minutes.

❧ Preheat the oven to 450°F (230°C). On a lightly floured surface, roll each round into a circle between 8 and 9 in (20 and 25 cm) across. Press a teaspoon of seeds into the top of each circle with the last few strokes of the rolling pin. Place as many as will fit in a single layer on a large baking sheet. Bake for 6 minutes, until blistered and lightly browned around the edges.

❧ Remove from the oven and rapidly turn the breads over. Bake for 4 minutes more, until lightly browned. *Lavosh* can be baked in relays, like cookies. Cool completely on a rack, then store airtight.

MAKES EIGHT 8-INCH ROUNDS

California Pizza

THE GOLD COUNTRY
AND SIERRA NEVADA

THE GOLD COUNTRY AND SIERRA NEVADA

A long the western foothills of the Sierra Nevada, a chain of gold rush towns echoes with tales of argonauts and mountain men, of fortunes won and lost and a wave of immigrants who changed the face of California forever. Months after gold was discovered at Sutter's Mill, about forty miles from Sacramento, workmen from San Francisco to Los Angeles dropped their tools, left the cows in the barns and the oranges on the trees and headed for the Sierra foothills. Sailors jumped ship and shopkeepers closed their doors, leaving behind families and businesses to join the frenzied rush to the gold country. Within ten years, the state's population swelled by almost three hundred thousand. Many of the newcomers came by clipper ship, eighteen thousand long miles around Cape Horn. Others barely made the trek by prairie schooner, on horse or on foot through the Rockies, over desolate alkali flats and through the awesome Sierra Nevada gateway to Sacramento. As the gold-seekers poured in, towns with names like Rough and Ready, Chile Bar, Hangtown and Fiddletown seemed to sprout overnight. This region of California saw more action between 1848 and 1860 than any other area of the western United States, save the boom supply towns of San Francisco and Sacramento.

Much of the gold country, a huge slice of eastern California that rises up to the single largest mountain

Previous pages: Crowned with a golden cloak of light, Half Dome towers above the granite walls of Yosemite National Park. Left: Mist follows the meandering path of the Merced River as it winds along the floor of a lush Sierra valley.

Protected from the threat of hunters, two mule deer feed on the abundant vegetation at Yosemite's floor. The first inhabitants of Yosemite Valley called it Ahwahnee, "the deep grassy valley."

range in the country, was virtually ignored by the early Spanish settlers. Being neither hunters nor trappers, they took one look at the steep canyons and snowy peaks, named them the Sierra Nevada and left them untouched. So the wholesome and sometimes eclectic cuisine identified with the area today traces its origins to the deep purple elderberries that grow wild, along with blackberrries, *piñon* nuts, plentiful game, salmon and sweet mountain trout that sustained the local Indians. Regardless of their culinary origins, most of the newly arrived Chinese, Irish, German, English, South American, French, Canadian, Scottish, Italian and American gold miners were subjected to a steady diet of pork and beans and sourdough bread in their early California days. Gold miners were actually nicknamed "sourdoughs" because they carried sourdough starters—self-perpetuating leavening—with them, baking bread in the most ingenious ways. One account describes "stick bread," fashioned on sticks slowly rotated over campfires and baked to that distinctive, chewy sourdough texture; others baked their bread in a kind of Dutch oven set over hot coals, and still others shaped and baked the dough in the same tin pans they used for mining.

DAME SHIRLEY WRITES FROM THE MINES

Some historians believe that the first sourdough starter was brought to California by the Basques. Others say it was carried up from Mexico, either by Mexican gold miners or by French bakers fleeing the country after political conflicts sent them north. Whatever the origin, what matters most is that it lives on, to be transformed into fragrant loaves and dunked into *cioppino* or broken with fresh crab. Fortunately, some highly skilled European bakers were among the gold rush immigrants, and they eventually opened several of the brick-oven bakeries that still operate in San Francisco.

The miners who struck pay dirt could lure a good cook to the mining camps, for a price. Soon they had access to brandied peaches and canned hams and oysters and the best of champagnes, clarets and ales—and even chocolate, once young Domingo Ghirardelli gave up mining and set up shop in the towns of Hornitos, Columbia and Melones.

Some of the most intriguing accounts of life in gold rush camps and kitchens were left by a refined young woman from Massachusetts named Louise Amelia Knapp Smith Clapp, also known as Dame Shirley. She joined her "fiddlefooted" husband, Dr. Fayette Clapp, on the east fork of the Feather River in the autumn of 1851. They were at the far north end of the gold country, a region of sparkling alpine lakes and moss-covered logs, just hours from the then "officially unexplored territories" and markings on maps that indicated "perpetual snow" where the Sierras cradle the far reaches of the Mother Lode. Supplies had to be brought in by pack mule until the small town called Rich Bar was built on the site.

Dame Shirley's letters home revealed as much about food (or the lack of it) in the grimy camps as they did about her adventurous spirit. The population was about ninety percent male and Shirley, though warned about Indians and miners, "laughed merrily at the mournful prognostications" of those who declared "that it was absolutely indelicate, to think of living in such a large population of men . . . " or that if the Indians did not kill her, the ennui would. Dame Shirley, however, lived to chronicle weeks without butter, potatoes, onions or fresh meat, and the special menus that made up for it—"oyster soup; fresh salmon, caught from the river; roast beef and boiled ham; fried oysters; potatoes and onions; mince pie and pudding made without eggs or milk; Madeira, nuts and raisins," prepared by her enterprising cook, Ned (who was eventually lured away by wealthier miners). Later, when supplies were more plentiful, a Spanish friend served a special breakfast and thrilled Dame Shirley with "cans of peaches; watermelons from the garden . . . venison with a fragrant, spicy gusto, as if it had been fed

The Sierras are a place of stunning visions, small and grand. Encased in a crystal casket of ice, a pine cone rests on the forest floor.

A group of hikers near Glacier Point in Yosemite National Park roughs it California-style with a simple picnic and a fine bottle of champagne.

on cedar buds; beef cooked in the Spanish fashion; preserved chicken and almost every possible vegetable bringing up the rear. . . ."

The simplified tail end of the gold rush saga is that more people struck out than struck it rich. Thousands of those who stayed went on to farm crops throughout the state. In time, they refined their native cuisines to take advantage of the local bounty, adding delicious layers of creativity to the California melting pot. Today the "gold chain," also known as the Forty-Niner Trail, is strewn with homey bed-and-breakfast inns and restored hotel dining rooms where specialties include roasted duck with fig and apple-raisin sauce, or walnut and banana pancakes, served with grapes fresh from the arbor. Inns and home cooks take advantage of fresh berries and small orchards with all kinds of tree fruit for old-fashioned condiments and cobblers as well as French tarts and American pies. People are often surprised to find good Chinese food in some of these very Western towns, but much of the large Chinese population who worked the mines and later the railroads stayed on to feed anyone with a hankering for steamed dumplings and fresh, fragrant stir-fries.

East of the Forty-Niner Trail, the Shenandoah Valley (named by early emigrants from Virginia) is dotted with small vineyards, many of which are known for the red volcanic soil that yields rich, spicy Zinfandel grapes.

AN ENGLISH DINNER IN YOSEMITE

As the altitude rises to the east of the gentle foothills, farms and orchards along Highway 49 thin out and give way to the Sierra Nevada. Granite peaks that enfold wondrous valleys and lakes, including Yosemite and Lake Tahoe, the Sierra Nevada cascade along nearly two-thirds of the state's eastern border for four hundred miles. The physical grandeur of Yosemite has yet to be captured in words. A monumental valley, carved by glaciers, graced with alpine meadows and giant sequoias, it is a national treasure. Nothing compares with the sensation of seeing it with your own eyes, savoring that first glimpse of the sheared side of Half Dome or the dizzying view from Glacier Point. Breathe the alpine air, walk along a waterfall, with icy spray soaking through every pore of your skin, or just sit quietly under the stars—but soon you will want to eat. Food here is simple and fresh. Restaurants and lodges serve abundant trout and prime rib and satisfying, hearty vegetarian casseroles.

One food event, however, is quite elaborate. People draw from a lottery to book a year in advance to attend the traditional Bracebridge Dinner at the Ahwahnee Hotel in the heart of the valley. It started in 1927 when Ansel Adams, the photographer, and a band of merrymakers thought that the Ahwahnee was a perfect setting for a California dinner that would be based on a reenactment of the Christmas dinner at Squire Bracebridge's old English manor, as described by Washington Irving in his *Sketch Book*. The menu has evolved over the years, and the chefs at the Ahwahnee say that "a typical menu is far from typical." Selections in 1987 included *crêpes* of pheasant with juniper berry sauce; truffle and wild mushroom sauce with snow peas; orange roughy Florentine; and a salad of fresh winter greens from the Monterey Bay area served with vinaigrette.

FRUITS AND VEGETABLES

Farm workers harvest spinach in the fertile fields of the Salinas Valley, inland from Santa Cruz.

FRUITS AND VEGETABLES

"As for vegetables, ours is the richest market in the world." So said the chef at San Francisco's Palace Hotel in 1885. And he may as well have added "fruits." Turn-of-the-century menus in both southern and northern California offered fruits and vegetables at every course. Simple appetizers of celery, olives or sliced cucumbers; vegetable courses of stewed carrots, sliced tomatoes and buttered asparagus were common. Prune-stuffed duck, raisin-studded rice, and squab with crabapple jelly joined the entrées. And for dessert as well as breakfast, green figs with cream, stewed prunes, compote of pears, Paradise Valley oranges and Sweetwater persimmons fed patrons at the Hotel Del Coronado in San Diego, where everything grew within a short rail journey, if not in local gardens.

Although the state was indeed rich in produce a century ago, the sheer volume and variety of fruits and vegetables grown and consumed in California today is staggering. The state's list of two hundred and fifty agricultural products is among the most diversified in the world. And the wonder of it is, California's thirty-three million acres of farmland account for only three percent of the country's farmland. Yet, that three percent produces fifty percent of the nation's fruits, nuts and vegetables. Some of them grow in significant quantities only in California: artichokes, avocados, broccoli, dates, figs, raisins, nectarines, olives, kiwifruit and prunes among them. And chances are, when you bite into a voluptuous strawberry or a roasted garlic clove, you are tasting a product of California's sunshine and soil. It all started with the Spanish missionaries and was carried on by

immigrants who settled in California after the gold rush of 1849. Today, growers range from huge cooperatives and commercial producers to small truck farmers and burgeoning groups of organic and specialty farmers.

RAMBLING BERRIES TO BEANS AND RICE

Most early California Indians lived as hunter-gatherers and flavored their acorn mush with the fruits of wild grape and blackberry vines and strawberry plants that rambled over the land. Wild onion, garlic, watercress and miner's lettuce popped up around the damp edges of waterways and in rich valley soil, and all were put to use. When the Spanish missionaries arrived in the mid-1700s, they came bearing seeds and cuttings for beans, *chiles*, squash and corn, which were to become staples. They also brought olive and grape cuttings, tomatoes, figs, peaches and apricots. For the most part, their early farming efforts were confined to small crops, and what they did not eat fresh was dried for long journeys. Although they grew a good variety of fruits and vegetables, many of the missionaries and, later, the rancheros tended to stick with squash and pinto or red beans with almost every meal. They flavored them with fat, onions and *chiles* and served them with *tortillas* and plenty of meat. The rancheros, who gave most of their land over to cattle, did enjoy a hearty all-vegetable stew called *colache*. Based on pumpkin or winter squash, it was seasoned with garlic, peppers and bacon fat.

Everything, including the diets of the early Californios, changed when thousands of immigrants stayed after the

Previous pages: Baked Zucchini with Cheese (left, recipe page 186)
and Green Beans with Tomatoes (right, recipe page 182)

The Farmers' Market in Los Angeles began as a wholesale produce market that has since grown to be a vast retail complex offering the best fresh fruits and vegetables from the south.

At least five varieties of onions are produced in California, and much of the crop is freeze-dried for use in spices and seasonings.

gold rush. Italians, Chinese, Armenians and farmers of almost every other country settled in California and grew the foods they knew and loved from their native countries. Arugula, artichokes, eggplant, melons, figs, prunes . . . and bushels more.

Today, California's network of shipping and distribution is so refined that every area has access to anything that grows here. In the rural farmlands of the central coast and Central and Imperial valleys, cooks might be more inclined to turn the excess bounty into preserves and condiments, though the many farmers' markets that come to the cities now provide everyone with enough produce to do the same. California cooks also like to dry fruits whole or turn them into sweet, chewy fruit leathers—sun- or oven-dried sheets of puréed fruit, rolled up and enjoyed like candy. And anyone one who likes to cook outdoors knows the warm, slightly smoky appeal of fresh fruits and vegetables brushed with olive oil and sizzled lightly on the grill. Other California favorites include Japanese-inspired *tempura*—crisp vegetables fried in a feathery light batter. Armenian or Greek *dolmas*—stuffed grape leaves—hold savory bites of rice, ground lamb and tender pine nuts seasoned with fresh mint and lemon juice, and the possibilities go on and on. Juicy, crunchy, spicy, tart, sweet—fruits and vegetables bring all these dimensions to the California melting pot, and ours is indeed "the richest market in the world."

BAKED SPINACH WITH MUSHROOMS

This dish is easy to prepare ahead and reheat; keep in mind that anything with spinach goes well with fish. It is also a good bed for a topping of poached eggs, as a tasty luncheon or supper dish.

4 bunches (about 2 lb/1 kg) spinach
8 tablespoons (4 oz/125 g) butter
1 lb (500 g) mushrooms, sliced
salt
freshly ground black pepper
¼ cup (1 oz/30 g) all-purpose (plain) flour
2 cups (16 fl oz/500 ml) milk
½ cup (2 oz/60 g) chopped toasted walnuts
½ cup (2 oz/60 g) dry breadcrumbs

❧ Remove the stems from the spinach and wash it well. Put the leaves in a large pot—just with the water that clings to them—and set over medium heat. Cover and cook for 5 to 10 minutes, stirring once or twice, until tender and wilted. Spread the spinach on a plate and let sit until cool enough to handle. A handful at a time, squeeze the spinach firmly to remove excess moisture, then chop it coarsely. Place in a large bowl and set aside.

❧ Melt 4 tablespoons (2 oz/60 g) of the butter in a skillet over moderate heat. Add the mushrooms and cook for 10 to 15 minutes, tossing frequently, until tender. If the mushrooms have exuded their juices, boil them rapidly over high heat, tossing frequently, until the liquid has evaporated. Season with salt and pepper and add to the bowl with the spinach.

❧ Preheat the oven to 350°F (180°C) and butter a shallow 6-cup (48-fl oz/1.5-l) baking dish.

❧ Melt the remaining 4 tablespoons of butter in a medium saucepan. Add the flour and cook, stirring constantly, for about 2 minutes. Whisk in the milk and bring to a boil. Season with salt and pepper to taste, reduce the heat and simmer for

*Wild Rice with Wild Mushrooms (top right)
and Baked Spinach with Mushrooms (bottom)*

about 5 minutes, stirring frequently. Stir the sauce into the spinach and mushrooms, add the walnuts and spread the mixture evenly in the prepared baking dish. Sprinkle with the breadcrumbs and bake for about 20 minutes, until bubbling.

SERVES 6

MUSHROOM AND SPINACH TARTS

Because such a variety of mushrooms is found in California's markets now, it is a pity not to make use of them. These individual tarts never fail to please, either served as a first course or as a luncheon main course, and they are even good cold, on a picnic.

1 recipe basic pastry dough (see *empanadas*, page 38)
4 tablespoons (2 oz/60 g) butter
1 lb (500 g) mushrooms, either *chanterelles* or regular cultivated
    mushrooms, chopped
salt
freshly ground black pepper
8 oz (250 g) fresh spinach, chopped and cooked to yield
    ½ cup (4 oz/125 g), squeezed as dry as possible
4 oz (125 g) cream cheese
½ cup (4 fl oz/125 ml) heavy (double) cream
1 egg

❧ Preheat the oven to 425°F (220°C).

❧ Prepare the dough and roll it out about ⅛ in (3 mm) thick. Cut as many 5-in (13-cm) rounds as you can and fit them into 4-in (10-cm) tart shells. Press the scraps together, reroll them and continue until you have lined 6 tart shells with dough.

❧ Heat the butter in a large skillet over moderate heat. Add the mushrooms and season with salt and pepper. Cook for 15 to 20 minutes, until any mushroom juices have evaporated. Add the spinach and cook for a minute more. Add the cream cheese and stir until melted, then stir in the heavy cream and boil for 2 minutes. Scrape the mixture into a bowl and let it sit for 15 minutes. Beat in the egg.

❧ Spoon the mixture evenly into the tart shells and bake for 10 minutes, then reduce the heat to 350°F (180°C) and bake for about 30 minutes more, until the filling is set and lightly browned. Serve warm or at room temperature.

SERVES 6

WILD RICE WITH WILD MUSHROOMS

Wild rice, which has a distinctive nutty flavor and chewiness all its own, is expensive. It is really not rice at all, but the seed of an aquatic grass that once grew mostly in Minnesota and is now cultivated in northern California's Sacramento Valley. Serve it when you want to splurge; it is a natural with game, especially duck. Wild mushrooms are not available everywhere, so you may substitute regular mushrooms if you wish.

8 tablespoons (4 oz/125 g) butter
¼ cup minced (finely chopped) shallots or green
    (spring) onions
1 cup (5 oz/155 g) wild rice
3 cups (24 fl oz/750 ml) chicken stock (see glossary)

Mushroom and Spinach Tart

salt
freshly ground black pepper
½ lb (250 g) wild mushrooms, such as *chanterelles*, sliced
¼ cup (1 oz/30 g) chopped, toasted almonds
2 tablespoons chopped parsley

🍂 Melt 4 tablespoons of the butter in a large saucepan and add the shallots. Cook over medium heat for about 3 minutes, until softened. Add the rice and cook for 2 to 3 minutes more, stirring. Add the chicken stock, season with salt and pepper to taste and bring to a boil. Reduce the heat, then cover the pot and simmer for 45 minutes.

🍂 While the rice cooks, melt the remaining 4 tablespoons of butter in a skillet over moderately high heat. Add the mushrooms, sprinkle with salt and pepper and toss for several minutes, until lightly browned.

🍂 When the rice has been cooking for 45 minutes, stir in the mushrooms and continue cooking, covered, for 15 minutes more, or until the liquid is absorbed and the grains are tender but still slightly chewy. Even after long cooking, the grains remain slightly firm. Stir in the almonds and parsley and serve.

SERVES 6

Red Beans and Rice (left) and Fried Parsley (right)

California
FRIED PARSLEY

Fried parsley is one of those things you might feel dubious about. One taste will make you a convert. It may be prepared in two ways, either plain or dipped in batter. Plain fried parsley is green and crisp and cooks in seconds. Batter-fried parsley is golden and crunchy and has a pleasing yeasty flavor—given by the beer in the batter. Try doing some of each. Either one goes well with fish or veal, and should be eaten fresh and hot.

4 cups (8 oz/250 g) parsley sprigs
1 egg
¼ cup (2 fl oz/60 ml) vegetable oil
¾ cup (6 fl oz/180 ml) beer
1 cup (4 oz/125 g) all-purpose (plain) flour
salt
¼ teaspoon freshly ground black pepper
oil for frying

❦ Wash and dry the parsley sprigs. Spread them out on a clean towel while you prepare the batter. They must be thoroughly dry or the oil will splatter.
❦ Beat together the egg, oil and beer. Add the flour, ½ teaspoon salt and the pepper, and blend until smooth. Cover and let the batter stand for about an hour.
❦ In a heavy pan, heat about 1½ in (4 cm) of oil to 375°F (190°C). For batter-fried parsley, dip several sprigs at a time briefly into the batter, then drop them in the hot oil. Fry for about 2 minutes, until golden, then drain on absorbent paper towels. Sprinkle with salt, if desired, and serve.
❦ For plain fried parsley, simply drop a small handful of sprigs into the hot oil—stand back, it splatters—and fry just a few seconds, until the sprigs are crisp.

SERVES 4

San Francisco
RED BEANS AND RICE

This recipe for a wholesome south-of-the-border combination comes from a cook in San Francisco. It is good as a main course, with tortillas, *or for breakfast when topped with a poached or fried egg, or as an accompaniment to a Mexican meal. Serve, if appropriate, with sour cream or* guacamole.

1 lb (500 g) dry red kidney beans or pinto beans
1 onion, chopped
salt
freshly ground black pepper
3 cups (6 oz/185 g) hot cooked rice
2 tomatoes, peeled, seeded and chopped
¼ cup (½ oz/15 g) chopped cilantro (coriander/Chinese parsley)

❦ Wash and sort through the beans for debris and grit. Cover with cold water and bring to a rolling boil. Boil for 1 minute, then cover and let stand for 1 hour. Drain well, then cover with fresh water, add the onion, 1½ teaspoons salt and ½ teaspoon pepper and simmer, partially covered, for about 1 hour, or until beans are just tender, but not mushy. If necessary, add more water to keep the beans covered. Remove from the heat and let the beans stand in their cooking liquid for 15 minutes, then drain thoroughly.
❦ In a large warm bowl, toss the beans (which will still be warm) with the hot rice. If you wish to hold the mixture at this temperature, set the bowl, partially covered, over a pan of simmering water, tossing the contents occasionally.
❦ Just before serving, fold in the tomato and cilantro and season with additional salt and pepper to taste.

SERVES 6

Sonoma
COLACHE

This is a winner—hot, warm or at room temperature. It is surprisingly good and appeals even to those who do not care for pumpkin. According to the late Helen Evans Brown, who was very knowledgeable about Californian—and West Coast—cookery, this was one of the few vegetable dishes in which the rancheros indulged. It is an old recipe for an all-vegetable stew, and you may vary the ingredients to suit what is available. It is also a good dish to carry to a picnic or barbecue.

2 lb (1 kg) pumpkin or winter squash
¼ cup (2 fl oz/60 ml) bacon drippings or melted butter
1 onion, chopped
2 garlic cloves, minced (finely chopped)
1 green bell pepper (capsicum), seeded and cut into 1-in (2.5-cm) squares
1 Anaheim *chile*, or other mild green *chile*, cut into 1-in (2.5-cm) squares
4 tomatoes, about 1 lb (500 g), peeled, seeded and coarsely chopped
½ lb (250 g) green beans, cut into 1-in (2.5-cm) pieces
1½ cups (6 oz/185 g) fresh or frozen corn kernels
2 teaspoons chili powder
1 cup (8 fl oz/250 ml) water or chicken stock (see glossary)
salt
freshly ground black pepper

🦃 Peel the pumpkin or winter squash and cut it into 1-in (2.5-cm) cubes, discarding the seeds and fibrous center. Heat the bacon drippings or butter in a large skillet or Dutch oven over moderate heat, add the squash and cook for 5 minutes, tossing or stirring frequently. Add the onion and cook, stirring occasionally, for about 5 minutes longer.

🦃 Add the garlic, pepper, *chile*, tomatoes, beans, corn and chili powder and stir to combine. Add the water or stock, 1 teaspoon salt and ½ teaspoon pepper, then cover and cook over low heat until the vegetables are tender, about 20 minutes. Season with salt and pepper, if necessary.

SERVES 6–8

Santa Maria
BARBECUE BEANS

These beans in a tomato-based sauce are similar to those you might eat at a Santa Maria barbecue in southern California. The smokiness of bacon gives the illusion of a barbecue flavor, and they are very good with a variety of meats from the grill, especially ribs and chicken.

1 lb (500 g) dry red kidney beans or pinto beans
1 onion, chopped
½ lb (250 g) bacon, diced
2 garlic cloves, minced (finely chopped)
2 medium tomatoes, peeled, seeded and chopped or ¾ cup (6 fl oz/180 ml) canned tomatoes, drained and chopped
¼ cup (2 fl oz/60 ml) chili sauce (American-style)
1 tablespoon brown sugar
1 tablespoon prepared mustard
1 teaspoon salt
freshly ground black pepper

🦃 Wash and sort through the beans for grit and other debris. Cover them with cold water, bring to a rolling boil and boil for 1 minute. Cover and remove from heat. Let the beans stand for 1 hour. Drain well, cover with fresh water, add the onion and simmer, partially covered, for about 1 hour, or until the beans are tender.

🦃 Meanwhile, cook the diced bacon until crisp. Remove with a slotted spoon and set aside. Pour all but a tablespoon of the fat from the pan and return to the heat. Add the garlic, tomato, chili sauce, brown sugar, mustard, salt and pepper. Bring just to a boil, stir in the bacon, then set aside off the heat.

🦃 When the beans are tender, drain them in a colander, reserving the liquid. Return them to the pot and add the bacon-and-tomato mixture. Add enough cooking liquid so that the beans are barely covered. Bring to a boil, then reduce the heat and simmer, partially covered, for 45 minutes to 1 hour.

SERVES 6

Barbecue Beans

Colache

Fresno

DOLMAS

The Greek culinary influence has given us such delights as shish kabobs, moussaka, avgolémono and dolmas. The latter are made of grape leaves rolled around a savory stuffing that usually contains rice, onions, pine nuts, mint and ground lamb. The leaves can be found in supermarkets, in the pickle section, packed in brine in small jars—and you will be surprised how many leaves fit in one jar. Dolmas are wonderful for a buffet and may be served hot or cold, with yogurt for dipping.

1 jar (8 oz/250 g) grape leaves (about 50)
½ lb (250 g) ground (minced) lamb
½ cup (4 fl oz/125 ml) olive oil
2 large onions, chopped
1 cup (5 oz/155 g) long-grain rice
¾ cup (6 fl oz/180 ml) water
1 teaspoon salt
½ teaspoon freshly ground black pepper
½ cup (2 oz/60 g) toasted pine nuts
3 tablespoons lemon juice
2 tablespoons chopped parsley
3 tablespoons chopped fresh mint
3 tablespoons currants (optional)
1 large potato, cut into slices about ½ in (12 mm) thick
1 cup (8 fl oz/250 ml), or more, chicken stock (see glossary)
plain (unflavored) yogurt

🐚 Cover the grape leaves with cold water and let them soak for an hour to remove some of the saltiness. Drain thoroughly and remove any stems.

🐚 To prepare the stuffing, cook the ground lamb in a skillet, breaking it up with a fork, until it loses its pinkness. Drain off any fat and transfer the lamb to a bowl.

🐚 Return the skillet to moderate heat and pour in ¼ cup (2 fl oz/60 ml) of the olive oil. Add the onions and cook for about 10 minutes, stirring frequently. Add the rice and cook for about 5 minutes more, stirring. Add the water, salt and pepper, then cover and cook over low heat for about 10 minutes, until the liquid is absorbed.

🐚 Remove from the heat, scrape the rice into the bowl with the lamb and let the mixture cool to room temperature. Stir in the pine nuts, lemon juice, parsley, mint and currants, if used.

🐚 A few at a time, place the grape leaves on your work surface, vein-side up. Place about a tablespoon of filling in the center of each. Fold the stem end over the filling, fold the sides to the center, then roll the leaf up tightly, forming a neat package.

🐚 Lay the potato slices flat in a large skillet or Dutch oven. The slices may overlap. The potato prevents the *dolmas* from sitting directly on the bottom of the pan. Arrange the *dolmas* in layers, seam-side down, over the potatoes, then pour in the remaining ¼ cup of olive oil and sufficient chicken stock to cover them. Set a heatproof platter or plate on top so they remain submerged and stationary.

🐚 Bring the liquid to a boil, then turn the heat to low, cover and simmer for 30 to 45 minutes, or until the leaves are tender. Remove from heat and let them sit for 10 minutes. Then remove the *dolmas* from the liquid and serve them warm, at room temperature or cold, with yogurt for dipping. The potato slices may be discarded or eaten separately.

MAKES ABOUT 50 DOLMAS

*Broccoli with Olive Sauce (left, recipe page 173)
and Dolmas (right)*

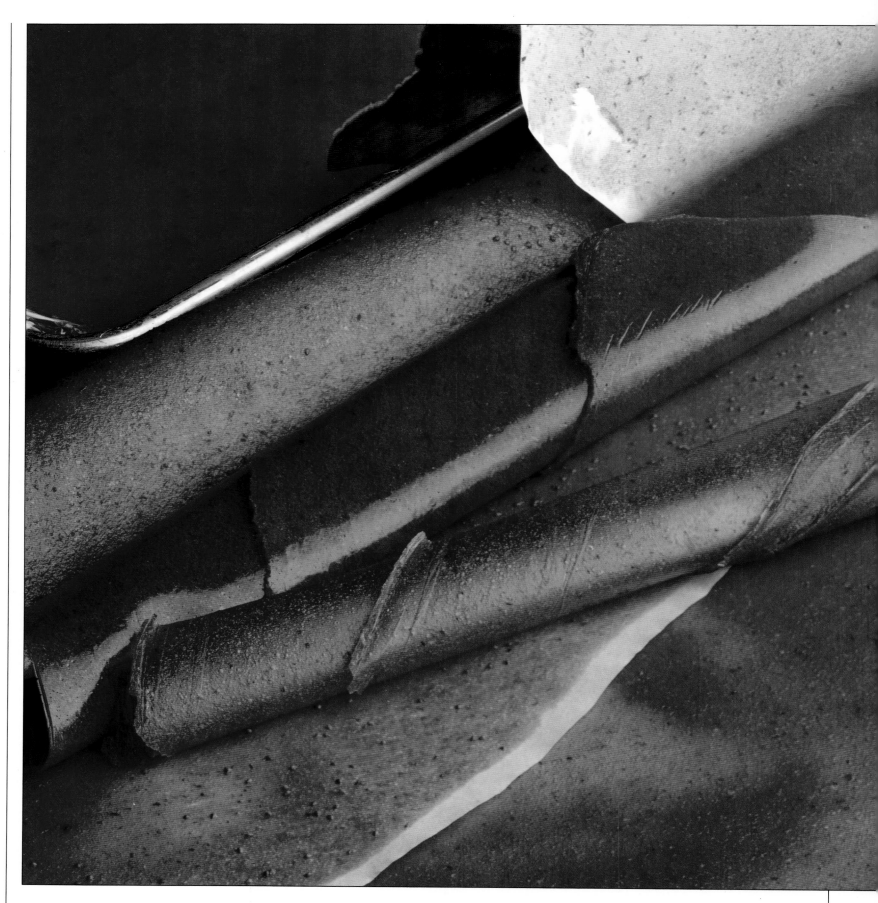

California

FRUIT LEATHER

Fruit leathers are made by puréeing fresh fruit with sugar, spreading the mixture out in a thin layer and letting it dry—either in the sun (the time-honored way), or in the oven (faster, and you do not have to worry about insects). Sweet and flavorful, a properly dried fruit leather will keep for about a month at room temperature, making it good for camping and hiking. Note that the oven is not preheated and that it must remain accurately at its lowest setting, so that the plastic wrap does not get too hot.

5 cups (1 lb/500 g) sliced ripe strawberries, peaches,
    apricots or plums

½ cup (4 oz/125 g) sugar
2 tablespoons lemon juice

🦋 Put the fruit in a saucepan, add the sugar and lemon juice, and cook over moderate heat, stirring constantly, just until the mixture boils and the sugar dissolves. Using a slotted spoon, transfer the fruit to a blender or food processor. Pour the cooking liquid into a medium-sized bowl. Purée the fruit until it is smooth, then add it to the liquid. Let the mixture cool until tepid.

🦋 Cover two large baking sheets or jelly-roll pans with wide plastic wrap, letting it come up the edges, but not hang over the sides. Pour the purée into the prepared pans, spreading it about ⅛ in (3 mm) thick. Place in the oven and turn to its

Fruit Leather

lowest setting—no more than 150°F (65°C). Leave the door slightly ajar. Check periodically to be sure the plastic wrap has not fallen into the purée. The leather is ready in about 5 hours, or when it can easily be peeled from the plastic wrap.

To dry the fruit in the sun, cover the pans with a fine-mesh screen or a double thickness of cheesecloth (muslin), pulled snugly across the top, and place them in the sunlight. The fruit will take about 20 hours of sunlight, or 2 to 3 days to dry. Bring the pans in at night.

Let the leather cool completely. To store, roll the leather up with the plastic wrap (it will be easy to unroll and peel off later), and keep in an airtight container.

MAKES 2 SHEETS, ABOUT 8 IN (20 CM) SQUARE

Gilroy
FRIED ONION RINGS

Though Gilroy is known for its annual Garlic Festival, onions are also grown in the vicinity. These onion rings are lighter than most, because they are simply tossed in seasoned flour before being fried, and not dipped in a thick batter. Don't be put off by the prospect of deep frying, either. Done properly, with fresh oil, the results are unlike those from any other cooking method. These rings go well with hamburgers and steaks and, because they are soaked in milk before they are fried, they lose some of the raw sting. (The milk is not wasted; it may then be used in a soup or sauce.)

3 large, mild onions, such as red (Spanish) or Bermuda onions
4 cups (32 fl oz/1 l) milk
1 cup (4 oz/125 g) all-purpose (plain) flour
salt
oil for frying

Peel the onions and slice them horizontally ¼ in (6 mm) thick. Separate the slices into rings and put them in a large shallow dish. Pour on the milk and let the onions stand for 30 minutes, stirring them occasionally.

Pour off the milk. Combine the flour with 1 teaspoon of salt. In a large pan heat about 1½ in (4 cm) oil to 375°F (190°C). Toss the drained onion rings in the flour to coat them completely.

Drop them into the hot oil several at a time and fry until golden on both sides, about 2 to 3 minutes. Drain on absorbent paper towels and sprinkle with more salt if you wish. Keep warm in a 200°F (95°C) oven if necessary until you have enough to begin serving.

SERVES 4–6   *Photograph page 175*

Fresno
BROCCOLI WITH OLIVE SAUCE

With a lemony olive sauce, this dish is a pleasant and unusual change from plain buttered broccoli. Like all members of the cabbage family, broccoli should not be overcooked. Serve it while it is still bright green and slightly crunchy. This is particularly good with roast beef or lamb.

4 tablespoons (2 oz/60 g) butter
3 tablespoons all-purpose (plain) flour
1½ cups (12 fl oz/375 ml) milk
½ teaspoon salt
½ teaspoon freshly ground black pepper
½ cup (2 oz/60 g) chopped ripe black olives
3 tablespoons lemon juice
2 lb (1 kg) broccoli
2 tablespoons chopped parsley

Make the sauce before cooking the broccoli: melt the butter in a saucepan, add the flour and cook over medium heat, stirring, for 2 minutes. Whisk in the milk, salt and pepper, then bring to a boil. Reduce the heat and simmer for about 2 minutes. Stir in the olives and lemon juice; set aside.

Cut away and discard the tough stems of the broccoli. Cut into florets all about the same size, with stems 1 or 2 in (2.5 or 5 cm) long.

Drop into a large pan of boiling salted water. Bring back to a boil over high heat and cook for 5 minutes, or less, until barely tender.

While the broccoli cooks, bring the sauce back to a simmer and stir in the parsley. Drain the broccoli well and arrange on a platter. Spoon the sauce over and serve.

SERVES 6   *Photograph pages 170–171*

San Francisco

VEGETABLES TEMPURA

Vegetables dipped in batter and fried until golden are unique. Tempura is not something you would cook every day, especially when you can find it in Japanese restaurants. But when you do feel like making your own, with fresh vegetables and good oil for frying, you can be sure of first-rate results, which are sometimes hard to find when you dine out.

BATTER

1¼ cups (10 fl oz/310 ml) ice water
1 egg
1 tablespoon soy sauce
1 cup (4 oz/125 g) cake (soft-wheat) flour (see glossary)
½ teaspoon salt
¼ teaspoon baking soda (bicarbonate of soda)

DIPPING SAUCE

⅔ cup (5 fl oz/160 ml) chicken stock (see glossary)
⅓ cup (3 fl oz/80 ml) soy sauce
3 tablespoons *mirin* (sweet rice wine, see glossary) or sweet sherry
2 tablespoons freshly grated ginger
1 tablespoon sugar

VEGETABLES

oil for frying
½ lb (250 g) small mushrooms, or large mushrooms, halved
½ lb (250 g) Japanese eggplant, about 6, halved or quartered
½ lb (250 g) broccoli florets
½ lb (250 g) asparagus tips

❧ To make the batter, beat together in a medium bowl the water, egg and soy sauce until smooth. Combine the flour, salt and baking soda. Add to the water mixture and stir with a fork until barely blended; do not combine thoroughly. The batter should be lumpy, with streaks of unblended flour. Set the batter bowl in a larger bowl of ice water to keep it cold.

❧ To make the dipping sauce, whisk together the chicken stock, soy sauce, *mirin*, ginger and sugar. Set aside.

❧ Heat about 2 in (5 cm) of oil in a deep kettle or Dutch oven to 360°F (185°C). A few at a time, dip the vegetables in the batter and gently slip them into the oil without crowding the pan. Fry for 2 or 3 minutes, turning once or twice, until golden and puffy. Drain for a moment on absorbent paper towels, then continue frying the remaining vegetables the same way. Serve as soon as possible with the dipping sauce.

SERVES 6

Vegetables Tempura

Fried Artichoke Hearts (top) and Fried Onion Rings (bottom, recipe page 173)

Castroville

FRIED ARTICHOKE HEARTS

Artichokes prepared in many ways are featured at the Giant Artichoke, a restaurant in coastal Castroville, the "Artichoke Capital of the World"—as the sign at the entrance of town proclaims. Serve these artichokes with lemon wedges and something for dipping, such as melted butter or mayonnaise. Beer, by the way, gives the batter a wonderful yeasty flavor.

2 boxes (9 oz/280 g each) frozen artichoke hearts, thawed
1 egg
3 tablespoons vegetable oil
½ cup (4 fl oz/125 ml) beer
¼ cup (2 fl oz/60 ml), more or less, milk
1 cup (4 oz/125 g) all-purpose (plain) flour
salt
oil for frying

lemon wedges
melted butter or mayonnaise, for dipping

❧ Separate the artichoke hearts and pat them dry; you should have about 40 halves and quarters.
❧ To prepare the batter, beat the egg and oil together, then whisk in the beer and ¼ cup milk. Add the flour and ½ teaspoon salt and beat until smooth. Cover and let the batter stand for 1 hour. After that time, if the batter is very thick, thin it with a little milk.
❧ Heat about 1½ in (4 cm) of vegetable oil in a heavy pot or skillet to 375°F (190°C). A few at a time, dip the artichoke hearts into the batter to coat them, then drop them gently into the hot oil. Fry for about 2 minutes, until golden. Drain on absorbent paper towels, sprinkle with salt and serve as soon as possible.

SERVES 6

Pajaro Valley

APPLE FRITTERS

Apples have been grown on the West Coast since the 1820s and commercially in the cool, coastal Pajaro Valley since 1854. The Martinelli family, of Watsonville, has certainly helped make the area famous for its cider. Apples are often used in pies, crisps and cobblers, but you rarely see fritters—apple wedges dipped in batter and fried until crisp and golden. They are special and are particularly good with roast pork and ham.

4 firm apples, such as Golden Delicious or
   Newtown Pippin
2 tablespoons lemon juice
1 cup (4 oz/125 g) all-purpose (plain) flour
1 teaspoon baking powder
½ teaspoon salt
2 tablespoons sugar
1 cup (8 fl oz/250 ml) milk
3 tablespoons melted butter
2 eggs, separated
oil for frying
powdered (icing) sugar in a sieve

❧ Peel the apples, halve and core them and cut each half into 6 or 8 wedges. Toss with the lemon juice and set aside; do not worry if they darken a little.

❧ Stir and toss together the flour, baking powder, salt and sugar. Beat together the milk, butter and egg yolks. Add to the dry ingredients and stir until smooth. Beat the egg whites until they stand in soft peaks, then fold them into the batter.

❧ Heat about 1½ in (4 cm) of oil to 370°F (188°C).

❧ A few at a time, dip the pieces of apple into the batter to coat completely, then gently lower them into the hot oil. Cook for about 1 minute, turn them over and cook for about 30 seconds more, or until golden, and a fritter is tender when pierced.

❧ Drain on paper towels. Keep warm if necessary in a 250°F (120°C) oven until you have enough to serve—but the sooner they are eaten, the better. Just before serving, sprinkle generously with powdered sugar.

SERVES 4–6

Napa Valley

RED WINE APPLESAUCE

The name says it all—applesauce in which red wine replaces the water, giving it an interesting flavor and color. I first had this in the Napa Valley, with barbecued pork.

8 tart apples, about 4 lb (2 kg)
¾ cup (6 fl oz/180 ml) dry red wine
⅓ cup (3 oz/90 g) sugar
1 bay leaf
3 tablespoons butter

❧ Peel, core and slice the apples, dropping them into a large saucepan as you work. Add the red wine, the sugar (using more or less, depending on the tartness of the apples) and the bay leaf. Cover and cook over medium heat, stirring occasionally, for about 15 to 20 minutes.

❧ As the apples soften and become tender, mash them with the back of a spoon or potato masher. Remove the bay leaf. If you want a thicker applesauce, boil it uncovered, stirring almost constantly, to reduce slightly. If you like a very smooth sauce, put it through a food mill. Stir in the butter and add more sugar to taste.

SERVES 4–6

*Red Wine Applesauce (top)
and Apple Fritters (bottom)*

Asparagus with Orange Butter Sauce

Riverside

ASPARAGUS WITH ORANGE BUTTER SAUCE

The flavors of oranges and asparagus have an affinity for each other. This buttery sauce with a sharp, fresh flavor is made like a hollandaise but is flavored with orange rather than lemon. It is also particularly good with poached or grilled salmon.

1 lb (500 g) asparagus
3 egg yolks
4 tablespoons (2 fl oz/60 ml) orange juice
½ cup (4 oz/125 g) unsalted butter, melted and hot
1 teaspoon grated orange zest
salt

❧ Trim the asparagus and, if the butt end is tough, peel the outer skin with a vegetable peeler. Bring a large pot of salted water to a boil, but prepare the sauce before cooking the asparagus.

❧ In a small heavy pan, whisk the egg yolks with 2 tablespoons of the orange juice until creamy. Set the pan over *medium* heat and whisk constantly for about 3 minutes, until the yolks are thickened and you see faint wisps of steam rising. You will also begin to see the bottom of the pan between strokes. Do not let the eggs get too hot or they will scramble. Immediately remove from the heat and continue whisking for a few seconds. Slowly whisk in the hot butter in a thin stream. Blend in the remaining 2 tablespoons of orange juice and the zest; the sauce should be fairly thick. Set the pan in a larger pan of warm—not hot—water, or near a faint heat, such as a pilot light, while you cook the asparagus.

❧ Drop the asparagus into the boiling water, bring it back to a boil over the highest heat, and cook for between 3 and 5 minutes, until the spears are just tender and droop slightly when lifted. Drain thoroughly and serve with the sauce.

SERVES 4

Napa Valley

GRILLED HERBED EGGPLANT

Japanese eggplant are long and skinny—about 4 inches in length and the diameter of a quarter. They cook quickly, are good hot from the grill or at room temperature, and may also be prepared successfully indoors, under the broiler.

⅓ cup (3 fl oz/80 ml) olive oil
2 tablespoons chopped fresh herbs, such as basil, oregano or thyme, or 2 teaspoons dried herbs
1 tablespoon lemon juice
1 lb (500 g) Japanese eggplant, about 6–8
salt
freshly ground black pepper

❧ Whisk together the olive oil, herbs and lemon juice. Trim the eggplant and halve them lengthwise. Score the cut side several times with the point of a knife and brush lightly with the oil mixture.

❧ Place, cut-side down, on the grill 4 to 6 in (10 to 15 cm) from hot coals. Sprinkle lightly with salt and pepper and cook for about 5 minutes. Turn them over, brush again with the oil mixture, sprinkle with salt and pepper and cook for about 5 minutes more, brushing once or twice with the oil.

❧ To cook indoors, brush the eggplant with herbed oil, salt and pepper and broil (grill) cut-side up, about 4 in (10 cm) from the heat for 5 minutes, or until lightly browned. Turn, brush again with the oil, sprinkle with salt and pepper and cook until the skin side darkens slightly—brushing once or twice more with the oil.

SERVES 6   *Photograph pages 10–11*

Imperial Valley

BRUSSELS SPROUTS WITH ALMOND BUTTER

Most of our Brussels sprouts are grown on the cool central California coast between Moss Landing to the south and Half Moon Bay to the north. They are most plentiful from October through February. Their distinctive cabbagelike flavor is enhanced by nuts—even cooked chestnuts (a combination that would surely make a fine holiday vegetable), and the toasty taste of this dish is a hearty complement to cold-weather foods, such as roast turkey, pork and game.

1½ lb (750 g) Brussels sprouts, washed and trimmed
4 tablespoons (2 oz/60 g) butter
½ teaspoon salt
freshly ground black pepper
⅓ cup (1½ oz/45 g) toasted sliced almonds
2 tablespoons chopped parsley

❧ With a sharp knife, cut a ½-in (12-mm)-deep cross in the stem end of each sprout. Drop them into a large pot of boiling salted water, cover the pan and, when it returns to a boil, remove the cover. Cook for about 5 minutes, or until the sprouts are fairly tender when pierced. Drain, then cover with cold water and let them sit for 3 minutes to cool, and drain again. Pat them dry with paper towels and cut each sprout into halves or quarters.

❧ A few minutes before serving, melt the butter in a large skillet over moderate heat. When the foam has subsided and the butter is on the verge of browning, add the sprouts. Season with salt and pepper, then stir and toss for several minutes,

until the vegetables are heated through. Add the almonds and parsley, and cook for 1 minute more.

SERVES 6

Ukiah

GRILLED PEACHES AND PEARS

After you have removed the main course from the barbecue, and the coals are still warm, take advantage of the residual heat and grill some fruit. It is a healthy way to finish any meal. They take only minutes to cook and are equally good hot or at room temperature. Serve, if you wish, with sour cream or crème fraîche *(see glossary).*

⅓ cup (3 fl oz/80 ml) melted butter
1 tablespoon sugar
1 teaspoon ground cinnamon
3 firm ripe pears, peeled, halved and cored
3 firm ripe peaches, peeled, halved and pitted

❧ Stir together the butter, sugar and cinnamon.
❧ Prepare a barbecue fire, or use an existing fire, with the grilling rack between 4 and 6 in (10 and 15 cm) from the heat.
❧ Grill the fruit for about 10 minutes, turning 2 or 3 times and basting occasionally with the butter mixture, until lightly browned and heated through. Remove to a platter and serve hot, warm or at room temperature.

SERVES 6

Grilled Peaches and Pears

Brussels Sprouts with Almond Butter

California
GREEN BEANS WITH TOMATOES

I cannot think of a meat or poultry dish that this summery combination would not complement. Cook the beans thoroughly—they should not be crunchy. If ripe summer tomatoes are not available, canned plum tomatoes are a suitable alternative.

1 lb (500 g) green beans
¼ cup (2 fl oz/60 ml) olive oil
2 large tomatoes, peeled, seeded and chopped, or 1½ cups (12 oz/375 g) canned plum (egg) tomatoes, drained and chopped
1 garlic clove, minced (finely chopped)
salt
freshly ground black pepper
2 tablespoons grated Parmesan cheese
¼ cup (½ oz/15 g) small fresh basil leaves or 2 tablespoons chopped fresh basil or 1 teaspoon dried basil

❧ If the beans are large, break them in half. Drop them into a large pan of boiling salted water and cook until tender, about 5 to 8 minutes, depending on their size. Drain thoroughly.
❧ Heat the olive oil in a large skillet, add the drained beans and toss to coat. Add the tomatoes and garlic, and stir and toss to blend. Boil rapidly for a minute or two if necessary to evaporate any exuded tomato juices. Season with salt and pepper to taste, then add the cheese and basil and combine thoroughly.

SERVES 4   *Photograph pages 160–161*

Gilroy
ROASTED WHOLE GARLIC

A whole head of garlic, after long cooking, becomes smooth, as soft as butter and not a bit sharp. The individual cloves can easily be squeezed out of their skins and spread on crackers or crusty bread. Serve as a first course, or as a garnish for a meat or poultry platter.

4 whole heads garlic
salt
freshly ground black pepper
¼ cup (2 fl oz/60 ml) olive oil

❧ Preheat the oven to 225°F (110°C).
❧ With a small, sharp knife make an incision around the circumference of each head of garlic at the middle, piercing the skin without cutting through the cloves. Peel off the outer layer of papery skin from the top half of the bulb only, exposing the tops of the cloves. Put the garlic in a baking dish, sprinkle generously with salt and pepper and drizzle with the olive oil.
❧ Bake for about 20 minutes, then cover the baking dish with foil and continue baking for about 1 hour longer, basting occasionally with the oil in the pan, until the garlic is very soft when squeezed.

SERVES 4   *Photograph pages 10–11*

Berkeley
BLACK BEAN CAKES

Black beans make a good soup, as well as frijoles refritos *(refried beans), but when you want something really different, try the cakes which were invented and made famous by Jeremiah Tower of Stars restaurant in San Francisco, when he opened the Santa Fe Bar and Grill in Berkeley. Mr. Tower serves them as a*

first course, topped with sour cream, salsa *and cilantro. They are also good mingled with the juices of a roast, such as the Napa Valley leg of lamb on page 97. (He warns that no matter how ghastly the uncooked mixture looks, it will taste just fine.)*

½ lb (250 g) black or turtle beans (*frijoles negros*)
6–8 cups (48–64 fl oz/1.5–2 l) chicken stock (see glossary)
1 medium carrot, peeled and chopped
1 celery stalk, chopped
freshly ground black pepper
1 tablespoon *ancho chile* powder (see glossary)
1 tablespoon ground cumin
1 *jalapeño* (hot green) *chile*, stemmed, seeded and minced (finely chopped)
½ cup (1 oz/30 g) chopped cilantro (coriander/Chinese parsley)
1 teaspoon salt

Black Bean Cakes

¼ cup (2 fl oz/60 ml) olive oil or rendered duck fat or lard
cilantro (coriander/Chinese parsley) sprigs
sour cream
tomato *salsa* (see recipe, page 207)

🐦 Sort through the beans for grit and pebbles and rinse them. Cover with plenty of cold water and soak them overnight.

🐦 Drain the beans well and combine in a large saucepan with 6 cups (48 fl oz/1.5 l) stock and the carrot and celery. Bring to a boil over moderate heat, then reduce the heat and boil gently, partially covered, until the beans are tender, 1 to 1½ hours. Add additional stock if it falls below the surface of the beans. Pour the beans into a colander and let them drain for about 2 hours—they must be thoroughly dry. (The liquid can be used for soup.)

🐦 Purée 3 cups (1½ lb/750 g) of the beans through a food mill or meat grinder and combine with the pepper, *chile* powder, cumin, *chile*, cilantro and salt. (Any leftover beans can be used in soup or salad.) The mixture will appear dry and stiff. Divide it into 4 equal balls.

🐦 Between 2 sheets of waxed paper, gently press and pat each ball into a round disk about ⅛ in (3 mm) thick and 5 in (13 cm) in diameter; set aside.

🐦 Heat ¼ cup of the oil in a large skillet, preferably one with a nonstick surface or of well-seasoned cast iron. When the oil is quite hot, put in as many cakes as you can without crowding them and cook for about 2 minutes on each side. Transfer to a warm platter, add more oil to the pan if necessary, and cook the remaining cakes the same way. Garnish with cilantro sprigs and serve with sour cream and *salsa*.

MAKES FOUR 5-IN (13-CM) CAKES

Los Angeles
REFRIED BEANS

These twice-cooked beans are a classic in Mexican cooking. They are first simmered in water, then drained, mashed and "fried" with their own cooking liquid and some fat. They go well with so many things from south of the border, including tamales, enchiladas, nachos *and tacos.*

1 lb (500 g) pinto or red kidney beans
1 onion, chopped
salt
½ teaspoon freshly ground black pepper
¼ cup (2 fl oz/60 ml) bacon dripping, vegetable oil or lard
1–2 cups (4–8 oz/125–250 g) grated Monterey Jack (mild melting) or Cheddar cheese
2 teaspoons chili powder

✿ Wash and sort through the beans for grit and other debris. Cover the beans with cold water, bring to a rolling boil and boil for 1 minute. Cover and remove from the heat and let stand 1 hour.

✿ Drain well, cover with fresh water, then add the onion, 1 teaspoon salt and the pepper. Bring to a boil and simmer, partially covered, for about 1 hour, until the beans are tender. If necessary, add more water to keep the beans covered. Drain thoroughly, reserving the cooking liquid.

✿ Heat the bacon dripping, oil or lard in a large skillet. Add a quarter of the beans and mash them with the back of a spatula. Add about ½ cup (4 fl oz/125 ml) of the cooking liquid and blend well. Continue adding and mashing beans and liquid alternately until all the beans are used; they should be creamy, not dry. Add the cheese and stir until smooth, then season with chili powder, and additional salt if necessary.

SERVES 6

California
STUFFED CHAYOTE

A pear-shaped member of the squash family native to Central America, chayote *is also known as mirliton and vegetable pear. It is particularly good for stuffing because it holds its shape and is compatible with so many fillings, from a bold sausage mixture to a more delicate creamed crab or shrimp. You will be surprised how long it must cook to become tender.*

4 *chayotes*, about 2 lb (1 kg) total
2 tablespoons olive oil
1 onion, chopped
1 lb (500 g) bulk sausage meat
1 cup (4 oz/125 g) dry breadcrumbs
½ teaspoon dried sage
salt
freshly ground black pepper
¼ cup (2 fl oz/60 ml) heavy (double) cream or leftover gravy
3 tablespoons melted butter

✿ Boil the *chayotes* in salted water to cover until they are just tender when pierced; this may take up to an hour. Drain, then cover with cold water and let them stand for several minutes to cool.

✿ Drain again and cut the *chayotes* in half lengthwise. Scoop out the innards, leaving a shell about ¼ in (6 mm) thick. Squeeze the scooped-out flesh in the corner of a towel, to remove excess moisture. Chop coarsely and place in a bowl. Heat the olive oil in a skillet over moderate heat. Add the onion and cook, stirring, for about 5 minutes. Scrape into the bowl with the squash. Return the skillet to the heat and in it cook the sausage meat, breaking it up with a spatula, until it

Sweet and Sour Carrots

loses its pinkness. Drain off the fat and add the sausage to the bowl with the other ingredients. Add the breadcrumbs and sage and toss to combine. Season to taste with salt and pepper. Blend in the cream or gravy.

✿ Preheat the oven to 350°F (180°C).

✿ Mound the stuffing into the *chayote* shells, place them in a baking pan, drizzle the tops with melted butter and bake for about 25 minutes.

SERVES 4

Imperial Valley
SWEET AND SOUR CARROTS

Of Chinese influence, these carrots go especially well with any salted or smoked meat, such as corned beef or sausages. To peel the pepper, it is not necessary to roast it—just shave off the skin with a vegetable peeler.

1 lb (500 g) carrots
1 tablespoon vegetable oil
1 tablespoon cornstarch (cornflour)
3 tablespoons cider vinegar
2 tablespoons sugar
¼ cup (2 fl oz/60 ml) tomato sauce or tomato purée
1 tablespoon soy sauce
1 green bell pepper (capsicum), peeled and thinly sliced
salt
freshly ground black pepper

✿ Peel the carrots and cut them into diagonal slices ¼ in (6 mm) thick. Drop into a pot of boiling salted water and cook for 5 minutes; they should remain slightly firm. Drain well.

✿ Heat the vegetable oil in a large skillet. Add the carrots and toss frequently for about 5 minutes.

✿ Stir together the cornstarch and vinegar, then add the sugar, tomato sauce and soy sauce. Pour the sauce over the carrots and add the green pepper. Cook a few minutes longer, until the sauce is slightly thickened and glistening. Season to taste with salt and pepper.

SERVES 4

Refried Beans (top right) and Stuffed Chayote (bottom)

Monterey

BAKED ZUCCHINI WITH CHEESE

It does not take a gardener to know that wherever you plant zucchini, it will surely be your leading crop. Summer squash can be watery, but grating, salting and squeezing it gets rid of much of the liquid and also seems to concentrate the flavor. Combined with a white sauce, some herbs and cheese, it goes well with any meat or poultry—and this is a good way to use up those larger squash that got away from you.

2 lb (1 kg) zucchini (courgette)
1 medium onion, finely chopped
salt
3 tablespoons olive oil
freshly ground black pepper
2 tablespoons butter
2 tablespoons all-purpose (plain) flour
¾ cup (6 fl oz/180 ml) milk
2 garlic cloves, minced (finely chopped)
1 tablespoon chopped fresh marjoram or 1 teaspoon
    dried marjoram
1 cup (about 4 oz/125 g) Teleme cheese, grated or finely diced

🐦 Grate the zucchini and toss it in a colander with the onion and 1 teaspoon salt. Set the colander in a bowl and let it stand for 30 minutes. Then, a handful at a time, squeeze the mixture as firmly as you can, to extract more water (this liquid may be added to a soup).
🐦 Heat the olive oil in a large skillet. Add the zucchini and onion and toss over moderately high heat for about 5 minutes, until tender. Season with salt and pepper. Preheat the oven to 350°F (180°C) and oil a baking dish of about 6-cup (48-fl oz/1.5-l) capacity.
🐦 Melt the butter in a small saucepan, add the flour and cook, stirring, for 2 minutes. Whisk in the milk, bring to a boil and season with salt and pepper to taste. Stir in the garlic and marjoram. Fold the sauce into the grated zucchini. Pour into the prepared baking dish, sprinkle with the cheese and bake for 20 minutes, until bubbling and lightly browned. Let it stand for 5 minutes before serving.

SERVES 6   *Photograph pages 160–161*

Monterey

CREAM-BAKED TOMATOES

Whole tomatoes, baked with an herbal crumb topping and some cream, which becomes a ready-made sauce, make a side dish that will go with any meat or poultry.

4 medium tomatoes, about 1 lb (500 g)
1 medium onion, chopped
½ cup (2 oz/60 g) dry breadcrumbs
¼ cup (2 fl oz/60 ml) melted butter
½ teaspoon salt
¼ teaspoon freshly ground black pepper
1 tablespoon chopped fresh tarragon or basil, or 1 teaspoon
    dried tarragon or basil
1 cup (8 fl oz/250 ml) heavy (double) cream

🐦 Preheat the oven to 325°F (165°C).
🐦 Slice off the top ½ in (12 mm) of each tomato and scoop out the central core. Place the tomatoes cut-side up in a glass baking dish large enough to hold them with some room in between.
🐦 Stir and toss together the onion, breadcrumbs, butter, salt

and pepper, and tarragon or basil. Heap the mixture evenly in the tomatoes, mounding it on top. Pour the cream into the baking dish. Bake for 20 to 30 minutes, until the tomatoes are soft but not mushy. Remove to a warm platter. Pour the cream and any juices into a saucepan and boil rapidly until they have thickened and reduced slightly. Pour around the tomatoes and serve as soon as possible.

SERVES 4

California

JERUSALEM ARTICHOKE PURÉE

Jerusalem artichokes, also known as sunchokes (they are in the sunflower family), are potato-shaped tubers with a knobby, gnarled skin. Though they grow in many parts of the world, including California, cooks are often unfamiliar with them and do not know how to prepare them. The flavor is subtle, and because they tend to be watery, steaming is better than boiling. Cook until tender, then toss them in butter and parsley, or serve them cold in a salad, or make this purée, which may be prepared ahead and reheated in a double boiler, to serve with beef, pork or lamb.

1 lb (500 g) Jerusalem artichokes
4 tablespoons (2 oz/60 g) softened butter
¼ cup (2 fl oz/60 ml) heavy (double) cream
salt
freshly ground black pepper

🐦 Peel the artichokes, removing as much of the skin as you can, but do not worry about shaving off every bit. Steam them whole, in a tightly covered pan over boiling water, until barely tender, for about 15 minutes. Do not let them become mushy.
🐦 Purée them in a food processor or through a food mill, beat in the butter and cream, and season with salt and pepper to taste. Reheat if necessary before serving.

SERVES 4

San Joaquin Valley

PESTO TOMATOES

If you are a backyard gardener, remember that home-grown basil proliferates like mad in a warm climate. And, as I learned from a gardening friend, you can keep leaf-eating insects away by interspersing the basil plants with fragrant marigold plants. Make this simple salad when summer tomatoes are at their peak.

1 cup (2 oz/60 g) fresh basil leaves
½ cup (4 fl oz/125 ml) olive oil
½ cup (2 oz/60 g) freshly grated Parmesan cheese
2 tablespoons white wine vinegar
1 garlic clove, minced (finely chopped)
½ teaspoon salt
several leaves of butter lettuce, or a few handfuls of mixed
    baby lettuces
4 large, ripe tomatoes, sliced

🐦 To make the *pesto*, combine the basil, oil, cheese, vinegar, garlic and salt in a blender or food processor and process until smooth. You will have about ¾ cup (6 fl oz/180 ml).
🐦 Line a platter with the lettuce and lay the tomato slices on top. Spoon the *pesto* over, and serve.

SERVES 6–8   *Photograph pages 10–11*

Jerusalem Artichoke Purée (top)
and Cream-Baked Tomatoes (bottom)

THE BAY AREA AND WINE COUNTRY

THE BAY AREA AND WINE COUNTRY

It is no wonder that around the San Francisco Bay, the California coast looks as though it has had a few nibbles taken out of it. The Golden Gate opens to one of the most glorious and eclectic food and wine regions in the entire United States. Exceptional offerings of food and drink seem to beckon at every turn, and the setting is a wonder of natural and man-made beauty.

Along the coastal shelf, rolling fog often obscures the dramatic views. Misty and cool, it washes over towering redwood and eucalyptus trees and envelops coastal and inland areas in a cozy silence, interrupted only by low foghorns. But when it lifts—and it always does—craggy headlands and sheltered coves, lush green meadows, landmark bridges and hilly cities emerge.

Within this compact region, the culinary offerings are by turns exotic, ethereal and perfectly simple. The Spanish-Mexican influence, though strong, is less evident here than it is in southern California. Rather, the area in general leans more to the European (especially Italian and French) and Asian—and, these days, toward a distinct northern California style. In cities and on farm trails throughout the land, scores of specialty cheese and sausage makers, some of the country's finest bakers and chocolatiers, coffee roasters, oyster farmers, winemakers, brewmasters, vinegar and olive oil producers, organic and

Previous pages: A brilliant sunset reflects in the water off the rocky Sonoma coast, an area that contrasts sharply with the quiet wine-growing landscapes inland. Left: A rosy dawn slides across the steep hillsides of San Francisco.

191

specialty vegetable and fruit growers, and brilliant chefs of every race ply their crafts and trades. Some are descendants of families who arrived with the gold rush and the railroads. Others have migrated from every other state in the country, and from the far corners of the world, drawn to communities that treat the business and pleasure of food and wine as part of the essential fabric of life.

To picture the region, imagine a large chunk, rather than a few nibbles, taken out of the coast north, south and inland of the Golden Gate. Begin around the pumpkin patches at Half Moon Bay, as the coast meanders north to San Francisco and nearby Berkeley and Oakland. The line runs past Stinson Beach, through tiny Olema and around Point Reyes, the site of a sprawling old cattle ranch and now a national seashore. Nearby, Jersey cows graze in pastoral dairy country. To the north, the waters of Tomales Bay wash over carefully tended oyster farms. Jenner, where a comforting bowl of clam chowder is always waiting in a little restaurant by the sea, marks the coastal stopping point of this region. Inland, Healdsburg, Calistoga and Angwin cap the north and east boundaries as the region opens up to the magnificent wine country—Napa and Sonoma valleys.

The southernmost reaches of Napa and Sonoma lie close to northern inlets of San Francisco Bay, where some vineyards are strategically positioned to take advantage of the cool breezes that nurture the development of grapes for complex varietal wines. Other vineyards thrive in the warmer inner folds of these world-famous valleys. Long and narrow, the Napa Valley is defined by the low, gentle Mayacamas Mountains and a valley floor blanketed with vineyards and bright fields of wild mustard. The Sonoma Valley centers around the historic Sonoma town square, where the California wine industry began. As it stretches north and south, the Sonoma Valley includes several wineries just outside the town square as

Children frolic on a playground near San Francisco's Chinatown, home to the largest number of Chinese people outside Asia and teeming with Asian culinary delicacies and restaurants.

well as others in the Russian River Valley. From the Pacific Ocean, breezes are drawn along the river and over the surrounding ridges. As the warm air rises, breezes cool nearby grapevines during the long, hot days of summer.

Over the Benicia Bridge and to the south, in Alameda and Contra Costa counties and the Livermore Valley, there is a slightly warmer climate and a few wineries, among them some venerable establishments that date from the late 1800s.

Together, California's winemakers, nearby specialty produce growers, chefs and consumers have created a minor agricultural renaissance that has been a key factor in the development of what is known as California cuisine. The term has been used, some would say overused, for the past several years to describe the way cooks throughout the state have refined or reworked classical recipes to take advantage of the ever-increasing supply of high-quality California-grown or -made ingredients. Some of the more common foodstuffs identified with the new style are classic items such as sun-dried tomatoes, dozens of varieties of fruits and vegetables (grown for quality and harvested young), goat cheeses, duck sausages made with fresh herbs, smoked chicken and Pekin ducks, baby lamb and unusual mushrooms. The shopping list is long, often reminiscent of France and Italy, and outside California may seem exotic. Californians, always a creative and adventuresome lot, have indulged in considerable experimentation in pairing ingredients, sometimes going overboard with miniature vegetables and overstylized presentations. Now, as happens with good trends that eventually become part of the culture, things are smoothing out and there is a confident sense of refinement. The plates are still beautifully presented, but self-conciousness is giving way to practicality and an awareness of the way people really like to eat—with good portions of fresh foods and honest, exciting flavors. And to go with the foods, plenty of local wines.

Sonoma Valley is one regional cradle of edible and potable delights. Dotted with the orchards, farms and workshops of dedicated market gardeners who are passionate about growing produce with the fullest flavor, making fresh cheese, raising meat, game and poultry to offer in small, rather than mass, quantities, the area is purveyor to chefs throughout the state. But anyone who is so inclined can get a Farm Trails map from the local Chamber of Commerce and spend a day sampling and buying varieties of apples, berries, melons, edible blossoms, jams and vinegars and cheeses—as much as they can carry. Farmers' markets that inspire fresh, healthy meals are regular weekly events throughout the region.

Wine plays a major role in California's agricultural and culinary development. California vintners have not only held their own since they astonished the wine world at a tasting organized in 1976 by the *Académie du vin* in Paris (in which a Napa Valley Cabernet Sauvignon and three California Chardonnays were awarded top honors in a blind tasting by French judges), they have taken up the gauntlet and educated both professional and amateur cooks in the finer points of enjoying good wine with good food—especially good California food.

San Francisco itself is a city of overwhelming gustatory temptations, brimming with appetizing sights, sounds and smells: the steam of a *cappuccino* machine; the open door of a *trattoria* wafting garlicky aromas out to the street; cleavers chopping cilantro and *chiles* in the Mission district; pork roasting on a spit; woks the size of manhole covers sizzling with shrimp and crab. Here, cooks find

The scenery of California echoes that of the rest of rural America, as in this rustic setting of barn and field in Sonoma County.

perfection in a lively fresh crab, steamed and served in its sweet, succulent glory—unfettered by complicated sauces—or the first bite of a magically light *sacripantina* cake from an Italian bakery in North Beach or a typically *nouvelle* concoction of mixed origins, such as grilled salmon with *wasabi-saki* Hollandaise and French caviar served in a restaurant that looks like an art gallery.

You need not be a chef or even go to a restaurant to enjoy all the specially grown or handmade foods available in the Bay Area. People in most neighborhoods, whether Chinese or Hispanic, Italian, Japanese or Russian, have only to go from market to market, filling their baskets. Each group has a defined district, but the wonderful thing is that the districts spill over into one another and often influence the mainstream supermarkets. You can find mangoes and papayas, fresh water chestnuts and persimmons, Italian regional breads, freshly made *tortillas*, fresh ricotta and mozzarella—whatever the menu calls for—at some market in San Francisco or the East Bay.

From its earliest days, San Francisco has basked in a reputation for great and plentiful food and lusty appetites. In *Bonanza Inn*, an account of the early days of the famous Palace Hotel, the authors were justifiably boastful, explaining that around 1885, "the Palace was mainly responsible for spreading abroad a knowledge of distinctly Californian foods. Mountain and valley quail were often on its menu, as were duck, venison, and in the earlier period, grizzly steaks. Rainbow trout was for years a specialty, along with sole, bass, and presently abalone." Since then, it seems the city hasn't missed a beat—even in the wake of the famous fire and earthquake of 1906, when "a sidewalk kitchen yielded up a fine meal of oysters on the half shell, crab *à la poulette* . . . Roman punch, dessert and coffee," as prepared and enjoyed by the members of the Chit-Chat Club. According to the spir-

ited classic *A Cook's Tour of San Francisco*, by Doris Muscatine, these gentlemen held such dinners on a regular basis and, like many San Franciscans, would not think of allowing natural or unnatural disasters to dampen their spirits or appetites.

Berkeley and Oakland, visible and easily accessible across the Bay Bridge from San Francisco, are both home to many of California's most renowned restaurants. The most famous of all must be Chez Panisse. Several local chefs have emerged from its kitchen and opened their own restaurants. In fact, the kitchen at Chez Panisse turned out to be a catalyst for a series of culinary changes in California, beginning in the 1970s. Many of the signs are evident in the proliferation of specialty growers and producers in all areas of the state and in the way people are cooking at home with fresher, more esoteric foods.

Within the confines of a few streets in Berkeley are bakeries and cheese shops, charcuteries, excellent fish and meat markets, wine merchants and all manner of ethnic markets—enough to please any cook. Here also is some of the best Southern barbecue, big farmers' markets, brew pubs and authentic Thai and Indian food. Oakland offers its own Chinatown and a refurbished Old Oakland in which are preserved some special reminders of another era, such as G.B. Ratto & Company. Known as Ratto's, it is an old-fashioned grocery, delicatessen, wine and cookware store established in 1890. And little has changed since then. A visit here is almost like stepping back in time, except that the variety of international food items lining the store's shelves is pure twentieth century. Ratto's makes its own oak-barrel-aged wine vinegar and bottles its own olive oil. The store's wood-planked aisles are lined with tubs of pastas and grains and its shelves packed with hard-to-find spices and exotic delicacies from around the world.

CONDIMENTS AND PRESERVES

A natural counterpart to the wine industry, locally produced vinegars fill the shelves of a fancy grocer.

CONDIMENTS AND PRESERVES

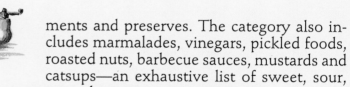

California fruits, vegetables and nuts offer tantalizing possibilities to any cook with an itch to "put food by." Whether the inspiration comes from an apricot tree laden with juicy, plump fruit falling to the ground or from an herb garden flush with fresh basil, it follows a long-standing tradition.

Many cooks may have visions of giant pots, tongs and water-bath processing when it comes to jams and jellies, but those belong to just one version of the art of condi-

A native American fruit, the strawberry has gained a worldwide audience. Thousands of crates are air freighted from California to Europe each year.

ments and preserves. The category also includes marmalades, vinegars, pickled foods, roasted nuts, barbecue sauces, mustards and catsups—an exhaustive list of sweet, sour, spicy, pungent and savory accompaniments.

The idea of condiments is certainly not unique to California, but the types of condiments and the foods with which they are paired often express a distinct West Coast style that sometimes flouts tradition and, at others, improves on it. For instance, a red pepper marmalade to savor with cold sliced pork, white wine barbecue sauce for lighter meats, *jalapeño* jelly with cheese, a handful of rosemary-flavored roasted walnuts with cocktails—all are delicious and original.

Condiments and preserves have been part of California cooking since the mission days, when the padres and their Indian cooks made vinegars and pickles and preserves for lean times, for trading and simply to make the best of an abundance of produce. Before the days of crockery and jars, mission cooks made a concentrated fruit jam called *cajeta*—sugar and fruit pulp cooked and stirred slowly, then turned onto a wooden tray and spread about an inch and a half thick. It was set out in the sun to dry, then cut up and wrapped in dry corn husks to be tucked away in tightly woven Indian baskets and stored in a cool larder. The confection was often just cut into squares, like a candy. To make jam for *tortillas* or bread, it was heated slowly, with a little water. Traditionally, *cajeta* was made from prickly pears, mission grapes, figs and quinces. Whole fruits were also preserved by sun-drying, which intensifies the flavor and imparts an entirely new character and chewy consistency to peaches, plums, apricots, grapes and myriad other fruits.

Previous pages: Brandied Peaches and Apricots (in large jars, recipe page 208), Oven Apricot Jam (in medium jars, recipe page 207) and Nectarine Butter (in small jars, recipe page 210)

No mission or rancho barbecue was complete without huge pots of *salsa* to go with all those charred sides of beef. The big demand for such condiments and preserves grew with the gold rush of 1849, when miners who virtually lived on beans and dried biscuits were willing to pay dearly for a jar of brandied peaches or crisp pickles to carry back to their outposts. It was from this demand and the growing availability of produce that the California canning industry emerged.

Since then, every region and ethnic group has contributed a relish or condiment to the California pot. The flavors run the gamut: Chinese plum sauce for roasted duck; *kim chee*, or spicy Korean cabbage; homemade *teriyaki* sauce; Indian chutneys; mustards of every shade—the list is truly endless. From the late 1800s on, California menus have always included a generous selection of such condiments. Turn-of-the-century menus at the Hotel Del Coronado in San Diego offered sweet pickled figs, olives and salted almonds, mint sauce for the lamb, cranberry sauce for roast turkey, apple sauce for suckling pig, guava jelly and crabapple jelly for roast teal duck and broiled squab, and anchovy sauce for boiled black bass. In 1990 the menu at a popular San Francisco restaurant offered Jamaican tomato chutney with Delta crawfish cakes, spicy peanut sauce for chicken *satay*, two *salsas* for griddled corn cakes with black beans, and orange mint jelly for lamb.

Flavored vinegars have long been popular, despite the misconception that they are something new. Recipes for raspberry vinegar and for other fruit and herb vinegars were included in farm country cookbooks published in the early 1900s. A cookbook of recipes from a grape festival held in northern California in 1940 is packed with recipes for such delectables as apple catsup (with cinnamon and ginger), watermelon pickles, green tomato pickles, pickled figs and spiced currants, all of which reflect the creative culinary spirit that Californians—pardon the expression—relish.

Oranges from southern California were shipped to the East as early as 1877, and the citrus industry has since played a critical role in California's agricultural economy. In the last few decades, orchards have been swallowed by the ever-onward spread of suburban Los Angeles.

The olive was first brought to California by the Spanish to use in making oil. Today the California black olive industry is a multimillion-dollar business.

Watsonville

BREAD AND BUTTER PICKLES

This is a good, well-balanced recipe that turns out crisp, sweet, old-fashioned pickles, so I have never tried any other. They are perfect for tucking into hot dogs and hamburgers.

16 cups (128 fl oz/4 l) thinly sliced unpeeled pickling
     cucumbers, not waxed*
4 yellow onions, peeled and cut into ½-in (12-mm) chunks
4 garlic cloves, peeled
⅓ cup (3 oz/90 g) pickling (pure uniodized) salt (see glossary)
cracked ice
5 cups (2½ lb/1.25 kg) sugar
1½ teaspoons ground turmeric
1½ teaspoons celery seeds
2 tablespoons mustard seeds
3 cups (24 fl oz/750 ml) cider vinegar

☙ In a large stainless steel or glass bowl, combine the cucumbers, onions and garlic. Add the pickling salt and toss to coat. Cover with 2 to 3 in (5 to 7.5 cm) of cracked ice and refrigerate for 8 hours or overnight.

☙ Drain thoroughly, then rinse and drain again. In a large pot or Dutch oven, combine the sugar, turmeric, celery seeds, mustard seeds and vinegar. Stir over medium heat until the sugar dissolves. Add the vegetables, raise the heat to high and bring just to a boil.

☙ Ladle the pickles into hot sterilized jars, leaving ½-in (12-mm) headspace. Wipe the rims with a clean, damp cloth, then seal with metal lids and rings. Process in a boiling water bath for 10 minutes (see glossary).

*The wax can be removed if the vegetable or fruit is soaked for 2 or 3 minutes in warm dishwashing detergent suds, wiped dry with a towel and then rinsed thoroughly.

MAKES 7–8 PINTS (112–128 FL OZ/3.5–4 L)

Tulare

PICKLED PEACHES

An old-fashioned way of preserving peaches, these are a nice companion for roast duck or pork. The peaches are also good for dessert, with a topping of sour cream and a sprinkle of sugar.

3 cups (1½ lb/750 g) sugar
2 cups (16 fl oz/500 ml) white vinegar
3 cinnamon sticks, broken up
2 teaspoons whole cloves
1-in (2.5-cm) piece peeled fresh ginger root, grated
16 medium-sized peaches, about 3½ lb (1.75 kg)

☙ In a large pan, combine the sugar, vinegar, cinnamon sticks and cloves. Bring to a boil, then cover and simmer for 20 minutes. Stir in the ginger. Set aside.

☙ A few at a time, drop the peaches into a pot of boiling water for about 15 seconds. Run them under cold water, then peel them. Halve the peaches and remove the pits.

☙ Bring the syrup back to a boil, add the peach halves and simmer gently for 8 to 10 minutes, until the fruit is tender but not mushy. With a slotted spoon, transfer the peaches to hot sterilized jars, making sure that each jar contains a few cloves and a piece of cinnamon stick, then fill with the syrup to within 1 in (2.5 cm) of the top. Seal with metal lids and rings and process in a boiling water bath for 15 minutes (see glossary).

MAKES 5–6 PINTS (80–96 FL OZ/2.5–2.8 L)

*Bread and Butter Pickles (top)
and Pickled Peaches (bottom)*

Pickled Red Onions (left) and Garlic Olives (right)

Benicia
PICKLED RED ONIONS

An advantage of these sharp, crunchy onion pickles is that there is no waiting—they can be eaten the day they are made and they keep for weeks. They are the creation of Judy Rodgers, the chef at the Zuni Café in San Francisco. She originally served them with hot dogs and hamburgers at the Union Hotel in Benicia, a small town north of Berkeley that was, briefly, the state capital in 1853–54, before the government moved to Sacramento.

3 large red (Spanish) onions, thinly sliced
1½ cups (12 fl oz/375 ml) white vinegar
1 cup (8 oz/250 g) sugar
2 cinnamon sticks, broken into pieces
1 teaspoon whole cloves
1 teaspoon whole mustard seeds
1 bay leaf
6 whole allspice
¼ teaspoon red pepper flakes

🦋 Place the onions in a large bowl, cover them with boiling water, and let them stand for 15 minutes.
🦋 In the meantime, combine the vinegar, sugar, cinnamon sticks, cloves, mustard seeds, bay leaf, allspice and pepper flakes in a saucepan. Bring to a boil, then reduce the heat and simmer, covered, for 5 minutes.
🦋 Drain the onions thoroughly and return them to the bowl. Pour the hot vinegar mixture over them and let the onions stand until cool. Store in tightly capped jars in the refrigerator.

MAKES 3 PINTS (48 FL OZ/1.5 L)

Gilroy
GARLIC OLIVES

Hot and garlicky, these will satisfy your craving for a salty nibble with drinks. They are also nice on a relish tray or on a picnic. Make them several days ahead.

2 cups (10 oz/315 g) ripe black olives, pitted or not, well drained
4 garlic cloves, mashed
½ teaspoon red pepper flakes
¾ cup (6 fl oz/180 ml), more or less, olive oil

🦋 Place the olives in a pint (16 fl oz/500 ml) jar along with the garlic and pepper flakes. Pour in enough olive oil to cover, then cover the top of the jar with a double thickness of cheesecloth (muslin) held snugly in place with a rubber band. Let the mixture sit at room temperature for 2 or 3 days, then cover tightly and refrigerate for longer storage. The chilled olive oil might congeal; just bring the olives to room temperature before serving.

MAKES 1 PINT (16 FL OZ/500 ML)

Rosemary Walnuts (recipe page 202)

Santa Clara
CHERRY AND BERRY PRESERVES

The West Coast produces sweet cherries primarily; sour varieties are grown in the East. The first cherries in California were probably planted by the Russians in the early 1800s. Their season never seems long enough, so buy them when you can and make this sweet, deep purple preserve.

1 lb (500 g) sweet cherries
3 tablespoons water
1 lb (500 g) raspberries
¼ cup (2 fl oz/60 ml) lemon juice
5 cups (2 ½ lb/1.25 kg) sugar
½ cup (4 fl oz/125 ml) liquid pectin

✿ Wash the cherries and pit them. Place them in a large saucepan with the water, then cover and set over medium heat. Cook, stirring frequently, for about 20 minutes.

Cherry and Berry Preserves served with bran muffins and biscuits

✿ Add the berries and the lemon juice and bring the mixture back to a boil. Add the sugar and bring to a full, rolling boil— one that cannot be stirred down—and boil for 3 minutes. Remove from heat and stir in the pectin. Pour into hot, sterilized jars and seal.

MAKES ABOUT 3 PINTS (48 FL OZ/1.5 L)

San Joaquin Valley
ROSEMARY WALNUTS

Fresh rosemary has a strong, flowery flavor and will grow like fury either as a potted plant or in an herb garden. A few rosemary walnuts, savory and salty, are good with cheese or tossed with beans or rice or in a green salad. They also make a seductive nibble with drinks (you can never eat just one) and are delicious when stuffed inside dates (see the recipe for olive-stuffed dates on page 40).

2 tablespoons walnut oil (see glossary) or vegetable oil
2 cups (about 8 oz/250 g) walnuts, in halves or
    large pieces
2 teaspoons coarse or kosher salt
2 tablespoons chopped fresh rosemary

✿ Preheat the oven to 350°F (180°C).
✿ Spread the oil on a baking sheet and set it in the oven for a few minutes to heat slightly. Add the nuts and toss to coat, then sprinkle with the salt and rosemary and toss again.
✿ Bake for 15 to 20 minutes, stirring and tossing frequently, until the nuts are light brown. Let them cool completely, then store in a tightly covered jar.

MAKES ABOUT 2 CUPS (8 OZ/250 G) *Photograph page 201*

Riverside
CITRUS MARMALADE

A rather tart marmalade, flecked with green, orange and yellow, this has a slightly bitter edge and is a perfect companion for whole-grain toast.

2 oranges
1 grapefruit
1 lemon
1 lime
5 cups (2½ lb/1.25 kg), more or less, sugar
3 tablespoons lemon juice

✿ With the fine side of the grater, grate the zest off all the fruit; set aside.
✿ Put all the fruit into a large saucepan, add water to cover and boil gently for about 30 minutes. Drain, reserving 2 cups (16 fl oz/500 ml) of the water, and cut the fruit into pieces. Pick out any seeds, then put the pieces through the coarse blade of a grinder or chop them coarsely in a food processor. Add the reserved water to the fruit pulp, and measure; you will have about 5 cups (40 fl oz/1.25 l). Add an equal volume of sugar and the grated zest.
✿ Pour into a large kettle or Dutch oven. Stirring often, cook the marmalade for about 30 minutes. To test for the jell point, put a spoonful on a saucer and set it in the freezer for a couple minutes; if it gets thick, the marmalade is done. Stir in the lemon juice, then pour into hot, sterilized jars and seal.

MAKES SIX 6-OZ (180-ML) JARS

Citrus Marmalade

GRAPE AND RHUBARB CONSERVE

Conserves are similar to jams and preserves, but are usually made with two or more fruits and often embellished with nuts and raisins. Though rhubarb is not of great commercial importance, it is grown in California, having been brought across the plains from New England. Use the stalks only; the leaves contain poisonous oxalic acid.

2 lb (1 kg) red seedless grapes
1 lb (500 g) rhubarb
6 cups (3 lb/1.5 kg), more or less, sugar
½ orange, seeded and finely chopped
½ lemon, seeded and finely chopped
½ cup (3 oz/90 g) raisins
1 cup (8 oz/250 g) walnut pieces

❧ Wash the grapes and remove them from their stems. Chop them coarsely in small batches in a food processor. (Grapes are difficult to chop by hand.) Wash the rhubarb well and cut it into 1-in (2.5-cm) pieces. Combine the rhubarb and grapes and measure; you will have about 6 cups (48 fl oz/1.5 l). Add an equal volume of sugar and the orange, lemon and raisins.
❧ Bring to a boil in a large kettle or Dutch oven, then reduce the heat and boil gently, stirring frequently, until slightly thickened, about 1 hour. Add the walnuts during the last 5 minutes of cooking. Pour into hot, sterilized jars and seal.

MAKES ABOUT 4 PINTS (64 FL OZ/2 L)

HONEY AND RED WINE FIGS

Here is a recipe for whole ripe figs preserved in a syrup of honey, wine and citrus juices. Do not use mushy fruit. The figs should be firm but ripe. And do not peel them; unpeeled figs hold their shape better. You will probably have some syrup left over, which is good on ice cream.

1 cup (8 fl oz/250 ml) honey
1 cup (8 fl oz/250 ml) dry red wine
½ cup (4 fl oz/125 ml) orange juice
¼ cup (2 fl oz/60 ml) lemon juice
2 lb (1 kg) figs
½ cup (4 fl oz/125 ml) rum

❧ In a large saucepan combine the honey, wine and juices. Bring to a boil, reduce the heat and simmer for 10 minutes. Add the figs and simmer gently for about 10 or 15 minutes, just until they are very tender when pierced. With a slotted spoon, carefully spoon the figs (but not the syrup) into hot, sterilized jars.
❧ Rapidly boil the syrup down until you have about 1 cup, then stir in the rum. Pour the syrup over the fruit and seal the jars with metal lids and rings. Process for 15 minutes in a boiling water bath (see glossary).

MAKES ABOUT 2 PINTS (32 FL OZ/1 L)

Honey and Red Wine Figs served with Cornish game hens

Grape and Rhubarb Conserve
served with oatmeal

RASPBERRY VINEGAR

Fruit vinegars have been around for centuries, though they came back in style in the seventies with the growing interest in American food and California cuisine. Before that, they had been neglected for generations, except by backyard gardeners who wisely and economically made their own. Raspberry vinegar is especially beautiful, with a good balance of acid and sweet—provided you do not scrimp on the berries. Use it on fruit salads, sprinkle it over sugared berries or stir a spoonful into a glass of iced soda water for a refreshing drink.

3 cups (14 oz/440 g) raspberries
2 cups (16 fl oz/500 ml) white wine vinegar
1 tablespoon sugar

❦ Sort the berries, discarding any that are moldy. Rinse and drain them well, then spread them on absorbent paper towels and let them sit for about 30 minutes, to dry thoroughly.
❦ Crush the berries lightly and place them in a sterilized 1-quart (32-fl oz/1-l) jar. Pour in the vinegar, cover tightly and shake. Let the mixture stand for two weeks, shaking the jar daily.
❦ Pour the mixture through a cheesecloth (muslin)-lined sieve set over a bowl. Press gently on the berries to extract as much liquid as you can. Discard the seedy pulp.
❦ Combine the strained vinegar and the sugar, bring to a simmer and simmer gently for 3 minutes. Let the mixture cool

mildly acid taste. Serve green salsa as you would a tomato salsa (see recipe below), or whenever you want a zippy accompaniment to eggs, tortilla chips or enchiladas.

12 fresh *tomatillos*, chopped, about 3 cups (24 fl oz/750 ml), husks discarded (see glossary)
1 red (Spanish) onion, peeled and cut into chunks
3 garlic cloves, peeled and cut into pieces
2 large Anaheim (mild green) *chiles*, seeded and cut into pieces
1 *jalapeño* (hot green) *chile*, seeded and cut into pieces
½ cup (1 oz/30 g) cilantro (coriander/Chinese parsley) sprigs
salt

❦ Put the *tomatillos*, onion, garlic, *chiles* and cilantro in a food processor. Process just until coarsely chopped, then season with salt to taste.

MAKES ABOUT 3 CUPS (24 FL OZ/750 ML)

Los Angeles
TOMATO SALSA

Salsa is an uncooked, piquant sauce of Mexican extraction, light and refreshing with the pleasant sharpness of onion and vinegar. Though traditionally served with Mexican food, salsa also points up the flavor of fried and scrambled eggs or omelets and just about anything with cornmeal, such as the recipe for prawns and polenta on page 64. If you like it fiery, add another jalapeño or two.

4 tomatoes, about 1½ lb (750 g)
1 medium red (Spanish) onion, chopped
1 large green (spring) onion, chopped
2 garlic cloves, minced (finely chopped)
2 *jalapeño* (hot green) *chiles*, seeded and minced (finely chopped)
2 tablespoons chopped cilantro (coriander/Chinese parsley)
2 tablespoons wine vinegar
1 teaspoon salt

❦ Chop the tomatoes coarsely and toss them in a bowl with the red and green onions, garlic, *chile*, cilantro, vinegar and salt. Adjust the flavors to suit your taste, adding more salt, cilantro, vinegar or garlic if desired.
❦ Chill before serving.

MAKES ABOUT 2 PINTS (32 FL OZ/1 L)

Watsonville
OVEN APRICOT JAM

California produces the lion's share of this country's apricots for canning, drying and eating fresh, and this is one fruit that tastes even better when cooked. Though the long baking time may seem daunting, this is a nearly effortless jam. It needs only an occasional stir. It is not too thick and makes a pleasing topping for vanilla ice cream.

3 lb (1.5 kg) apricots
5 cups (2½ lb/1.25 kg), more or less, sugar

❦ Halve and pit the apricots. Put them through the coarse blade of a grinder or chop them almost to a pulp with a food processor.
❦ Measure the purée into a 9- x 13-inch (23- x 33-cm) baking pan; you will have about 5 cups (40 fl oz/1.25 l). Add an equal volume of sugar and stir to blend. Place in a 275°F (135°C) oven and bake for 3 hours, stirring every 45 minutes or so.
❦ Pour the jam into hot, sterilized jars and seal.

MAKES EIGHT 6-OZ (180-ML) JARS   *Photograph pages 194–195*

Tomato Salsa (center) and Green Salsa (top right)

to room temperature, then strain the vinegar through a coffee filter or a sieve lined with absorbent paper towels into a sterilized pint (16 fl oz/500 ml) jar. Cap tightly.

MAKES 1 PINT (16 FL OZ/500 ML)   *Photograph page 12*

Los Angeles
GREEN SALSA

The Spanish name, salsa verde, means "green sauce," literally. The color comes from tomatillos, a small, green, Mexican fruit with a papery husk, similar to a large gooseberry and with a

Walnut Creek

APPLE AND MELON CHUTNEY

This is a wonderful chutney, full of crunch and flavor. The recipe comes from Marion Cunningham, who uses a combination of honeydew melon and green apple, but firm pears are good in it too.

12 cups (3 lb/1.5 kg) fruit, peeled, seeded and diced
    (leave melon in 1-in/2.5-cm cubes)
2 cups (10 oz/315 g) raisins
1 cup (8 oz/250 g) peeled fresh ginger, cut into
    small chunks
4½ cups (2¼ lb/1.12 kg) sugar
3 cups (24 fl oz/750 ml) cider vinegar
1½ teaspoons whole allspice
1½ teaspoons whole cloves
2 pieces cinnamon stick, 2 in (5 cm) each

❧ Combine the fruit, raisins, ginger, sugar and vinegar in a large Dutch oven or kettle. Tie the allspice, cloves and cinnamon sticks in a piece of cheesecloth (muslin), smash the bundle a couple times with a mallet or hammer to break the spices up, and add to the fruit mixture.

❧ Bring the mixture to a boil, stirring occasionally. Reduce the heat to low and let the mixture simmer for about 2 hours, or until darkened and thickened.

❧ Remove and discard the spice bag. Spoon the mixture into hot sterilized jars, leaving ½-in (12-mm) headspace, and seal with metal lids and rings. Process in a boiling water bath for 10 minutes (see glossary).

MAKES 4 PINTS (64 FL OZ/2 L)

Tulare

BRANDIED PEACHES AND APRICOTS

Brandied fruits go well with cake and ice cream, yet these are not so terribly alcoholic that you couldn't use them on your hot cereal too. Make sure that the fruit is firm but ripe, and without bruises.

2½ cups (1¼ lb/625 g) sugar
3¼ cups (26 fl oz/800 ml) water
1 lb (500 g) peaches
1 lb (500 g) apricots
½ cup (4 fl oz/125 ml), more or less, brandy

❧ Combine the sugar and water in a large saucepan and bring to a boil. Boil for 10 minutes, then set aside.

❧ Dip the peaches and apricots in boiling water for a few seconds, then run them under cold water and slip off the skins. Halve and pit them.

❧ Bring the syrup back to a boil and add the fruit. Simmer gently just until the fruit is tender when pierced, about 5 to 7 minutes.

❧ Pack the fruit into hot, sterilized pint (16 fl oz/500 ml) jars. Add ¼ cup (2 fl oz/60 ml) brandy and a couple of pieces of cinnamon stick to each jar. Finish filling the jars with some of the hot syrup, leaving ½-in (12-mm) headspace. (You will not use all the syrup.) Seal with metal lids and rings, and process in a boiling water bath for 10 minutes (see glossary).

MAKES 2 PINTS (32 FL OZ/1 L)   *Photograph pages 194–195*

Apple and Melon Chutney

California
TRADITIONAL BARBECUE SAUCE

Here is a basic recipe for the sweet and spicy ketchup-based sauce that is traditionally brushed on ribs and chicken. Because it contains sugar, it burns easily and is best brushed on during the last 5 or 10 minutes of cooking, so that it forms a light glaze. Pass the remaining sauce at the table.

2 tablespoons vegetable oil
1 onion, chopped
1 garlic clove, minced (finely chopped)
1¼ cups (10 fl oz/310 ml) ketchup (tomato sauce)
½ cup (4 fl oz/125 ml) cider vinegar
⅓ cup (3 fl oz/80 ml) Worcestershire sauce
⅓ cup (2 oz/60 g) brown sugar
1 tablespoon chili powder
several drops hot red pepper (Tabasco) sauce

❧ Heat the oil in a medium saucepan, add the onion and garlic and cook gently for 10 minutes. Add the ketchup, vinegar, Worcestershire sauce, brown sugar, chili powder and red pepper sauce. Let the mixture simmer for about 20 minutes, stirring occasionally, until it is slightly thickened. Let cool, then refrigerate, tightly covered.

MAKES ABOUT 2½ CUPS (20 FL OZ/625 ML)

California
TERIYAKI SAUCE

Teriyaki was brought to California from Hawaii and is good for barbecued chicken, thin steaks and large shrimp, when you want to give them a Polynesian flavor. Food that has been marinated in teriyaki sauce for 2 or 3 hours before grilling develops a rich brown color and takes on a pleasant sweet and salty flavor.

½ cup (4 fl oz/125 ml) soy sauce
½ cup (4 fl oz/125 ml) dry sherry
½ cup (4 fl oz/125 ml) vegetable oil
¼ cup (2 oz/60 g) sugar
2 large garlic cloves, minced (finely chopped)
1 tablespoon grated fresh ginger

❧ In a bowl whisk all the ingredients together and let the sauce stand for at least 1 hour before using, so that the flavors blend.

MAKES ABOUT 1¾ CUPS (14 FL OZ/430 ML)

St. Helena
WHITE WINE BARBECUE SAUCE

This is lighter than the traditional barbecue sauce above, and not so spicy. It is good on chicken and veal and, because it contains very little sugar, may be brushed on food every 20 minutes or so throughout cooking and will not burn.

¼ cup (2 fl oz/60 ml) olive oil
1 onion, finely chopped
1 cup (8 fl oz/250 ml) dry white wine
½ cup (4 fl oz/125 ml) red or white wine vinegar
2 tablespoons Worcestershire sauce
2 tablespoons sugar
¼ teaspoon red pepper flakes

grated zest of 1 lemon
1 teaspoon salt

❧ Heat the oil in a saucepan, add the onion and cook gently for 5 minutes. Add the wine, vinegar, Worcestershire sauce, sugar, pepper flakes, lemon zest and salt. Bring to a boil, then reduce the heat and simmer, partially covered, for about 20 minutes. Let cool, then refrigerate tightly covered.

MAKES ABOUT 2 CUPS (16 FL OZ/500 ML)

Gilroy
BASIL AND GARLIC VINEGAR

Flavored vinegars are often expensive to buy but easy to create at home, and you have the option of making them as strong or as mild as you wish. This one is especially good for green salads or, combined with olive oil, for the dressing on a salad composed of buffalo-milk mozzarella, tomato slices and basil leaves.

24 or more basil leaves
6 garlic cloves, or more, peeled and mashed
2 cups (16 fl oz/500 ml) white wine vinegar

❧ Wash the basil leaves and spread them on absorbent paper towels to dry thoroughly.
❧ Scald (sterilize) a quart (32 fl oz/1 l) jar and let it cool to room temperature. Gently bruise the basil leaves with your fingers, but do not cut them up. Place them in the jar along with the garlic cloves. Bring the vinegar just to a simmer and pour it into the jar. Cover with a double thickness of cheesecloth (muslin) held snugly with a rubber band, and let the mixture stand overnight.
❧ The next day, cap the jar and let it stand for two weeks, giving it a shake daily. Strain the vinegar into a freshly scalded pint (16 fl oz/500 ml) jar, cap and store at room temperature.

MAKES 1 PINT (16 FL OZ/500 ML)   *Photograph page 12*

Tulare
NECTARINE BUTTER

California produces over ninety percent of this country's nectarines, which are at their peak from June through early fall. They resemble peaches in flavor and appearance, but without the fuzz, and make wonderful pies, ice creams and this thick fruit butter to spread on your morning toast.

3 lb (1.5 kg) nectarines
1½ cups (12 fl oz/375 ml) water
2½ cups (1¼ lb/625 g) sugar, more or less
1½ teaspoons ground cinnamon
½ teaspoon ground cloves
3 tablespoons lemon juice

❧ Drop the nectarines into boiling water for 15 seconds, then run them under cold water and peel off the skins. Halve and pit them, and cut each half into several pieces. Place in a kettle or Dutch oven with the water and cook over medium heat, stirring frequently, until the fruit is soft. Purée in a food mill or food processor and measure the pulp; you will have about 5 cups (40 fl oz/1.25 l). Add ½ cup (4 oz/125 g) sugar for each cup of pulp and return to the saucepan.
❧ Add the cinnamon, cloves and lemon juice and bring to a boil, stirring constantly. Reduce the heat and boil slowly, stirring frequently, until the mixture is thick. Be patient, this can take up to 1½ hours. Pour into hot, sterilized jars and seal.

MAKES FOUR 6-OZ (180-ML) JARS   *Photograph pages 194–195*

Traditional Barbecue Sauce (top right), White Wine Barbecue Sauce (left) and Teriyaki Sauce (bottom right)

Madera

FIG JAM

Figs are a luxury. They are not in season for long and quite dear when they are. If you have a tree, or know someone who does, try this jam. The yield is quite small but the flavor is sweet and concentrated. Spread on a shortbread cookie, it will remind you of a fig bar.

2 lb (1 kg) fresh figs
1 small lemon
1 orange
2½ cups (1¼ lb/625 g) sugar

❧ Wash the figs well, but there is no need to peel them. Remove the stems and cut each fig into 4 or 5 pieces. Slice the lemon and orange as thinly as you can and pick out the seeds. Cut the slices into quarters.
❧ Combine all the fruit with the sugar in a Dutch oven or large saucepan and bring to a boil. Reduce the heat and simmer, stirring frequently, until the mixture has reduced and thickened slightly, about half an hour. Pour the mixture into hot, sterilized jars and seal.

MAKES ABOUT FIVE 6-OZ (180-ML) JARS

Watsonville

SUNSHINE STRAWBERRY PRESERVES

This jam is sometimes called "strawberry sunshine" because, after a brief stovetop warming, it is cooked by solar power alone. Ruby red and sweet, with a fresh strawberry essence, these preserves will keep in the refrigerator for weeks. If evenings are cool while they are "cooking," move them inside, and if clouds persist, place them in a warm oven, about 150°F (65°C), until thick—this is faster than the outdoor method.

4 cups (1 lb/500 g) small strawberries, or large berries, halved
4 cups (2 lb/1kg) sugar
¼ cup (2 fl oz/60 ml) lemon juice

❧ In a large saucepan place alternating layers of berries and sugar. Let them stand for about 1 hour, until the berries have exuded some juice.
❧ Add the lemon juice, slowly bring to a boil, then simmer for 5 minutes, stirring almost constantly. When you taste it, you should feel no granules of sugar on your tongue.
❧ Pour the mixture onto 2 large nonaluminum pans or platters and cover snugly with mosquito netting or cheesecloth (muslin), taking care that the fabric does not rest on the jam. Place in a warm spot, moving the pans to follow the sun if necessary, for 3 or 4 days, stirring occasionally, until you have a thick syrup and plump berries.

MAKES ABOUT 2 PINTS (32 FL OZ/1 L)

*Sunshine Strawberry Preserves (center)
and Fig Jam (top right)*

Monterey

MUSHROOM RELISH

Fresh raw vegetable relishes are a traditional part of the American table and an important element in Californian cooking too. With their cool crunch, they help round out a meal, enhancing meat and poultry. This cold relish is, by the way, blissful tossed with hot pasta for a quick supper; the flavors and textures are wonderful.

1 lb (500 g) mushrooms
2 medium red (Spanish) onions, finely chopped
4 celery stalks, finely chopped
1 teaspoon salt
¼ cup (2 fl oz/60 ml) white vinegar or cider vinegar
1 tablespoon sugar
1 teaspoon dry mustard
½ teaspoon freshly ground black pepper

🦋 Wipe the mushrooms clean if necessary, then chop them very fine either by hand or in a food processor. A handful at a time, squeeze them firmly in the corner of a kitchen towel to remove much of their liquid (it may be added to a soup or sauce). Do not omit this step, or you will have a watery relish.
🦋 Place the squeezed mushrooms in a bowl. Squeeze the chopped onion, too, then add it to the mushrooms. Add the celery and salt, toss to combine, then let the vegetables stand for about 20 minutes. Drain off any accumulated liquid.
🦋 Add the vinegar, sugar, mustard and pepper and combine. Chill before serving.

MAKES ABOUT 1 PINT (16 FL OZ/500 ML)

Santa Clara

RED PEPPER MARMALADE

This is so good that it will surprise you. Cardinal red and quite sweet, pepper marmalade is good with cold sliced beef and pork, and also as a spread for crackers, with a soft goat cheese. This recipe yields a manageable amount that can be stored in the refrigerator for up to several weeks, so you do not have to fuss with sterilized jars and water bath processing.

2½ lb (1.25 kg) red bell peppers (capsicums)
1 tablespoon salt
1 cup (8 fl oz/250 ml) cider vinegar
2 cups (1 lb/500 g) sugar

🦋 Stem and seed the peppers and put them through the coarse blade of a grinder, or chop them coarsely in a food processor (take care not to purée them). Toss with the salt and let them stand for 2 hours.
🦋 Drain and discard any accumulated juices and combine the peppers in a saucepan with the vinegar and sugar. Bring to a boil, then reduce the heat and simmer for 1 hour, stirring now and then.
🦋 Let the marmalade cool to room temperature, then store, tightly covered, in the refrigerator.

MAKES ABOUT 2½ CUPS (20 FL OZ/625 ML)

*Red Pepper Marmalade and Jalapeño
Pepper Jelly (recipe page 217)*

Mushroom Relish, served over ravioli

Riverside

BAKED ORANGE SLICES

Baked, spiced orange slices go well with a holiday turkey, duck or goose. As a friend remarked, the house smells like Christmas while they bake. They will keep for ages in the refrigerator and should, in fact, be made several days before serving.

4 oranges, about 1½ lb (750 g), preferably seedless
1½ cups (12 oz/375 g) sugar

¾ cup (6 fl oz/180 ml) cider vinegar
¾ cup (6 fl oz/180 ml) water
¼ cup (2 fl oz/60 ml) corn syrup
1 cinnamon stick, broken in pieces
1 teaspoon whole cloves

❧ Place the whole oranges in a pan and cover with water. Bring to a boil, then simmer gently for about 15 minutes, until they are tender but not mushy. Drain and, when cool, cut with a serrated knife into ½-in (12-mm) slices. Pick out any seeds.

Baked Orange Slices (left) and Persimmon Jam (right)

🌸 Pour the remaining syrup along with the cinnamon and cloves into the jar with the oranges, and store tightly covered in the refrigerator.

MAKES 1 QUART (32 FL OZ/1 L)

Sacramento

PERSIMMON JAM

Persimmon growing is not a major industry and the autumn harvest is short, but those who love them can't seem to get enough and know that the purée freezes perfectly to have on hand for puddings and cookies. For this jam, use persimmons that are ripe and as squishy as a water balloon.

5 or 6 persimmons
2 cups (1 lb/500 g) sugar
3 tablespoons lemon juice
¼ teaspoon ground cloves

🌸 Cut the persimmons into small pieces and force them through a strainer to remove the tough skin. You will need 2 cups (16 fl oz/500 ml) of pulp. Combine it in a saucepan with the sugar, lemon juice and cloves.
🌸 Simmer slowly for 20 to 30 minutes, stirring almost constantly and not letting the mixture come to a hard boil, until it is slightly thickened. Pour into a hot, sterilized jar or jars, and seal.

MAKES ABOUT 1 PINT (16 FL OZ/500 ML)

El Centro

JALAPEÑO PEPPER JELLY

This is not an emphatically hot jelly, but a moderately hot one that goes well with meats, poultry and smoked fish. In the old-fashioned California tradition, it was served with softened cream cheese, as spread for crackers. When handling hot peppers, it is advisable to wear rubber gloves and avoid touching your face; jalapeños can be very irritating to the skin and eyes.

2 green bell peppers (capsicums)
20 *jalapeño* (hot green) *chiles*, about 10 oz (315 g)
1½ cups (12 fl oz/375 ml) cider vinegar
1 teaspoon salt
4½ cups (2¼ lb/1.12 kg) sugar
¾ cup (6 fl oz/180 ml) liquid pectin

🌸 Remove the stems from the bell peppers and *chiles*, halve them and scrape out all the seeds and ribs. Put the peppers and *chiles* through the coarse blade of a grinder or chop them coarsely in a food processor.
🌸 Combine the chopped peppers with the vinegar in a saucepan, bring to a boil, then reduce the heat and simmer for 15 minutes. Pour the mixture into a colander lined with several layers of cheesecloth (muslin) and let it drain into a bowl; do not squeeze it or press it to extract more juice, lest you make the jelly cloudy—just let it drip unaided until most of the juice has drained. Discard the pulp.
🌸 You will need 1¼ cups (10 fl oz/310 ml) of the extracted pepper juice; if you are short, add water. Pour it into a large saucepan, add the salt and sugar and, over high heat, bring to a full boil—a boil that cannot be stirred down. Boil hard for 1 minute, then stir in the pectin. Bring back to a full rolling boil and boil for 1 minute, stirring constantly. Remove from the heat and rapidly skim off any foam. Pour the mixture into hot, sterilized jars, and seal.

MAKES ABOUT FIVE 6-OZ (180-ML) JARS *Photograph page 214*

🌸 Combine the sugar, vinegar, water, corn syrup, cinnamon stick and cloves. Boil for 5 minutes.
🌸 Preheat the oven to 350°F (180°C).
🌸 Place the orange slices slightly overlapping in an 8-in (20-cm) square glass or enamel baking dish (do not use aluminum). Pour the sugar mixture over them.
🌸 Bake for about 1½ hours, basting frequently, until the syrup is thick. Let cool, then stack the slices in a wide-mouthed quart (32 fl oz/1 l) jar.

THE FAR NORTH

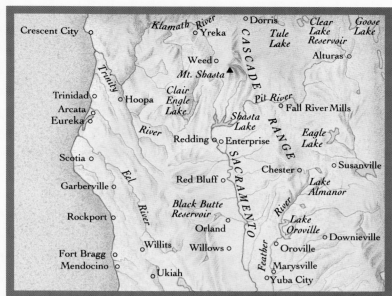

THE FAR NORTH

A zigzagging route along the rugged northern coast through damp pine forests and giant redwoods forms the western edge of this vast and varied region. Along the way, small fishing and logging towns hold on to the spirit that exemplifies northern California. Here, even the fences that line the highway have a special character. Most are pleasingly uneven. Made of grapestakes and split rails, their rustic silhouettes frame fields of wildflowers or stark vistas of sea and sky. Just sixty years ago, travelers on Highway 1 above Jenner had to stop every mile or so and open a sheep or cattle rancher's gate to continue north. Of course the highway is well paved and well traveled now, but life along the north coast is still more extreme, more tranquil and less developed than in many other areas of California. This is partly because much of the coast is protected as a natural (and national) treasure. Much of it is also inaccessible—except at low tide, when tide pools reveal a rich world of sea plants and creatures, many of which are being harvested for food.

As quiet and sparsely populated as the north coast is, even the small resort villages offer some exceptional dining. Salmon, trout and bass thrive in hundreds of nearby streams. To go with the succulent fish, an inspiring assortment of ingredients comes from over the hill, down in the valleys and along the roads that connect Highway 1 to Interstate Highway 101. Mendocino, Lake and northern Sonoma counties all hold warm "pocket" valleys, suited to wine grapes. These valleys are home to prized vineyards and wineries, both large and small. The Anderson, Potter and Yokayo valleys blossom with orchards, berry patches and specialty farms, much like

Previous pages: Isolated lighthouses dot the rugged northern coast, guiding ships through the rain and fog. Photo: Reg Morrison
Left: Fishing boats return to port along the coast near Fort Bragg. The fish and lumber industries form the backbone of the north coast economy.

221

those of Sonoma Valley, providing lamb, pears, apples, wild rice, sun-dried tomatoes, wild mushrooms, exotic lettuces and organic produce. A few small operating breweries offer high-quality ales as excellent refreshment along the way.

Beyond the valleys and the Coast Range, the remainder of this region is a wild and sparsely inhabited expanse called the Shasta-Cascade. Approximately the size of Ohio, it defines the northeastern corner of the state. It encompasses the far tendrils of the gold country around Whiskeytown Lake and Trinity, where the mining life was somewhat more arduous than it was down south. Winter blows hard through this magnificent mountain region. The Trinity Alps, the California Cascade Range and Klamath, Marble and Warner mountains embrace eight national and state parks and six national forests, where fishing, hiking, camping and skiing are the way of life. Mount Shasta, a 14,000-foot-high inactive volcano, looms over the landscape, visible for one hundred miles. The town of Shasta, about sixty miles southwest of the peak, was a gold boom town bringing in a hundred thousand dollars worth of gold dust a week in the 1850s. As in many other areas of the state, life there during and after the gold rush was partially shaped by the influences of gold-seekers from all corners of the world.

As Highway 1 winds north along the narrow shelf of land that begins around Jenner, towns are few and far between. Sheep stand quietly, perched on sheer cliffs looming above the road or on rocks that drop six hundred feet straight down to the sea. Weathered barns and the remnants of a Russian fort built in the mid-1800s are set off by pink coast rhododendrons and ocean waters that run gray, green or blue, depending on the light and fog. Fort Ross, built in 1812, was a self-sufficient outpost for the Russian-American Fur Company, a colony devoted to hunting sea otters and trading their pelts. To sustain this colony and their Alaskan outpost, the Russians raised poultry and cattle and grew wheat, potatoes and some leafy greens. Their diet was fairly bland, but good enough to fortify them until crop failures and grizzly bears depleted the food sources. The Russians left behind a compound of plain redwood structures, including the commander's house and a Russian Orthodox chapel, but not much else, save some architectural inspiration.

The icy waters around this area yield clams and abalone, and divers in wet suits are a common sight. The natural abalone are less abundant than they were a century ago, however. Then they were plentiful enough to feed construction gangs who built the logging railroads that served ports such as Timber Cove and Salt Point in the late 1800s. If the chefs were skilled and savvy about abalone, the hardworking gangs would enjoy sweet, tender steaks. Otherwise, they were subjected to some rather chewy meat—either improperly pounded or overcooked. That may have contributed to the early reluctance on the part of many Californians to enjoy this delicate treat. To be appreciated, abalone should be cut into thin slices, either as steaks or strips, then pounded to a tender consistency. Cooking should be simple and quick. You do not want to mask the flavor or overcook the meat. Most chefs in California recommend dipping abalone in a light milk batter and quickly sautéeing it. Add a squeeze of lemon or lime and perhaps some tartar sauce. The California abalone population was for many years endangered and none could be shipped out of the state (in its fresh form, at least). Today, it is enjoying a revival, especially along the central and southern coasts. Aquaculturists are also growing small three-inch abalone with great success, so once again there is enough to go around, though it still commands a high price.

A comfortably cluttered front porch in the Trinity River valley suggests the laid-back life of the north.

with the seasons, as all good menus do. The chefs work with what comes out of local gardens and streams, out of the fields and off the trees. Apricot muffins, wild berries and wild rice, omelets filled with smoked fish, or a salad of marinated grilled rabbit—anything could happen.

But back to the Anderson, Yokayo and Potter valleys, the lush strip that parallels the coast. The area around Ukiah is known for its luscious Bartlett pears, which thrive in the warm hills. Every September in a nearby little town called Boonville, the Mendocino County Fair is the showcase for over fifty varieties of local apples. Members of 4-H clubs show off their sheep and lambs, and a big rodeo draws people from all over the state. This is not the only county fair in California, but it is certainly one of the most genuine.

TO THE WILDERNESS

The Shasta-Cascade wilderness is rich in food for the soul, but if you want to partake of the best real foods of the region, take your fishing pole. Most campers bring their own food to supplement the catch of the day, cooked over their own campfires. Whitewater river runners on the Klamath River offer guests elaborate breakfasts of plump, pan-fried trout, stacks of sourdough pancakes topped with chopped nuts and maple syrup, and half-gallon-sized pots of coffee as a matter of course. Such robust meals reflect the region at its best—fresh, invigorating and ultimately satisfying.

While visitors to Eureka may fish for relaxation, many locals find it a way of life.

Antique bottles in a window reflect the colorful history of Weaverville, once a gold boom town in the Trinity Alps.

Heading north along the coast, the fog seems cooler, the air more invigorating, the redwood forests more dense. Lumber, rather than gold, was the source of north coast wealth in the last century. Railroads carried logs, as did elaborate systems of chutes and flumes that moved the logs from the precarious bluffs to the ships waiting below in the rocky, forbidding sea. Life in the fishing ports and lumber towns such as Point Arena, Mendocino and Fort Bragg also thrives on tourism these days, but still is suited to hearty foods to balance the chill of the fog. You will find trencherman portions at small pubs or inns. Many serve local specialties such as fresh grilled sausages with mustard and Mendocino County applesauce, or roast lamb with hot pepper jelly. Fishermen bring in plenty of trout from the countless streams that run through the area to the sea. Salmon, however, is the most plentiful fish—both for commercial and private purposes. One cook might grill the fish and serve it with roasted new potatoes and another might steam it in parchment with lemon grass and ginger. As is true throughout California, diversity is an underlying theme when it comes to cooking. But as is also true, you can always find impeccably fresh ingredients and innovative recipes to write home about. In the old stage and rail days, travelers who stopped at Trinidad or Eureka, which served as waterfront pack stations for the northern gold mines, dined on simple fare. Biscuits, bean soup, fried fish, rice pudding and brandied peaches were standard. Today, people drive half a day to visit Mendocino—just for the food at special places such as Cafe Beaujolais, which shows off sophisticated California country cooking at its best. The menu changes

DESSERTS

*A chocaholic dream come true—truffles of every description
wait for addicts in a Bay Area candy shop.*

DESSERTS

Dessert options seem to expand with the summer heat in California. As berries and tree fruits turn ripe and lush with natural syrup and juices, they inspire simple wonders of creativity—orange shortcake, for instance. Consisting of light, tender shortbread dough topped with southern California oranges drenched in orange liqueur and fin-

Green dates hang from a tree in the Coachella Valley, awaiting the golden face of the Mojave sun to ripen them into transparent amber globes.

ished with a drift of whipped cream, it captures the spirit of California sunshine and our sweet love affair with fresh fruits. In another gem of fruit-inspired creativity, deep purple plums from the Central Valley make a wonderful topping for a traditional upside-down cake.

From the turn-of-the-century days of fancy dining, cooks have enjoyed showing off California's crop of plump strawberries in strawberries Romanoff—berries topped with Cointreau- and brandy-flavored whipped cream. Strawberries are also routinely sliced over shortcake, piled high in sundaes or simply dipped in dark chocolate. The same early menus that offered strawberries Romanoff also suggested plain raisins, walnuts, figs or dates as dessert. The fruits were all so plentiful—and at that time, almost exclusive to California—that chefs liked to show them off in their naturally sweet, unadorned state, and they are especially good with a glass of port or a locally made fruit liqueur.

The repertoire of fruit desserts in California also includes intensely flavored sherbets and ices, whipped up with everything from lemons to kiwifruit and wild blackberries. Ice cream is as popular here as it is anywhere else. Often, it is made with fresh peaches, all kinds of berries or California nuts—almonds, walnuts and pistachios.

Fresh citrus zest is also used to its best advantage in the dessert course. Zest is simply the peel of lime, lemon, orange or grapefruit, usually removed with a sharp paring knife or zester—a small hand-held tool with four or five tiny, sharpened holes that make it easy to remove thin shreds of zest with a quick peeling motion. The volatile oils in the peel give a fresh, true, fruit flavor to creams, pastries, cookies, cakes and pies. (When removing the

Previous pages: Coffee Crunch Cake (left, recipe page 238) and Chocolate Malts (right, recipe page 231)

On a hot day in Indio (and most days are), nothing satisfies like a creamy date milkshake.

peel, be sure not to include any of the bitter white pith underneath.)

Walnuts, almonds and pistachios are essentials when it comes to the international dessert cart. Chinese almond cookies are routinely served with fragrant tea in any Chinatown tea room. Italian *biscotti*—hard, sweet cookies flavored with almonds or walnuts—are made for dipping in *espresso* or hot chocolate and are extremely popular in San Francisco, where no decent coffee house is without a big jar of *biscotti* on the counter.

All-American cookies packed with dates, nuts, currants, raisins and figs are year-round pleasures, too, and obviously inspired by the ingredients at hand.

Californians do eat desserts with nary a trace of fruit or nuts. From the early Spanish days come wondrous *churros*—light puffs of sweet dough, sprinkled with sugar and sold in Mexican bakeries from San Diego to San Francisco. A cup of hot chocolate with a fresh *churro* is quite possibly one of the most comforting desserts (or breakfasts) imaginable. A generation or so ago, classic desserts such as Blum's coffee crunch cake were popular at afternoon tea. Though the teatime custom fades in and out of favor, the appeal of soft angel food cake with a crunchy coffee candy coating will always be with us. Raisin, walnut and orange cake could only spring from California. And last but assuredly not least, chocolate reigns as a dessert choice in every region of the state. As devil's food cake, mousse, truffles, or plain candy bars from Ghirardelli, chocolate has been a favorite since the Spaniards introduced it with the missions.

All these desserts point to the fact that Californians are probably most inclined to follow tradition when, of all the courses of a meal, it comes to dessert. But, as is always the case in California, there are exceptions. Few are more colorful than pudding *à la Sultan*, as described in *Bonanza Inn*, an account of San Francisco's Palace Hotel written by the historians Oscar Lewis and Carroll D. Hall. "It was made of yellow corn flour, cooked in milk sweetened with brown sugar. Among its other ingredients were cinnamon, mint, sliced bananas, dates and the yolks of eggs. It was served with a hot rum sauce, flavored with anise seeds, 'green tea essence,' mint and sugar. . . . Pudding *à la Sultan* was regarded as a fitting climax to a Palace Christmas dinner. After so hearty a meal, it was wise to finish with something light."

Small independent creameries add a fresh twist to ice cream consumption in the Golden State.

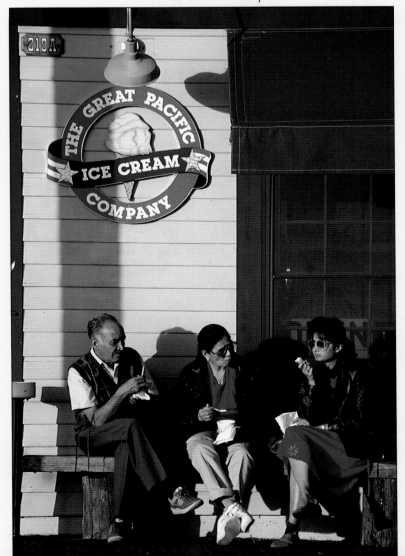

DATE AND RAISIN PIE

Raisins and dates are major California crops, with the entire United States supply of both crops coming from the Golden State. Together they make a sweet pie, with a tart edge from the buttermilk and vinegar, that is good enough to vie with mincemeat as a holiday tradition.

basic pie dough for a 9-in two-crust pie (see *empanadas*, page 38)
1 egg
1 cup (8 fl oz/250 ml) buttermilk
1 tablespoon cider vinegar
⅓ cup (3 oz/90 g) sugar
2 tablespoons all-purpose (plain) flour
½ teaspoon ground cinnamon
½ teaspoon ground nutmeg
¼ teaspoon salt
1 cup (5 oz/155 g) raisins
1 cup (5 oz/155 g) finely cut dates

🍂 Preheat the oven to 450°F (230°C). Roll out half the dough for a bottom crust and fit it into a 9-in (23-cm) pie pan. Roll out the remaining dough for a top crust and set it aside on a piece of waxed (greaseproof) paper.
🍂 Beat the egg, buttermilk and vinegar together; set aside. Stir and toss together the sugar, flour, cinnamon, nutmeg and salt. Stir in the buttermilk mixture and the raisins and dates. Pour into the prepared pie pan, set the top crust in place, then trim and flute the edges. Bake for 15 minutes, then reduce the heat to 350°F (180°C) and bake for 30 minutes longer, or until the crust is golden.

MAKES ONE 9-IN (23-CM) TWO-CRUST PIE

DATE AND PRUNE BREAD

There are many recipes for date breads, which are so good with tea or coffee, or topped with a spoonful of whipped cream. This one, which includes prunes, is sweet and moist and as good as any you will find.

1½ cups (12 fl oz/375 ml) boiling water
1½ cups (7 oz/220 g) finely cut dates
1½ cups (9 oz/280 g) finely cut prunes
½ cup (4 oz/125 g) butter, softened
1 cup (5 oz/155 g) brown sugar
2 eggs
1 tablespoon grated orange zest
3 cups (12 oz/375 g) all-purpose (plain) flour
2 teaspoons baking soda (bicarbonate of soda)
½ teaspoon salt
1 cup (4 oz/125 g) chopped walnuts

🍂 Preheat the oven to 350°F (180°C). Grease and flour two 8½- x 4½- x 2½-in (22- x 11- x 6-cm) loaf pans.
🍂 In a large bowl, pour the boiling water over the dates, prunes and butter. Stir until most of the butter is melted, then let the mixture cool to lukewarm.
🍂 Beat in the brown sugar, eggs and orange zest. Stir and toss together the flour, baking soda and salt. Add to the first mixture and beat until blended. Stir in the walnuts. Divide the batter between the prepared loaf pans and bake for 50 to 60 minutes, or until a broom straw or small wooden skewer inserted in the bread comes out clean. Let the loaves cool in the pans for 5 minutes, then turn out onto a rack to cool completely.

MAKES 2 LOAVES

Date and Raisin Pie

Date and Prune Bread (center) and Stuffed Date Rolls (recipe page 230)

Walnut Creek

STUFFED DATE ROLLS

This recipe for whole dates stuffed with a walnut half, coated with cookie batter and then baked and glazed comes from Marion Cunningham of Walnut Creek. They keep well in an airtight container and are marvelous for a celebration, afternoon tea or to give as a gift.

COOKIES

60 pitted dates
60 walnut halves or large pieces
6 tablespoons (3 oz/90 g) butter, softened

1 cup (5 oz/155 g) brown sugar
2 eggs
¾ cup (6 fl oz/180 ml) sour cream
2 cups (8 oz/250 g) all-purpose (plain) flour
½ teaspoon salt
½ teaspoon baking powder
½ teaspoon baking soda (bicarbonate of soda)

GLAZE

6 tablespoons (3 oz/90 g) butter
1½ cups (8 oz/250 g) powdered (icing) sugar
1 teaspoon vanilla extract (essence)
about ¼ cup (2 fl oz/60 ml) cold water

❧ While the first batch bakes, prepare the glaze so that you can brush it over the cookies while they are still warm. To make the glaze, melt the butter in a small saucepan and cook, swirling the pan by the handle, until the butter is lightly browned.

❧ Remove from heat and stir in the sugar, vanilla and enough water to make it runny.

MAKES ABOUT 60 COOKIES   *Photograph page 229*

Hollister

APRICOT CRISP

The area around Hollister, California, with its hot summer days, is particularly suited to apricot growing. To me, this fruit symbolizes the Fourth of July; that is about when the trees are at their peak of production, and this old-fashioned crisp with a crunchy oatmeal and brown sugar topping makes a fine Independence Day dessert. Serve it with whipped cream or ice cream.

6 tablespoons (3 oz/90 g) softened butter
½ cup (3 oz/90 g) brown sugar
½ cup (2 oz/60 g) all-purpose (plain) flour
½ cup (2 oz/60 g) uncooked oatmeal (rolled oats)
½ teaspoon ground cinnamon
¼ teaspoon salt
5 cups (about 2¼ lb/1.12 kg) pitted, quartered apricots
1 tablespoon quick-cooking tapioca
¼ cup (2 oz/60 g) sugar

❧ Preheat the oven to 350°F (180°C) and set out an 8-in (20-cm)-square baking pan.

❧ To make the topping, in a large bowl combine the butter, brown sugar, flour, oatmeal, cinnamon and salt. Using a pastry blender or your fingertips, rub the butter into the dry ingredients until the mixture resembles coarse crumbs and there are no visible lumps of butter; set aside.

❧ Toss the apricots with the tapioca and sugar until combined, then place them in the baking pan. Spread the topping evenly over the apricots. Bake for about 40 minutes, until the top is lightly browned and the juices are bubbling.

SERVES 6–8

Los Angeles

CHOCOLATE MALT

What has happened to the real chocolate malts that were thick and frosty, with the taste of good ice cream and lots of malt? With the complete automation of fast food, they seem to have disappeared, leaving us with concoctions that are much less flavorful and so emulsified that they hardly melt. Fortunately you can still make them the old-fashioned way at home.

¾ cup (6 fl oz/180 ml) milk
½ teaspoon vanilla extract (essence)
3 tablespoons chocolate syrup
3 tablespoons malt powder
2 scoops (about ⅔ cup/5 fl oz/160 ml) vanilla ice cream

❧ Combine all the ingredients in a blender and blend briefly, just until smooth and frothy.

SERVES 1   *Photograph pages 224–225*

Apricot Crisp

❧ Preheat the oven to 400°F (200°C) and set out some cookie sheets.

❧ Stuff each date with a walnut half or a large piece.

❧ In a large bowl, beat the butter and sugar until blended. Beat in the eggs, then the sour cream.

❧ Stir and toss together the flour, salt, baking powder and baking soda. Add to the first mixture and blend until thoroughly combined; you will have a very sticky batter.

❧ With your fingers, roll each nut-stuffed date in the batter, covering it as best you can—do not worry if it looks patchy— then place the dates about 2 in (5 cm) apart on ungreased cookie sheets. Bake for 10 minutes or until pale golden. Remove the cookies from the oven and transfer to racks.

Berkeley

Chez Panisse Almond Tart

Through the years this tart has been one of the most popular desserts in this famous Berkeley restaurant. It is thin and sweet, with a rich, chewy filling. The creation of Lindsey Shere, it is almost foolproof.

TART DOUGH

1 cup (4 oz/125 g) all-purpose (plain) flour
1 tablespoon sugar
¼ teaspoon salt
¼ teaspoon grated lemon zest
½ cup (4 oz/125 g) unsalted butter, chilled
½ teaspoon vanilla extract (essence)
1 tablespoon water, if needed

FILLING

¾ cup (6 fl oz/180 ml) heavy (double) cream
¾ cup (6 oz/185 g) sugar
2 or 3 drops almond extract (essence)
1 teaspoon Grand Marnier liqueur
1 cup (4 oz/125 g) sliced almonds

❧ To make the tart dough, in a food processor combine the flour, sugar, salt, lemon zest and butter (cut into small

Plum Upside-down Cake

pieces). Add the vanilla and process until the dough forms a ball that leaves the side of the bowl and whirls around on the blade. If the dough remains dry and will not form a ball, add the water and process for a few seconds longer. Pat it into a small cake, wrap in plastic and chill for about 30 minutes before using.

❧ Preheat the oven to 425°F (220°C).

❧ Roll out the dough on a floured surface and fit it into a 9-in (23-cm) tart pan. Prick all over with a fork, then press a piece of heavy-duty foil snugly into the tart shell. Bake for 8 minutes, then remove the foil and bake for about 4 minutes more, until the shell appears dry but has not browned. Reduce the oven temperature to 400°F (200°C).

❧ To make the filling, warm the cream and sugar in a small saucepan until the sugar has melted and the mixture is translucent. Blend in the almond extract and liqueur, then stir in the almonds. Pour the mixture into the tart shell, spreading it evenly.

❧ Bake for about 25 minutes, turning the tart once or twice if it is not browning evenly; the top should be a deep golden brown. Remove from the oven and, as soon as it is cool enough to handle, gently ease it from the pan. Serve with whipped cream.

MAKES ONE 9-IN (23-CM) TART

Fresno

Plum Upside-down Cake

This cake could be a county fair winner. It is rich and buttery, with a sweet caramel-like glaze over the plum halves. And it is made the old-fashioned way—in a skillet. Upside-down cakes, by the way, became famous because of a cooking contest sponsored in 1925 by the Dole Company, which first canned pineapple in 1903.

4 tablespoons (2 oz/60 g) butter
1 cup (5 oz/155 g) dark brown sugar
8 to 10 plums (1¼ lb/625 g), halved and pitted
½ cup (4 oz/125 g) vegetable shortening (vegetable lard)
⅔ cup (4 oz/125 g) sugar
1 teaspoon vanilla extract (essence)
2 eggs
1⅔ cups (7 oz/225 g) all-purpose (plain) flour
2 teaspoons baking powder
½ teaspoon salt
⅔ cup (5 fl oz/160 ml) milk

❧ Preheat the oven to 350°F (180°C).

❧ Melt the butter over moderate heat in a 9-in (23-cm) cast-iron or other ovenproof skillet. Add the brown sugar and cook, stirring constantly, until melted, thick and bubbly. Be careful—it is very hot. Rapidly arrange the plum halves, cut-side down, in one layer in the skillet, pressing them into the hot syrup; set aside.

❧ Beat the shortening in a large bowl, then add the sugar and beat until blended. Add the vanilla, then the eggs, and continue to beat until the mixture is well blended and fluffy. Stir and toss together the flour, baking powder and salt. Add to the creamed mixture along with the milk and beat for about 30 seconds, until the batter is perfectly smooth. Spread evenly over the plums.

❧ Set the skillet on a baking sheet (in case it bubbles over) and bake for 45 minutes, or until a toothpick inserted in the center of the cake comes out clean, and syrupy juices are bubbling around the edges. Remove from the oven and let the cake cool in the pan for 5 minutes, then turn it out onto a serving plate, fruit-side up.

MAKES ONE CAKE

Chez Panisse Almond Tart

Half Moon Bay

PUMPKIN TURNOVERS

Pumpkin can be more than just a holiday pie filling. These turnovers, with a filling of chopped candied pumpkin, raisins and spices enclosed in a sour-cream dough, are an adaptation of an early California recipe.

DOUGH

1½ cups (6 oz/185 g) all-purpose (plain) flour
½ teaspoon salt
6 tablespoons (3 oz/90 g) butter
½ cup (4 fl oz/125 ml) sour cream
2 tablespoons milk

FILLING

1 recipe candied pumpkin (see next page)
¼ cup (2 fl oz/60 ml) orange juice
⅓ cup (2 oz/60 g) raisins
¼ cup (2½ oz/75 g) brown sugar
1 tablespoon butter
½ teaspoon ground cinnamon
2 tablespoons heavy (double) cream

🍂 To make the dough, combine the flour and salt in a bowl. Drop in the butter and blend it into the flour until the mixture resembles coarse breadcrumbs. Add the sour cream and stir with a fork, then sprinkle the milk over and stir again until the

Place 2 generous tablespoons of the pumpkin filling in the center of each round and moisten the edges with water. Fold in half to enclose the filling, then press gently with a fork to seal. Brush each turnover lightly with cream. Place at least 1 in (2.5 cm) apart on the prepared baking sheet. Bake for 20 minutes, or until lightly browned. Remove from the pan and cool on a rack.

MAKES ABOUT 10 PASTRIES

Half Moon Bay
CANDIED PUMPKIN

In the early days, pumpkin was used more as a vegetable or in candies than as a pie filling. Since then, pumpkin has been humbled and relegated mostly to Thanksgiving. This unusual confection is very good and, cut into small pieces, is a pleasant topping for hot cereal or vanilla ice cream.

2 cups (16 fl oz/500 ml) water
2 cups (1 lb/500 g) sugar
4 or 5 thin slices of lemon, seeds removed
1 teaspoon aniseed
2 lb (1 kg) pumpkin or other winter squash

To make the syrup, combine the water, sugar, lemon slices and aniseed in a saucepan. Bring to a boil, then boil for 10 minutes.
While the syrup boils, prepare the pumpkin or squash: peel it and scrape away the seeds, then cut it into strips about 1 in (2.5 cm) wide and 2 in (5 cm) long. Add the strips to the boiling syrup and cook gently until tender when pierced, about 15 minutes. Let the pumpkin cool to room temperature, then chill it thoroughly before serving.

MAKES ABOUT 4 CUPS (32 FL OZ/1 L)

Los Angeles
TORREJAS

Torrejas *(corn wafers) are unlike any shortbread you probably know. Dark and crumbly with a distinctive taste, they are made with* masa harina, *the finely milled corn flour used in* tortillas, *and brown sugar, which gives them a caramel-like flavor. They keep for weeks and, in early California,* torrejas *were often taken on journeys. Sugar and butter were scarce, so they were made with honey and pork lard. Today we have choices, but if you have some good home-rendered lard, it will impart a crisp, sandy texture and make the wafers meltingly tender.*

2 cups (1 lb/500 g) butter or lard, or a mixture
2 cups (11 oz/345 g) brown sugar
4 cups (1 lb/500 g) *masa harina* (see glossary)
1 teaspoon salt

Preheat the oven to 350°F (180°C); set out cookie sheets.
In a large bowl, beat the butter or lard until smooth and creamy. Add the sugar and beat well. Stir and toss together the *masa harina* and salt. Add to the first mixture and beat just until completely blended.
Turn the dough out onto a lightly floured surface, then press, pat and roll it to a thickness of ½ in (12 mm). Cut into rounds with a floured 2-in (5-cm) cutter and place the rounds about 1 in (2.5 cm) apart on ungreased cookie sheets. Reroll the remaining dough and cut more rounds from the scraps until all the dough is used. Prick each cookie 3 times with a fork. Bake for about 20 to 25 minutes, until the wafers are pale gold around the edges; don't overbake. Remove from the baking sheets and cool on a rack.

MAKES ABOUT 36 WAFERS *Photograph page 236*

Pumpkin Turnovers (left) and Candied Pumpkin (right)

dough holds together. Form into a cake about 1 in (2.5 cm) thick, wrap in plastic and refrigerate while you make the filling.
Preheat the oven to 425°F (220°C) and cover a large baking sheet with foil.
Drain the candied pumpkin well and chop it (including any of the lemon slices) finely. Set aside. Combine the orange juice, raisins, sugar, butter and cinnamon in a small saucepan, bring to a boil and simmer for 1 minute. Remove from the heat and stir in the pumpkin. Set aside.
On a generously floured surface, roll out the dough ⅛ in (3 mm) thick. With a 4½-in (11-cm) cutter, cut as many rounds as you can. Push the scraps together, reroll them and cut more rounds; you will need 10 in all.

Ventura

ORANGE SHORTCAKE

Why make shortcake only with strawberries? Bright segments of orange, macerated in orange liqueur, give this dessert a light, summery quality. It is also very good for breakfast. The shortcake dough, incidentally, is based on one that we made for many summers in James Beard's cooking classes in Oregon. Heavy cream, which makes a light and tender cake, is the secret.

FRUIT

8 to 10 large seedless oranges, about 4 lb (2 kg)
⅓ cup (3 fl oz/80 ml) orange liqueur
⅓ cup (3 oz/90 g) sugar

SHORTCAKE

2 cups (8 oz/250 g) all-purpose (plain) flour
3 tablespoons sugar
1 tablespoon baking powder
1 teaspoon salt
¼ cup (2 oz/60 g) grated orange zest (from 4 of the oranges)
1¼ cups (10 fl oz/310 ml), more or less, heavy (double) cream

sweetened whipped cream

✿ Grate the zest from 4 of the oranges and set aside. With a sharp knife, peel each orange, cutting deeply enough to remove the white pith and expose the fruit all around. Cut away the sections between the membranes, letting them

*Orange Shortcake (top) and
Torrejas (bottom, recipe page 235)*

drop into a bowl; discard the membranes. Drain the orange sections well in a colander (you may drink the juice), then toss them in a bowl with the orange liqueur and sugar; set aside.
✿ Preheat the oven to 425°F (220°C).
✿ To make the shortcake, in a bowl stir and toss together the flour, sugar, baking powder and salt. Add the orange zest and combine, then pour in 1¼ cups of cream and stir vigorously with a fork. The dough should be cohesive. If it is dry and shaggy, add more cream to make it hold together.
✿ Turn out onto a lightly floured surface and knead gently about 10 times. Pat the dough into a circle 6 to 7 in (15 to 18 cm) across and ½ to ¾ in (1.25 to 2 cm) thick and place on a baking sheet. Bake for about 30 minutes, until lightly browned and puffy.
✿ Remove from the oven and while still warm, split the shortcake horizontally. Do not worry if it breaks; you can cover cracks with whipped cream.
✿ Spoon the oranges and liqueur over the bottom layer, spread with a large spoonful of whipped cream, then set the top in place. Pass additional whipped cream at the table.

SERVES 6

California

RAISIN, WALNUT AND ORANGE CAKE

This is a California-style fruitcake, chock-full of raisins, nuts and grated orange zest. Containing no candied fruit or liquor, it usually appeals even to those who claim they don't like fruitcake. Tightly wrapped, it remains fresh and moist for about a week; for longer keeping, it should be frozen.

2½ cups (10 oz/315 g) cake (soft-wheat) flour (see glossary)
1½ teaspoons baking powder
1 teaspoon salt
2 cups (10 oz/315 g) golden raisins (sultanas)
2 cups (10 oz/315 g) seedless muscat or dark raisins
2 cups (8 oz/250 g) chopped walnuts
1 cup (8 oz/250 g) butter, softened
1 cup (8 oz/250 g) sugar
1 tablespoon vanilla extract (essence)
5 eggs, beaten together
¼ cup (2 oz/60 g) grated orange zest

✿ Preheat the oven to 300°F (150°C). Grease two 8½- x 4½- x 2½-in (22- x 11- x 6-cm) loaf pans. Line them with foil pressed snugly over the bottom and sides, then grease and flour the foil.
✿ In a large bowl, stir and toss together the flour, baking powder and salt. Add the raisins and nuts, and toss to combine and coat with flour. If you are using muscats, which tend to be sticky, be sure they are mostly broken apart.
✿ In another large bowl, beat the butter and sugar together until blended. Beat in the vanilla. Add the combined dry ingredients to the butter mixture alternately in three stages with the eggs, beating vigorously after each addition. With the last addition, add the orange zest.
✿ Spread the batter evenly in the prepared pans; they will be almost full. Bake for 1½ to 2 hours, or until a broom straw or thin wooden skewer inserted in the center of a cake comes out clean. Remove from the oven and let the cakes cool in the pans for 30 minutes. Turn them out onto a rack, peel away the foil and cool completely before wrapping airtight.

MAKES 2 LOAVES

Raisin, Walnut and Orange Cake

Los Angeles
FORTUNE COOKIES

According to an article in Sunset magazine published in 1971, fortune cookies are probably not Chinese, but rather the invention of an enterprising young baker in Los Angeles in the 1920s. It can be said for certain that they are a challenge, and especially satisfying when they come out just right. The trick is in the forming: the cookies must be hot and pliable or they will break. Bake only a few at a time and be patient. You might have to make a batch or two before mastering the knack of folding them. If your hands are sensitive to heat, wear cotton— not rubber—gloves. The cookies can be folded without fortunes inside, but if you wish to include them, write or type messages on paper, then cut the fortunes into strips measuring ½ by 3 inches (1.25 by 7.5 cm).

1 cup (4 oz/125 g) all-purpose (plain) flour
½ teaspoon salt
2 tablespoons cornstarch (cornflour)
⅓ cup (3 oz/90 g) sugar
½ cup (4 fl oz/125 ml) vegetable oil
⅓ cup (3 fl oz/80 ml) egg white
⅓ cup (3 fl oz/80 ml) water

❧ Preheat the oven to 300°F (150°C) and line cookie sheets with foil; butter the foil.
❧ Combine and sift together the flour, salt, cornstarch and sugar. Add the oil and egg and stir until smooth. Add the water and stir until blended.
❧ Bake only 2 or 3 cookies at a time at first. Drop level tablespoons of the batter several inches apart on the prepared cookie sheet. With the back of a spoon, spread each blob evenly into a 4-in (10-cm) circle. Bake for about 10 minutes, or until the cookies are beginning to brown—do not overbake them.
❧ With a wide spatula, remove them from the oven one at a time and form them rapidly: flip a cookie upside down onto your hand. Put a fortune in the center and fold the cookie in half. Then fold each semicircle in half by bending it briefly over the edge of the pan so that it is creased down the middle, but the two sides do not touch. As the cookies are formed, gently set them in empty cardboard egg cartons to become cool and crisp, then store airtight.

MAKES ABOUT 18 COOKIES

San Francisco
COFFEE CRUNCH CAKE

There are many versions of this time-honored cake, made famous by Blum's, the once-popular haven for dessert lovers in San Francisco. It is simply an angel food cake, frosted generously with whipped cream, then coated with a brittle, crunchy coffee candy. It is heavenly. If you prefer, a sponge or chiffon cake may be used instead.

CRUNCHY COFFEE CANDY

1½ cups (12 oz/375 g) sugar
¼ cup (2 fl oz/60 ml) strong coffee
¼ cup (2 fl oz/60 ml) light corn syrup
1 tablespoon baking soda (bicarbonate of soda), sifted after measuring

FROSTING

3 cups (24 fl oz/375 ml) heavy (double) cream
3 tablespoons nonfat dry milk (milk powder)
¼ cup (2 oz/60 g) powdered (icing) sugar

2 teaspoons vanilla extract (essence)
one 10-in (25-cm) angel food cake (see following recipe)

❧ Line the bottom and sides of a jelly-roll pan with foil; set aside.
❧ To make the candy, combine the sugar, coffee and corn syrup in a saucepan of at least 16-cup (128-fl oz/4-l) capacity (the mixture will foam up when the soda is added). Bring to a boil and cook to the hard-crack stage (305°F/150°C on a candy thermometer). Remove from the heat, add the baking soda and stir to distribute; the mixture will foam, thicken and pull away from the pot. Pour onto the foil-lined pan and let cool and harden.
❧ Peel off the foil, then break the candy into irregular ¼- to ½-in (6- to 12-mm) pieces. Store airtight until ready to use.
❧ When you are ready to assemble the cake, make the frosting by whipping the cream with the dry milk, sugar and vanilla until it stands in peaks.
❧ Split the cake horizontally into 4 layers. Spread the cream generously between the layers, then frost the top and sides. Shortly before serving, sprinkle the crunch all over, pressing it down gently so it adheres. Serve as soon as possible. (The crunch will soften after several hours, though it still makes very good eating.)

Fortune Cookies

ANGEL FOOD CAKE

1 cup (4 oz/125 g) cake (soft-wheat) flour (see glossary)
1½ cups (12 oz/375 g) sugar
2 cups (16 fl oz/500 ml) egg whites (about 13 eggs)
1½ teaspoons cream of tartar
1 teaspoon vanilla extract (essence)
½ teaspoon salt

❦ Preheat the oven to 375°F (190°C) and set out an ungreased 10-in (25-cm) tube pan.
❦ Combine the cake flour with half the sugar, sift them together 3 times and set aside. Reserve the remaining sugar in a small cup or bowl.
❦ Put the egg whites in a large bowl and beat on the lowest speed of an electric mixer for 1 minute. Stop beating and add the cream of tartar, vanilla and salt. If you are using a standing electric mixer, gradually turn to medium speed; if it is a hand-held electric beater, gradually turn to top speed. Add the reserved sugar one tablespoon at a time. Continue beating until the whites stand in peaks that droop just slightly when the beater is lifted.

❦ Sift about one-third of the flour-sugar mixture over the beaten whites and fold it in until mostly incorporated. Sift half the remaining flour mixture on top and fold it in until mostly incorporated, then sift on the last of the flour mixture and fold it in until there are no unblended streaks.
❦ Immediately scoop the batter into the cake pan and smooth it with a rubber spatula. Bake for 35 to 45 minutes, or until a broom straw or thin wooden skewer inserted in the cake comes out clean. Remove the cake from the oven and immediately invert the pan.
❦ Let the cake cool completely upside down by placing the tube over the neck of a bottle or an inverted metal funnel.
❦ To remove the cake, insert a long, thin-bladed knife between the cake and the edge of the pan. Cut all around the side with a smooth motion, holding the knife flush against the pan. Cut the same way around the center tube. Gently use your fingers or a thin spatula to ease the cake from the bottom—don't worry about crushing the cake, it is really quite resilient and springy.

MAKES ONE CAKE, SERVING 12   *Photograph pages 224–225*

STRAWBERRIES ROMANOFF

Dishes incorporating strawberries and copious amounts of cream were common on hotel menus in old California. They included strawberry shortcake, strawberries and cream, and strawberries Romanoff, the latter usually consisting of a blending of various liqueurs with ice cream and whipped cream, with fresh strawberries folded in. It must be made just before serving and is good with Chinese almond cakes (see the recipe below).

2 cups (16 fl oz/500 ml) vanilla ice cream, softened slightly
1 cup (8 fl oz/250 ml) heavy (double) cream
¼ cup (2 fl oz/60 ml) orange liqueur
3 tablespoons brandy
8 cups (3 to 4 baskets; 2 lb/1 kg) strawberries, washed, patted
    dry, hulled and halved if they are large

Put the ice cream in a large chilled bowl and beat it briefly until it is smooth. In another bowl, whip the cream until it forms soft peaks, then scoop it on top of the ice cream. Add the orange liqueur and brandy and stir briefly just until blended. Fold in the strawberries and serve immediately.

SERVES 4–6

CHINESE ALMOND CAKES

These delicate cookies are like shortbread with an almond flavor and a cloak of sesame seeds. You often see them, along with fortune cookies, in Chinese bakeries. They make a wonderful conclusion to any meal, either occidental or oriental, when served with fresh or poached fruit.

1 cup (8 oz/250 g) butter, softened
⅔ cup (4 oz/125 g) powdered (icing) sugar, sifted
1 egg yolk
1 teaspoon almond extract (essence)
2 cups (8 oz/250 g) all-purpose (plain) flour
¼ teaspoon salt
¼ teaspoon baking powder
1 egg white
1 tablespoon water
3 tablespoons sesame seeds
40, more or less, blanched almonds

In a large bowl, beat together the butter and sugar until smooth and blended. Beat in the egg yolk and almond extract.
Stir and toss together the flour, salt and baking powder. Add to the butter mixture and beat until smooth and blended.
Preheat the oven to 375°F (190°C) and set out cookie sheets; do not grease them.
Roll generous tablespoon-sized bits of the dough between your palms into small balls; set aside.
In a small bowl, beat the egg white and water together. Dip half of each ball of dough into the egg white, then into the sesame seeds. Place, seed-side up, about 2 in (5 cm) apart on the cookie sheets. Use the bottom of a glass to flatten each cookie into a disk about 1½ in (4 cm) across. Push a whole almond into the center of each cookie. Bake for 15 to 20 minutes, or until the cookies are pale golden; they should not brown too much. Remove from the sheets and cool on racks.

MAKES ABOUT 40 COOKIES

FIG BARS

Fig trees flourished in the early California missions, and there are nearly eighteen thousand acres of orchards in the state. Old-fashioned fig bars are fun to make, and there is a sense of satisfaction to be gained from getting that filling inside the dough. They are certainly worth the effort, too, because they taste so much better than those you can buy.

DOUGH

1 cup (8 oz/250 g) softened butter
1 cup (8 oz/250 g) sugar
2 eggs
1 tablespoon vanilla extract (essence)
3 cups (12 oz/375 g) all-purpose (plain) flour
1 teaspoon salt
1 teaspoon baking powder
½ teaspoon baking soda (bicarbonate of soda)

FILLING

2 cups (1 lb/500 g) dried Mission (black) figs
½ cup (4 oz/125 g) sugar
1 cup (8 fl oz/250 ml) dry red wine

To make the dough, cream the butter and sugar together in a large bowl. Add the eggs and vanilla and beat until light and fluffy.
Stir and toss together the flour, salt, baking powder and baking soda. Add to the butter mixture and beat until completely blended. Turn the dough out onto a well-floured surface—it will be quite sticky—and pat it into a thick cake. Wrap in plastic and chill for at least 2 hours or overnight if you wish.
To make the filling, remove any stems and cut the figs into small pieces. Combine them in a saucepan with the sugar and red wine. Cook over medium heat, stirring frequently, for about 10 minutes, until the mixture boils and thickens. Purée in a food processor, then set aside to cool to room temperature.
Preheat the oven to 375°F (190°C) and grease some large cookie sheets. They must be at least 15 in (38 cm) long; be sure they will fit in your oven.
On a generously floured surface, roll half the dough into a rectangle measuring 14 in (35 cm) long and 7 in (18 cm) wide. (Keep the other half of the dough chilled until needed.) Do not worry if the dough crumbles or breaks as you roll it; just patch to your heart's content. Cut the dough in half lengthwise. Spoon one quarter of the filling evenly down each strip of dough, placing it just to the right of center, so that one side has filling and the other does not.
With a long spatula or pastry scraper, flip the clean side of dough over the filling, covering the filling completely. Seal the edges by pressing all around with your fingertips. Using a spatula to help you, gently push and roll the filled strips of dough onto the cookie sheets so that they are seam-side down. Press the strips down gently, spreading them out so they are about 1½ in (4 cm) across and bar shaped. Roll out and fill the other half of the dough the same way. (Bake one batch while you are filling and forming the other.)
Bake for 20 to 25 minutes, or until delicately browned. Do not overbake; the cookies should remain soft and moist. Let them cool on the baking sheet for about 10 minutes, then slide the strips onto a rack to cool completely. Cut each strip into 7 or 8 bars that are 1½ in (4 cm) long

MAKES ABOUT 30 BARS   *Photograph pages 242–243*

*Strawberries Romanoff (top)
and Chinese Almond Cakes (bottom)*

Long Beach
CALIFORNIA RANGER COOKIES

Old California cookbooks often include cookie recipes chock-full of chunky things such as nuts, dates, figs and raisins. They go by such names as rocks, billy goats and rangers.

1 cup (8 oz/250 g) vegetable shortening (vegetable lard) or
    softened butter
1 cup (8 oz/250 g) sugar
1 cup (5 oz/155 g) brown sugar
2 eggs
2 teaspoons vanilla extract (essence)
1 tablespoon milk
2 cups (8 oz/250 g) all-purpose (plain) flour
1 teaspoon salt
1 teaspoon baking soda (bicarbonate of soda)
½ teaspoon baking powder
2 cups (10 oz/315 g) uncooked oatmeal (rolled oats)
2 cups (10 oz/315 g) coarsely cut dates
2 cups (2 oz/60 g) cornflakes

❦ Preheat the oven to 350°F (180°C). Grease some cookie sheets.
❦ In a large bowl, cream together the shortening or butter and the sugars. Add the eggs, vanilla and milk and beat until smooth.
❦ Stir and toss together the flour, salt, baking soda and baking powder. Add to the first mixture and beat until completely mixed. Add the oatmeal, dates and cornflakes and mix well.
❦ Drop the dough by heaping teaspoons about 2 in (5 cm) apart on the prepared cookie sheets. Flatten each cookie slightly. Bake for about 12 minutes, or until lightly browned, then transfer the cookies to racks to cool completely.

MAKES ABOUT 90 COOKIES

Imperial Valley
CURRANT BARS

Currants look like small raisins and, in the United States, they are grown almost exclusively in California. They produce a mighty good bar cookie, soft and moist, that keeps well and is best made a day ahead.

1½ cups (7 oz/220 g) dried currants
1 cup (8 fl oz/250 ml) water
½ cup (4 oz/125 g) softened butter
2 tablespoons grated orange zest
1 egg, beaten
1 cup (8 oz/250 g) sugar
1¾ cups (7 oz/220 g) all-purpose (plain) flour
½ teaspoon salt
1 teaspoon baking soda (bicarbonate of soda)
1 teaspoon ground cinnamon
1 teaspoon ground nutmeg
1 teaspoon ground allspice
½ teaspoon ground cloves
½ cup (2 oz/60 g) chopped walnuts

❦ Preheat the oven to 375°F (190°C). Grease and flour a 9- x 13-in (23- x 33-cm) baking pan.
❦ Combine the currants and water in a large saucepan and bring to a boil. Remove from heat, add the butter and orange zest and stir until melted. Let the mixture cool until it is tepid.
❦ Beat in the egg and sugar. Stir and toss together the flour, salt, baking soda, cinnamon, nutmeg, allspice and cloves. Add to the currant mixture and beat until completely mixed. Stir in the chopped nuts. Spread the batter evenly in the prepared pan and bake for 35 minutes, or until a toothpick inserted in the center comes out clean. Let cool, then cut into bars measuring about 1 x 2 in (2.5 x 5 cm).

MAKES ABOUT 50 BARS

Fig Bars (top, recipe page 240), Currant Bars (left) and California Ranger Cookies (right)

KIWI SHERBET

Kiwifruit have been maligned because they were overused in the nouvelle cuisine of the seventies. They do have a cool tropical flavor, like a blend of bananas and peaches. All of the commercially produced kiwifruit in the United States comes from California. Kiwis flavored with a dash of Campari make a beautiful green sherbet that I first tasted at the Cafe Beaujolais in Mendocino. You may, if you wish, force the purée through a very fine mesh sieve to remove the tiny seeds, but this is a refinement and not essential.

⅔ cup (5 oz/155 g) sugar
⅓ cup (3 fl oz/80 ml) water
6 large kiwifruit, about 1¼ lb (625 g)
¼ cup (2 fl oz/60 ml) lemon juice
2 tablespoons Campari apéritif

🍷 Combine the sugar and water in a saucepan, bring to a boil and boil until the sugar dissolves. Chill before using.
🍷 Peel the kiwifruit and purée them in a blender or food processor. Add the sugar syrup, lemon juice and Campari and blend well. Freeze in an ice cream maker according to the manufacturer's instructions.

MAKES ABOUT 3 CUPS (24 FL OZ/750 ML)

Kiwi Sherbet (left) and Lemon Sherbet (right)

Poached Figs with Cream

Madera
POACHED FIGS WITH CREAM

Figs really do not ripen well after they have been picked, so ideally they should remain on the tree until they are ready, a requirement that makes those that are not eaten by birds fragile and expensive in the market. These figs are sweet and soft, good with a little of their red wine and lemon poaching syrup poured over them and served with a spoonful of heavy cream or crème fraîche. They keep for several days in the refrigerator.

2 cups (16 fl oz/500 ml) dry red wine
⅓ cup (3 fl oz/80 ml) lemon juice
1 cup (8 oz/250 g) sugar
1 cinnamon stick
4 whole cloves
12 figs, ripe but not mushy
crème fraîche (see glossary) or heavy (double) cream

✿ In a medium-sized saucepan, combine the wine, lemon juice, sugar, cinnamon stick and cloves. Bring to a boil, then cover and simmer for about 10 minutes.

✿ Add the figs to the hot liquid, keeping them in just one layer if you can. Poach gently—do not let them boil—for about 10 minutes, just until soft and tender. Let the fruit cool in the liquid for at least an hour, or in the refrigerator overnight before serving.

✿ Place the figs in individual bowls, pour some of the poaching liquid around them, and top each fig with a spoonful of *crème fraîche* or heavy cream.

SERVES 4

Riverside
LEMON SHERBET

Sherbets made with juice tend to become hard and icy, though a generous amount of sugar tempers that tendency. Egg whites give them a richness that will have you thinking there is cream in the mixture, even when there is none. Plain and simple, this is a sherbet without obstacles.

2 cups (1 lb/500 g) sugar
1 cup (8 fl oz/250 ml) water
2 egg whites, beaten until foamy
1 tablespoon grated lemon zest
1 cup (8 fl oz/250 ml) freshly squeezed lemon juice

✿ Bring the sugar and water to a boil, stirring until the sugar is dissolved. Chill thoroughly.

✿ Combine the sugar syrup with the egg whites, lemon zest and lemon juice. Freeze in an ice cream maker according to the manufacturer's instructions.

MAKES ABOUT 4 CUPS (32 FL OZ/1 L)

San Francisco
BLUM'S COFFEE TOFFEE PIE

This has been called a candy bar masquerading as a pie—it is really irresistible. The idea of filling a chocolate cookie crust with chocolate butter and topping it off with coffee-flavored whipped cream is credited to Blum's, a restaurant that was, in its time, a haven for the sweet lovers in San Francisco. The restaurant is not in business anymore, but you can make this at home. You will need an electric mixer for the long beating and several hours for the pie to chill before it is served.

CHOCOLATE DOUGH

1 cup (4 oz/125 g) all-purpose (plain) flour
½ cup (4 oz/125 g) butter, softened
¼ cup (1½ oz/45 g) brown sugar
1 square (1 oz/30 g) unsweetened (bitter cooking) chocolate, grated
1 teaspoon vanilla extract (essence)
2 tablespoons, or more, milk
¾ cup (3 oz/90 g) finely chopped walnuts

FILLING

½ cup (4 oz/125 g) butter, softened
¾ cup (6 oz/185 g) sugar
2 teaspoons powdered instant coffee
1 square (1 oz/30 g) unsweetened (bitter cooking) chocolate, melted
2 eggs

TOPPING

1½ cups (12 fl oz/375 ml) heavy (double) cream, chilled
6 tablespoons (3 oz/90 g) powdered (icing) sugar
1½ tablespoons nonfat dry milk (milk powder)
1½ tablespoons powdered instant coffee
1 tablespoon grated unsweetened (bitter cooking) chocolate

❧ Preheat the oven to 375°F (190°C) and set out a 9-in (23-cm) pie plate.
❧ To make the dough, combine the flour, butter, brown sugar and chocolate in a bowl and mix until well blended, using your fingertips, a pastry blender or a food processor. Add the vanilla, 2 tablespoons of milk and the walnuts and mix well. The mixture should form a cohesive—but not sticky—mass. If it is too dry, add a few drops more milk.
❧ This is a cookielike dough, not harmed by handling. The easiest way to get it into the pan is to take walnut-sized pieces and press them onto the bottom and sides of the pan, making sure you distribute them evenly, with no gaps or thin spots. Press the dough well up the sides too, then crimp the edges. Prick all over with a fork and press a piece of heavy-duty foil snugly into the pie shell. Bake for 8 minutes, then remove the foil and bake for about 10 minutes more, or until the shell is dry and crisp. Remove to a rack and let cool completely before filling.
❧ To make the filling, put the butter in the large bowl of an electric mixer and beat until fluffy. Beating on high speed, gradually add the sugar. Beat in the instant coffee and melted chocolate. Add 1 egg and beat on the highest speed for 5 minutes. Add the second egg and beat for 5 minutes more. Spread the filling evenly in the cooled pie shell, then cover and refrigerate for at least 6 hours, or overnight, before topping.
❧ To prepare the topping, combine the cream, powdered sugar, dry milk and instant coffee in a large bowl and beat with an electric mixer until stiff. Spread in peaks and swirls over the chilled pie and sprinkle with the grated chocolate. Refrigerate again for at least 2 hours before serving.

MAKES ONE 9-IN (23-CM) PIE

Blum's Coffee Toffee Pie

Southern California
PUCHITAS

Like torrejas, puchitas are a shortbread. Made with white flour and flavored with an anise-and-lemon infusion, they are refined, dainty cookies, and feasts and celebrations in early California were not complete without them. They keep well and are easy to make.

2 tablespoons water
1 tablespoon lemon juice
1 tablespoon aniseed
½ cup (4 oz/125 g) sugar
2¼ cups (9 oz/280 g) all-purpose (plain) flour
¼ teaspoon baking powder
½ teaspoon salt
1 cup (8 oz/250 g) butter
1 egg, beaten

❧ Combine the water, lemon juice and aniseed with 2 tablespoons of the sugar. Bring just to a boil, then reduce the heat and simmer, covered, for 5 minutes. Set aside to cool.
❧ Preheat the oven to 300°F (150°C) and set out cookie sheets.
❧ Into a large bowl, sift together the remaining sugar, the flour, baking powder and salt. Add the butter and blend it into the dry ingredients with your fingertips or a pastry blender until the mixture resembles coarse crumbs. Add the egg and the anise syrup—with the seeds—and stir until the dough holds together.
❧ Turn the dough out onto a floured surface and roll to a thickness of ½ in (12 mm). Cut rounds with a floured 2-in (5-cm) cutter and place them 2 in (5 cm) apart on ungreased cookie sheets. Continue rerolling and cutting the scraps until all the dough is used. Prick each cookie 3 times with fork and bake for 20 to 25 minutes, or until the cookies are barely colored around the edges. Remove from the sheets and cool on a rack.

MAKES ABOUT 24 COOKIES

Wine Jelly (top) and Puchitas (bottom)

Napa Valley
WINE JELLY

This is not a jelly to be spread on toast, but an old-fashioned dessert jelly, cool and softly set. With a spoonful of whipped cream and a crisp cookie, it is a refreshing way to conclude a meal. You may also make a jelly with sherry or Madeira.

2 envelopes (½ oz/15 g) unflavored gelatin, about 2 scant
    tablespoons
1 cup (8 oz/250 g) sugar
½ cup (4 fl oz/125 ml) cold water
1½ cups (12 fl oz/375 ml) boiling water

½ cup (4 fl oz/125 ml) fresh orange juice
3 tablespoons lemon juice
2 cups (16 fl oz/500 ml) dry white wine, such as a
    Sauvignon Blanc

🍂 Combine the gelatin, sugar and water in a small bowl and let the mixture stand for 5 minutes to soften.
🍂 Stir in the boiling water and cook over low heat for 5 minutes or until the sugar and gelatin are dissolved; do not boil. Stir in the orange juice, lemon juice and wine. Pour into a bowl or individual dishes and chill the jelly for several hours, until set.

MAKES 4 CUPS (32 FL OZ/1 L)

Los Angeles
BUÑUELOS WITH ANISE SYRUP

The name buñuelos *literally means "fritter," so there are many types of* buñuelos *and, like* churros, *they are often sold in Mexican bakeries. These are small circles of sweet dough, fried until airy and golden, then soaked in an anise-flavored syrup.*

DOUGH

¼ cup (2 oz/60 g) vegetable shortening
¼ cup (2 oz/60 g) sugar
2 eggs
1 teaspoon vanilla extract (essence)
1¾ cups (7 oz/220 g) all-purpose (plain) flour
2 teaspoons baking powder
1 teaspoon salt
¼ cup (2 fl oz/60 ml) milk
oil for frying

SYRUP

1 cup (8 fl oz/250 ml) water
½ cup (4 oz/125 g) sugar
1 cinnamon stick
2 pieces star anise (optional)
¼ cup (2 fl oz/60 ml) anise-flavored liqueur
powdered (icing) sugar

To make the dough, beat together the shortening and sugar, then add the eggs, one at a time, beating well after each addition. Beat in the vanilla.

Stir and toss together the flour, baking powder and salt. Add to the egg mixture along with the milk, and mix until you have a soft, smooth dough. Turn out onto a generously floured surface and knead about 10 times, sprinkling on a little more flour if necessary to keep the dough from being too sticky.

Roll out the dough ¼ in (6 mm) thick and cut into 3-in (7.5-cm) rounds. Set aside on a floured surface.

Heat about 2 in (5 cm) of oil in a skillet or kettle to 375°F (190°C). While the oil heats, prepare the syrup.

Combine the water, sugar, cinnamon stick and star anise in a saucepan, bring to a boil and boil for 5 minutes. Cover the pan and keep the syrup warm while you fry the *buñuelos*.

Fry about 6 *buñuelos* at a time in the hot oil, turning them often, for about 1½ minutes, until they are puffy and golden.

Drain on absorbent paper towels. While they are still warm, arrange the *buñuelos* slightly overlapping on a deep platter or pie plate. Stir the anise liqueur into the syrup and spoon it over the fritters. Dust with powdered sugar and serve as soon as possible.

MAKES ABOUT 12 FRITTERS

San Francisco
CHURROS

There are bakeries in the Mission district of San Francisco where they turn out hot churros *all day, cooking them in huge vats of fat in the back room. These golden ropes of fried cream-puff dough rolled in cinnamon sugar are so puffy and satisfying that it is hard to get enough of them. Good* churros *can make you famous, and their unique character makes them just right for a special breakfast.*

½ cup (4 fl oz/125 ml) water
½ cup (4 fl oz/125 ml) milk
½ teaspoon salt
½ cup (4 oz/125 g) butter
1 cup (4 oz/125 g) all-purpose (plain) flour
4 eggs
2 teaspoons vanilla extract (essence)
oil for frying
¾ cup (6 oz/185 g) sugar
1 tablespoon ground cinnamon

Combine the water, milk, salt and butter in a heavy saucepan. Heat the mixture slowly until the butter melts, then bring it to a full boil. Dump in the flour all at once, then cook over medium heat, beating constantly, for about 2 or 3 minutes.

Remove from the heat and add the eggs one at a time, beating vigorously after each addition until the mixture is smooth. Beat in the vanilla.

Heat about 2 in (5 cm) of oil in a skillet to 390°F (198°C). Combine the sugar and cinnamon on a platter; set aside.

Scoop the egg mixture into a pastry bag fitted with a ½-in (12-mm) round or star tip. Squeeze the bag over the hot oil, pushing out a rope of paste 4 in (10 cm) long, then cut it off with a knife, letting it fall gently into the oil. Rapidly form about 4 more *churros* in the same way. Turn them frequently until they are golden, about 2 minutes.

Remove with a slotted spoon and drain on absorbent paper towels. While the *churros* are still warm, roll them in the cinnamon sugar.

Fry and finish the remaining dough in the same way.

MAKES 24 CHURROS

Fresno
DATE PUDDING CAKE

Old favorites, pudding cakes have graced American—and Californian—tables for generations. Gooey and rich, with a spicy date-and-nut cake topping a sweet custard, this confection goes into the oven as one batter, and the transformation to cake and pudding occurs in baking. If you have a sweet tooth, this will appeal to you.

1½ cups (7 oz/220 g) finely cut dates
4 tablespoons (2 oz/60 g) butter, softened
2 cups (16 fl oz/500 ml) boiling water
2 eggs
1½ cups (6 oz/185 g) all-purpose (plain) flour
1½ cups (8 oz/250 g) brown sugar
1 teaspoon ground cinnamon
1 teaspoon baking soda (bicarbonate of soda)
½ teaspoon baking powder
½ teaspoon salt
½ cup (2 oz/60 g) chopped walnuts

Preheat the oven to 375°F (190°C) and grease an 8-cup (64-fl oz/2-l) baking dish.

Put the dates and butter in a large bowl and pour in 1 cup (8 fl oz/250 ml) of the boiling water. Stir until the butter melts, then let the mixture stand for about 5 minutes. Beat in the eggs and set aside.

Combine the flour with ½ cup (3 oz/90 g) of the brown sugar, the cinnamon, baking soda, baking powder and salt. Stir and toss together until blended. Add to the date mixture along with the walnuts and beat until blended.

Spread the batter evenly in the baking dish. Sprinkle with the remaining 1 cup (5 oz/155 g) of brown sugar, then pour the remaining 1 cup (8 fl oz/250 ml) of boiling water over the top.

Bake for 45 minutes, or until a toothpick inserted in the cake comes out clean.

SERVES 6–8   *Photograph page 251*

*Buñuelos with Anise Syrup (top)
and Churros (bottom)*

Date Pudding Cake (recipe page 248)

Benicia

UNION HOTEL
CHOCOLATE CAKE

In the words of one chocolate lover, this cake, which was once on the menu at the venerable Union Hotel in Benicia, a small town at the mouth of the Sacramento Delta, is so good that it can make you cry. It is a dark, rich, moist loaf, quickly and easily mixed with a spoon in a saucepan—you do not even need an electric beater. Sliced thickly, it requires no icing, just a spoonful of unsweetened whipped cream.

7 squares (7 oz/220 g) unsweetened (bitter cooking) chocolate
¾ cup (6 oz/185 g) butter
1½ cups (12 fl oz/375 ml) strong coffee
¼ cup (2 fl oz/60 ml) bourbon
2 eggs
1 teaspoon vanilla extract (essence)
2 cups (8 oz/250 g) cake (soft-wheat) flour (see glossary)
1½ cups (12 oz/375 g) sugar
1 teaspoon baking soda (bicarbonate of soda)
¼ teaspoon salt

TOPPING

2 cups (16 fl oz/500 ml) heavy (double) cream
2 teaspoons vanilla extract (essence)

❦ Preheat the oven to 275°F (135°C). Grease and flour two 8½- x 4½- x 2½-in (22- x 11- x 6-cm) loaf pans.

❦ Put the chocolate, butter and coffee in a heavy-bottomed pan of about 16-cup (128-fl oz/4-l) capacity. Place over low heat and stir almost constantly until the chocolate melts, then stir vigorously until the mixture is smooth and completely blended.

❦ Set aside to cool for about 10 minutes, then beat in the bourbon, eggs and vanilla.

❦ Combine the flour, sugar, baking soda and salt and sift them together. Add to the chocolate mixture and beat with a wooden spoon until well blended and smooth.

❦ Divide the batter evenly between the prepared pans and bake for 45 to 55 minutes, or until a broom straw or wooden skewer inserted in the center of a loaf comes out clean. Remove from the oven and let the cakes cool in the pans for 15 minutes, then turn them out onto a rack to cool completely.

❦ Before serving, combine the cream and vanilla and whip until it barely stands in peaks; it should be fluffy, but thin enough to run down the sides of the cake when you place a spoonful on each serving.

MAKES 2 LOAVES

Union Hotel Chocolate Cake

GLOSSARY

ABALONE: A large, single-shelled mollusk, abalone is found attached to rocks in California coastal waters. Because of its delicate taste and scarcity, it is an expensive luxury and, until recently, was not sold outside California. Small quantities of farm-raised abalone are now sent outside the state, though it is still costly. Keep in mind that, if not pounded thoroughly, abalone can be mighty tough and disappointing.

ANISE: There is no middle road with anise; you either like this licorice-flavored spice or you don't. The seeds (spelled *aniseed*) are frequently used to flavor cookies, breads, cakes and liqueurs. They are also good when toasted and added to chicken and veal stews. Star anise is a member of the magnolia family that looks like a small star and is more strongly flavored than aniseed, to which it is not botanically related. Imported from China, it is to be found, logically, in Asian markets. Use it whole or broken in pieces in pickles, beverages and sugar syrups.

ARTICHOKE: Artichokes are green, globe-shaped members of the thistle family introduced in California by Italian and Spanish settlers. They are grown primarily in Castroville where you can purchase them in any size, from that of a walnut—and entirely edible—to nearly as large as a football—and as tasty as the small ones, though not completely consumable. Instructions on how to cook and eat them are on page 88.

AVOCADO: There are many varieties but, because of the pear shape and thick, rough skin of the common Haas avocado, they were called alligator pears in the early days. Under the skin is a soft, pale green flesh, the taste of which can be described as both bacony and buttery. They combine well with fruits, vegetables and seafood, and may be found in many dishes, including salads, chilled soups, dips (see the recipe for *guacamole*, page 34), sandwich and omelet fillings, cold sauces, and may even be combined with sugar, lime juice and sweetened condensed milk to make a pie filling. They are best eaten raw, as cooking destroys their delicate flavor. Let hard avocados sit at room temperature for a few days, until they give to slight pressure.

BAMBOO SHOOTS: Young edible shoots from the tropical bamboo plant are used frequently in Asian cookery. Fresh bamboo shoots are a rarity, so you will probably purchase them canned. Brands vary, so try to find one with shoots that are white, crisp and clean tasting, and rinse them before using.

BARBECUE METHODS: There are two common ways of cooking on an outdoor fire; direct and indirect. The direct method involves cooking on the grilling rack directly above the hot coals—this is for hamburgers, steaks, chops, chicken parts and fish fillets. Indirect cooking, used with covered-kettle barbecues, is more leisurely, similar to using your oven. The hot coals are spread around the edge of the fire pan, so the food on the grilling rack above is surrounded by radiant heat, but not directly above it. This is the best way to cook roasts, whole chickens, turkeys and ducks, as well as large fish.

BLACK BEANS: About the same size and shape as the small white beans used for traditional Boston baked beans, black beans (also called turtle beans) are used frequently in South American and Caribbean cooking. Delicious in soups, they also make excellent refried beans as well as a California masterpiece, black bean cakes (see the recipe on page 182).

BULGUR: Bulgur is made from whole-wheat grains that are cooked, dried and cracked into tiny pieces. With a chewy texture and nutty flavor, bulgur has long been used in the Middle East and has gained popularity here as a side dish instead of rice or macaroni, and is the base of many stuffings, salads and hot cereals.

CANNING: Few of us nowadays are actually living off our acreage, so home canning is usually done more for fun than out of necessity. It's also satisfying to see jars full of homemade jams, jellies and preserves made with summer's bounty. To sterilize jars, boil them gently in water to cover for 10 minutes; leave them in the water until you are ready to fill them. Some recipes in this book instruct you to process the filled jars in a boiling water bath. This is a safeguard and ensures a better seal. As soon as the jars are filled and the screw bands attached, lower them into a large pot of boiling water, deep enough so the water will cover them by at least 1 inch. The pot should be fitted with a rack, so the jars don't touch the bottom, the sides, or one another. Cover the pot and start timing when the water returns to a boil. Uncover and boil gently for the specified time, then carefully remove the jars with tongs.

CHEESE: California produces some outstanding cheeses, so there's no reason to be monotonous. Brie and Camembert when properly aged are creamy, subtle and rich in flavor. Goat cheeses, also known as *chèvre*, are made in many shapes and sizes by several California producers. The flavor is distinctively tangy—some would call it barnlike—and the texture ranges from mild and creamy to fairly hard and dry, depending on the age of the cheese. It is good on pizzas and in salads of bitter greens. Monterey Jack, California's only native cheese, is made from cow's milk. Originally a spreadable, mild white cheese made by the Spanish missionaries, it has changed over the years. After the gold rush, it became identified with David Jacks of Monterey, who made and sold it in great quantities. Today, Monterey Jack is a mellow, semisoft cheese that comes plain and in many flavored variations. It is good for slicing on sandwiches or melting in *quesadillas*, *chiles rellenos*, quiches and omelets. Dry Monterey Jack, aged six months or more, is hard, dry and more sharply flavored. It is good for grating and cooking—use it as you would Parmesan. California Teleme is a natural, unripened cheese made from cow's milk, with a soft texture and mild, salty taste, unlike the European type that is made from goat's milk and cured in a salt brine.

CHILES: The subject of hot *chile* peppers is vast. There are several varieties and their heat enlivens many dishes. Capsaicin, the compound that gives *chiles* their incendiary quality, can be irritating to skin, so wear rubber gloves when handling them if you are sensitive, and don't touch your eyes until you've washed your hands.

Anaheim: Slender, pale green *chiles* about the diameter of a quarter (1 in/2.5 cm) and 6 to 8 inches (15 to 20 cm) long, Anaheim *chiles* are fairly mild once the seeds and internal ribs are removed. They are perfect for stuffing and are traditionally used for *chiles rellenos* (see the recipe on page 150).

Canned *chiles*: Available both mild and hot, canned *chiles* are roasted, peeled, and ready to use. They are a great convenience, and I've recommended them in many recipes where it isn't worth spending the time roasting and peeling fresh *chiles*.

Chili powder: Most commercial powders are a blend of dried ground *chiles*, cumin, oregano, salt and garlic, and are only mildly hot. They lend a characteristic flavor to many southwestern and Mexican dishes. Pure *chile* powders, made solely from ground dried *chiles* such as *anchos*, are much hotter and should be used with discretion.

Jalapeño: Dark green, plump and short (about 2 in/5 cm), *jalapeños* are very hot. Not quite as hot as *serranos*, their flesh is meatier and they are wider at the stem. Sun marks or striations running lengthwise down the skin indicate good quality and heat.

Serrano: Serranos are small, bullet-shaped *chiles*, between two and three inches long, with very hot veins and seeds. They are good for *salsas* and long-simmering soups and stews.

CILANTRO: Also called coriander or Chinese parsley, fresh cilantro resembles flat-leaf parsley in shape, and has a distinctive pungent, peppery flavor. It is used frequently in Latin American and Asian cooking. Ground coriander, the spice, is made from the dried seeds.

CLARIFIED BUTTER: Clarified butter is suitable for sautéing because, as the milk solids have been removed, it can be heated without burning to a higher temperature than unclarified butter and keeps for weeks, refrigerated in a tightly capped jar. To clarify butter, melt it slowly in a small saucepan without stirring. Skim and discard any white foam from the surface, then spoon the clear liquid into a container, leaving the milky residue in the bottom of the pan.

CORN HUSKS: There is no substitute for dried corn husks in *tamale* making, except perhaps banana leaves. As a *tamale* casing, dried corn husks both protect and flavor the filling within. They are sold in Mexican markets and some supermarkets.

CURRANTS: Zante currants, which are the only kind you are likely to find in the market, are made from small, dried grapes and look just like tiny raisins. Fresh currants, botanical relatives of the European gooseberry and also native to California, are tart, round, sparkly berries that may be red, black or gold (called "white"). Though fresh currants are not generally available, if you can find them, buy them: they are wonderful for jams and jellies.

CRÈME FRAÎCHE: Crème fraîche is thicker than whipping cream and has a slightly acid, nutty flavor similar to sour cream. Unlike sour cream, it can be boiled without curdling. Once a rarity, *crème fraîche* is now in many supermarkets, yet it is easy and less costly to make your own: Heat 1 cup of whipping cream in a small saucepan just until tepid—enough to take off the chill. Add 1 tablespoon buttermilk and transfer to a tightly capped jar; shake well. Remove the cap and cover the jar with cheesecloth. Let stand at room temperature until thickened, 12 to 24 hours (ultrapasteurized cream may take longer to thicken). Cover and refrigerate.

FIELD GREENS: Field greens are any of the leafy salad greens commonly sold as mesclun, a blend of several types of small, tender young leaves. Mesclun can be an extraordinary mix of colors, textures and flavors, variable by the season and what's in the garden. A common mix might include arugula or rocket, which has long slender leaves with a peppery flavor; chicory (also called curly endive or *frisée*), spiky and leafy with a bitter edge; *mâche* or lamb's lettuce, mild, and nutty tasting with small round leaves; *radicchio*, which resembles a small red cabbage, with sturdy, crunchy leaves and a sharp bitter flavor. Belgian endive and peppery watercress are also sometimes included.

FIGS: Many varieties, both fresh and dried, are available for cooking and eating out of hand. Those you are most likely to find are Mission or Black Mission (originally grown by the padres in the early California missions), which have a purplish black skin and reddish flesh, and Calimyrna, the commercial figs of California, which have a pale green skin and white flesh.

FISH: California waters are abundant in fish, and many types can be used interchangeably. A discussion of the numerous varieties and their preparation could be a book in itself, and indeed there are many volumes on the subject. The key to good tasting fish of any type is freshness, and the best guide to that is your nose: a fish should smell fresh—not fishy—as though it had just swum from the water. Among the fish used in this book are albacore, red snapper, salmon, swordfish and trout. A description of each is given in the appropriate recipe in the fish chapter.

FLOUR: Flour is the basis or foundation of most cookies, cakes and breads. All-purpose flour, a blend of hard and soft wheat flours, is used most frequently in this book. It doesn't matter whether the flour is bleached or unbleached. Cake flour, milled from soft wheat and highly refined, sometimes makes a lighter, more tender cake than all-purpose flour. I've used it only where a delicate texture really counts, so don't substitute all-purpose flour.

FRIJOLES: Frijoles is the Spanish word for beans. Its use indicates the strong Mexican influence on California cooking. The best-known dish is perhaps *frijoles refritos*—refried beans (see the recipe on page 185).

FRITTER: Fritters are pieces of uniformly cut fruits or vegetables, dipped in batter, and deep-fried to a delectable outside crispness. Fruit fritters—and almost any fruit will work—are good sprinkled with powdered sugar and served with honey or maple syrup. Vegetable fritters, Japanese style, are called *tempura*, and you will find them on page 174.

GINGER ROOT: Ginger root is a thick, brown, knobby fibrous root with a spicy aroma and a pungent, hot flavor. Peeled and minced, grated or finely chopped, it is used frequently in Asian cooking. Powdered or ground ginger, often called for in baking, is not interchangeable with fresh.

HERB VINEGAR: White wine vinegar is the usual choice for making herb-infused vinegars. There are many flavored vinegars on the market, but it is easy, and far more economical to do it yourself. The recipe for basil and garlic vinegar on page 210 can be adapted to other herbs, too, such as tarragon, dill, chives and mint.

JERUSALEM ARTICHOKE: Despite the name, these knobby tubers are no relation to the green globe artichoke. Light brown on the outside and white on the inside, Jerusalem artichokes (also called sunchokes) have a slightly sweet taste and may be eaten raw in salads or treated like a potato—fried, steamed, roasted, or mashed with butter.

JÍCAMA: Now available in most supermarkets, *jícama* is a major crop from Mexico. Brown and rough-looking, it is a large, roundish root with a thin skin. The texture is pleasingly crisp and somewhat juicy. It is usually peeled and eaten raw—cut in matchstick slices for salads, or cut in larger strips and served as an appetizer, sprinkled with lime juice and chili powder. Look for thin skin and scratch to see that the flesh is juicy. Peel with paring knife to remove the fibrous layer under the skin.

KIWIFRUIT: Formerly and elsewhere known as the Chinese gooseberry, kiwifruit is fuzzy brown on the outside and about the size of a large lime. Inside, the fruit is bright green with tiny, edible black seeds. The flavor is tart, reminiscent of cool melon and strawberry, with a juicy texture. It should be as soft as a ripe pear for eating. California kiwifruit is harvested in the late fall and represents ninety-five percent of all kiwifruit grown commercially in the United States.

LETTUCE: Leaf lettuce is California's number one crop, with the state producing about seventy-five percent of this nation's supply. Unlike many crops, it is picked throughout the year, with some of the workers migrating from north to south and back again, following the harvests around the state. Crisp, mild-flavored iceberg lettuce is king, though romaine, green leaf, red leaf, escarole, endive and butter lettuce are also grown. These sturdy leaf lettuces take better to assertive dressings than do delicate field greens.

MASA HARINA: The corn (maize) flour used for making *tortillas* and *tamales, masa* is made from whole corn grains soaked in lime water, dried and ground into a smooth flour. It is always available in Latin American food stores and mainstream supermarkets in many areas of California.

MIRIN: A sweet, almost syrupy rice wine used as a flavoring in Japanese cooking. Sweet sherry is an acceptable substitute.

MOLE: From the spanish term *molli,* meaning a sauce flavored with *chiles, mole poblano* is the most popular version of this intensely flavored, deep brown purée with a long list of ingredients, among them *chiles poblanos,* onions, tomato, garlic, ground almonds, chicken stock, ground coriander and sometimes, bitter chocolate. Often *mole* sauce is simmered with chicken or turkey or spooned over *enchiladas.*

OIL: The flavor and quality of oil for cooking varies tremendously, depending on the source.

Hot *chile* oil: An infusion, usually of vegetable oil or sesame oil flavored with hot red *chiles,* hot *chile* oil is used sparingly as a seasoning in Chinese cooking. Remember, it is fiery, and more than a few drops can be lethal.

Olive oil: California produces many first-rate olive oils, some fruity and strongly flavored, others delicate and subtle. Which you use depends on how much flavor you want to incorporate in a dish, so the way to purchase it is to buy what pleases you. Price does not always indicate the best quality, nor do the terms "virgin" and "extra virgin" on the label.

Peanut oil: Peanut oil is used frequently in Chinese cooking and favored for its mild, slight peanut flavor, as well as its ability to withstand the high temperatures of frying and sautéing without smoking.

Sesame oil: Like *chile* oil, this is a seasoning rather than a cooking oil, and should be used sparingly. It has a rich, nutty flavor and aroma and is frequently used in Chinese cooking.

Walnut oil: Walnut oil is wonderful in salad dressings. It is expensive and special, and doesn't keep as long as other oils—so be sure it is fresh. If in doubt, taste it.

OLIVES : Olive growing is a huge industry in California, and there are many varieties, all of them cured to be made palatable for consumption. Don't eat an olive right off the tree—it's a sharp and bitter experience you won't soon forget. Canned ripe olives are the most common. With a subtle, salty flavor, they make a great snack and certainly have their place in cooking. But stay out of an olive rut by exploring other types, such as salt-cured olives, which are oily, wrinkled and strongly flavored, and brine-cured olives, packed in a vinegar and salt solution.

PASTA: Pasta is the general term for an immense variety of noodles from every country. It can be made with durum wheat (semolina) or all-purpose flour and eggs, or with rice, soybean or buckwheat flour, and is often flavored with herbs or vegetables such as chives, spinach, beets and tomatoes.

PENNE: Penne are quill-shaped, medium-sized pasta tubes with thin ridges and ends cut on the diagonal.

POLENTA: Polenta is Italian cornmeal (yellow maize flour) porridge, or mush that may be prepared in a variety of savory ways. It is made by sprinkling coarse-ground cornmeal into boiling water and stirring the mixture with a whisk, and it is often served as a side dish, piping hot and topped with cheese. *Polenta* takes to many savory preparations and is often cooled and sliced, then baked in a casserole or sautéed with onions, peppers, or sausage.

SALSA: A fresh Mexican tomato sauce, generally based on chopped tomatoes or *tomatillos,* green *chiles,* onions and cilantro (coriander/ Chinese parsley), *salsa* enlivens numerous dishes, serves as a relish for grilled meats or fish, or stands on its own as a dip. *Salsa verde* is made from green *chiles* and *tomatillos*—no red tomatoes.

SALT: Table salt brings out the natural flavors of foods, and there is no substitute for it. Unless you are on a restricted diet, don't be fainthearted when a recipe says "salt to taste." Pickling salt is not iodized, as iodine can darken and cloud pickles. Rock salt is very coarse, large nuggets of salt that are generally used as a base for oysters when they are to be baked, as in Oysters Kirkpatrick (see the recipe on page 66).

SHELLFISH: Shellfish are either crustaceans (those with claws or a tail, such as crab, shrimp and prawns) or mollusks. Some mollusks are univalves, single-shelled creatures such as abalone; others are two-shelled bivalves, such as oysters and scallops.

SOURDOUGH: Sourdough generally refers to chewy, fragrant bread with a faintly tart taste and crumbly crust. It is made with a starter—a self-perpetuating leavening, originally created from a blend of liquid and flour, sparked by airborne yeast spores. Some sourdough bakeries in San Francisco can trace their starters back more than a century. Each time a batch of dough is made, a small quantity of the fermented dough is set aside as a starter for the next batch. Starter can also be made by adding yeast to a flour and water mixture rather than allowing natural fermentation to occur. This method, however, does not produce a *true* starter.

SQUAB: Squabs are small young pigeons with delicate, tender flesh. They are excellent stuffed and roasted or grilled.

STIR-FRY: To rapidly cook uniformly chopped vegetables, seafood and/ or meat in hot oil, either in a wok or skillet, turning with a spatula. Because of the short cooking time, the food retains flavors and crispness.

STOCK: Canned beef and chicken stocks are definitely a convenience, and bottled clam juice is a handy substitute for fish stock. These products are usually quite salty, so watch your seasoning and taste carefully, taking care not to oversalt. Canned stocks are often used with success, but there is no mistaking the natural flavor your own home-made stocks give to soups and sauces.

To make beef stock: Roast 5 pounds of beef shanks in a large roasting pan in a 450°F (180°C) oven for 30 minutes, turning them once. Transfer to a large pot and add 2 onions, peeled and halved, 3 whole carrots, 3 whole celery stalks, a bay leaf, a handful of parsley sprigs, 1 teaspoon salt and ½ teaspoon cracked peppercorns. Discard the fat from the roasting pan and deglaze the pan with 2 cups of water. Add to the pot along with 3 additional quarts of water, or enough to cover the ingredients by about 1 inch. Bring to a boil, then reduce the heat and simmer very gently, partially covered, for about 5 hours, skimming off any foam that rises to the surface for the first 30 minutes or so. If necessary add more water during cooking to keep the ingredients submerged. Strain through several thicknesses of cheesecloth and let cool, uncovered. Makes about 2½ quarts.

To make chicken stock: Place about 4 pounds chicken parts (backs, wings, necks, the remains of a roast chicken) in a large pot. Add 2 onions, peeled and halved, 2 whole carrots, 2 whole celery stalks, a handful of parsley sprigs, 1 bay leaf, 6 crushed peppercorns, 1 teaspoon dried thyme and 1 teaspoon salt. Pour in about 4 quarts of water, or enough to cover the ingredients by 1 inch. Bring to a boil, then reduce the heat and simmer gently, partially covered, for about 4 hours, skimming off any foam that rises to the surface for the first 30 minutes or so. If necessary, add more water during cooking to keep the ingredients just covered. Strain through several thicknesses of cheesecloth and let cool, uncovered. Makes about 3 quarts.

To make fish stock: Use white-fleshed fish. Dark, oily fish make an unpleasant stock. Rinse about 4 pounds combined fish heads (with gills removed) and meaty skeletons under running water and place in a large pot. Add 2 onions, peeled and sliced, 2 carrots, peeled and thinly sliced, 2 stalks celery, sliced, 1 bay leaf, 8 crushed peppercorns and 1 teaspoon salt. Add 2 cups dry white wine and about 3 quarts of water, or enough to cover the ingredients by 1 inch. Bring to a boil, then reduce the heat and simmer, uncovered, for about 45 minutes, skimming any scum from the surface. Strain through several thicknesses of cheesecloth and cool uncovered.

SUN-DRIED TOMATOES: Originally an Italian specialty, sun-dried tomatoes have become very popular in California cooking. Sliced tomatoes are literally dried in the sun and often packed in olive oil. The flavor is concentrated—rich and lingering—and a little goes a long way. California now produces its own versions, some made in dehydrators and some the time-honored way. Sun-dried tomatoes may be paired with basil and goat cheese, tossed with pasta, sprinkled on pizza or puréed for various dips and sauces. Dry-pack tomatoes may be reconstituted and used in cooking as you would use fresh tomatoes.

TAMALES: Tamales are bundles of *masa harina* (cornmeal/yellow maize flour) wrapped around a meat filling, folded in dried corn husks and steamed.

TOFU: Also known as bean curd, *tofu* is a high-protein cheeselike derivative of soy beans frequently used in Chinese cooking. The texture is smooth and the flavor bland, so it can be used in a variety of ways. It comes in white cakes packed in water and will keep for weeks in the refrigerator if the water is changed daily.

TOMATILLO: A *tomatillo* is a fruit that resembles a small green tomato, but is actually a relative of the Cape gooseberry. It is distinguished by a light colored, papery husk and mildly acidic taste, and is used for *salsa verde* (see the recipe on page 207).

TOMATOES: To peel a ripe tomato, drop it into boiling water for about 15 seconds, then plunge it into cold water. Cut out the stem end with a sharp knife and pull off the skin. To seed a tomato, cut it in half and gently squeeze out the seeds and juices from the interstices. Use your fingers or a small knife to scrape off any that remain.

TORTILLAS: Tortillas are the bread of Mexico. Made from corn or wheat flour, round and flat, *tortillas* are served in a basket, warmed, just as bread is served in a basket, to mop up sauces such as *mole*. More familiar to most Americans in their steamed or fried forms, *tortillas* are the foundation of *tacos, burritos, enchiladas, quesadillas, tostadas* and many other preparations. They are sold packaged in most supermarkets and handmade in Latin American communities throughout California.

UTENSILS: Perhaps because those pioneering days are not that far behind us, cooking in California has a simplicity of technique that does not require much in the way of fancy equipment and high-tech gadgets. Cookie sheets or baking trays differ slightly from jelly roll (Swiss roll) pans in that the former have no rims. A Dutch oven is a casserole with a lid, which ideally can be used both on the stovetop and in the oven, for soups, stews, long-simmered dishes and preserves. A kettle is any large, deep pan, primarily used for high-volume dishes with a lot of liquid, such as soups and stews. It is also useful for boiling pasta, sterilizing canning jars, and with a rack in the bottom will double as a boiling water bath. Pastry (piping) bags and tips (nozzles), which are vital to professional confectionary and cake making, but not to everyday cooking, are useful for squeezing lengths of *churro* dough into hot fat and, if you are handy with them, piping out blobs of cookie dough—

though this task is just as easily done with a spoon. A skillet or frying pan is used for browning, sautéing and stove-top cooking and, if ovenproof, will also double as a baking dish.

WATER CHESTNUTS: Water chestnuts are round, small bulbs with a crisp texture and a very mild flavor. They are sold fresh in Asian markets or canned in most supermarkets.

WILD RICE: Actually an aquatic grass, wild rice kernels look like thin rice grains but are a dark, shiny brown. They are cooked like white or brown rice, but with more liquid, and generally, for a longer period of time. When cooked, the outer shell opens to reveal a creamy interior. The flavor is nutty, the texture is slightly chewy. Wild rice was at one time grown only in Minnesota, but in recent years California has become the country's second largest producer.

ZEST: The outside rind of citrus fruit, zest contains volatile oils that give off fragrance and concentrated flavor. When removing the zest from oranges, lemons and limes, be careful not to take any of the bitter-tasting white pith from under the rind. Zest adds flavor to both savory and sweet foods.

ACKNOWLEDGMENTS

My thanks to Margaret D. Fallon, who came to my home several times weekly to test recipes, and faced each session with humor and enthusiasm. Her cooking skills and fine palate were invaluable in writing this book; Frances Bowles, whose knowledge of food and keen, skillful editing made this a much better manuscript; Michael J. Bauer, Food Editor of the San Francisco Chronicle, for his friendship and support; Marion Cunningham, for her good sense about home cooking and sound advice on cookbook writing; Wayne A. Strei, whose help on the glossary enabled me to meet my deadline; Mr. and Mrs. Prentis Hale, whose interest and support in my career have meant so much.

John Phillip Carroll

Virginia Rainey wishes to thank Judith Himelstein, Alan Schein, the Natural Resources and Bancroft Libraries at UC Berkeley and the Alice Statler Library at City College of San Francisco.

The publishers and photographers would like to thank the following people and organizations for their assistance in the preparation of this book:

Laurie Wertz; Barbara Roether; Richard VanOosterhout; Dawn Low; Sigrid Chase; Vida Merwin; Elizabeth Germaine; Kelly Newman; David Carriere; Susannah Clark.

Alex Cichy; Ann Nicholson Gardner; David Greenfield; Stephanie Greenleigh; Paul Lapping; Frances B. Larkey; Lorraine Puckett; Art Rosser; Bill Smith; Helen Spangenberg; Mr. and Mrs. J. Van Lott; Charles E. Williams.

Rapid Lasergraphics, San Francisco; Specialized Messenger Services, San Francisco; Samy's Camera, 2298 Third St., San Francisco, CA 94107; The New Lab, 10 Cleveland, San Francisco, CA 94103.

Props used in this book are from the following sources:
Beaver Bros. Antiques, 1637 Market St., San Francisco, CA 94103; Biordi Art Imports, 412 Columbus Ave., San Francisco, CA 94133; Chelsea Lane Antiques, 251 Rhode Island St., San Francisco, CA 94103; Claire Thomson Antiques, 495 Jackson Street, San Francisco, CA 94111; Cookin', 339 Divisadero St., San Francisco, CA 94117; Cottonwood, 3461 Sacramento St., San Francisco, CA 94118; Crate & Barrel, 125 Grant Ave., San Francisco, CA 94108; Fillamento Home Furnishings, 2185 Fillmore St., San Francisco, CA 94115; Forrest Jones Inc., 3274 Sacramento St., San Francisco, CA 94115; George V Collection Antiques, 340 Kansas St., San Francisco, CA 94108; J. Goldsmith American Antiques, 1924 Polk Street, San Francisco, CA 94109; Paul Bauer Inc., 120 Grant Ave., San Francisco, CA 94108; Pottery Barn, Stonestown Galleria, San Francisco, CA 94132; Set Your Table, 2258 Market St., San Francisco, CA 94114; Sue Fisher King Co., 3067 Sacramento St., San Francisco, CA 94115; Tiffany & Co., 252 Grant Ave., San Francisco, CA 94108; Virginia Brier Contemporary & Traditional Crafts, 3091 Sacramento St., San Francisco, CA 94115; Waterford/Wedgwood Store, 304 Stockton St., San Francisco, CA 94108; Wells Fargo History Museum, 420 Montgomery St., San Francisco, CA 94163; Williams-Sonoma, 150 Post St. San Francisco, CA 94108.